D1343616

TRAINS, COAL AND TURF

Transport in Emergency Ireland

PETER RIGNEY

IRISH ACADEMIC PRESS
DUBLIN • PORTLAND, OR

First published in 2010 by Irish Academic Press

2 Brookside.
Dundrum Road,
Dublin 14, Ireland

920 NE 58th Avenue, Suite 300
Portland, Oregon,
97213–3786, USA

www.iap.ie

British Library Cataloguing in Publication Data
An entry can be found on request

ISBN 978 0 7165 3009 1 (cloth)
ISBN 978 0 7165 3010 7 (paper)

Library of Congress Cataloging in Publication Data
An entry can be found on request

Typeset by FiSH Books, Enfield, Middx.
Printed in Great Britain by Good News Digital Books, Ongar, Essex

Contents

Abbreviations

ARP	Air Raid Protection
ASLEF	Associated Society of Locomotive Engineers and Firemen
BCDR	Belfast and County Down Railway
CME	Chief Mechanical Engineer
CP	The Portuguese railway company
DUTC	Dublin United Transport Company
ESAI	Engineering and Scientific Association of Ireland
ESRB	Emergency Scientific Research Bureau
GNR	Great Northern Railway
GOC	General Officer Commanding
GSR	Great Southern Railways
GS&WR	Great Southern & Western Railway (absorbed into GSR in 1924)
GWR	Great Western Railway (British)
LDF	Local Defence Force
LMSR	London Midland and Scottish Railway
LNER	London and North Eastern Railway
LSF	Local Security Force
MGWR	Midland Great Western Railway (absorbed into GSR in 1924)
NCC	Northern Counties Committee (Northern Ireland Arm of LMSR)
NIRTB	Northern Ireland Road Transport Board
NUR	National Union of Railwaymen
RENFE	The Spanish railway company
SHAEF	Supreme Headquarters Allied Expeditionary Force
SJ	The Swedish railway company
TDB	Turf Development Board
YMCA	Young Men's Christian Association

List of Illustrations and Plates

List of Tables

Acknowledgements

Many years ago, when researching for an undergraduate history dissertation on the history of railway trade unionism, I spoke to a number of retired locomotive drivers, mainly from around Inchicore. Their accounts of their working lives always included a description of the trials and tribulations they suffered during the Emergency. This awakened my interest in the period. Almost a quarter of a century later, the files of the General Manager of the Great Southern Railways came to the archive of the Irish Railway Record Society in Heuston Station. These files made possible the writing of the Ph. D thesis on which this book is based. I am therefore indebted to the officers of the society for the facilities accorded to me over the years, and in particular to Librarian, Tim Moriarty and to the Archivist, Brendan Pender.

I am also indebted to my supervisor Professor Eunan O'Halpin for his support and guidance throughout this project. The Centre for Contemporary History in Trinity College provided a most congenial place for writing and research. My thanks also to the staff of other libraries and archives I visited during my research; Trinity College; the National Archives; Military Archives, Cathal Brugha Barracks; ESB Archives; the Secretary's Office, CIÉ at Heuston Station; Louth County Archives; the British Library and the National Archives in Kew.

The writing of this book, and the thesis on which it was based would not have been possible without the knowledge I have acquired of the workings of the steam locomotive. For that knowledge I am grateful to a number of working and retired railwaymen. Dan and Tony Renehan and Pearse Mc Keown taught me most of what I know of how steam locomotives work, while the late Val Horan and the late Paddy Guilfoyle worked as firemen throughout the Emergency and shared their knowledge with me both in discussion and in correspondence.

A number of other people helped with the preparation of this book, both by providing useful leads or by reading drafts of the work in progress. My thanks are therefore due to Anna Bryson, David Dickson, Brian Hanley, Deirdre Keogh, Eve Morrison, Mary Muldowney, Mary McMillen-Rigney,

Daithi Ó Corráin, Greagóir Ó Dúill, Cormac Ó Gráda, Dan and Tony Renehan, Kathleen Rigney, Gregg Ryan, Brian Solomons and Pádraig Yeates. Gerry Beesley, David Carse, Gerry Hampson and Seán Kennedy provided illustrations.

Peter Rigney
April 2010

Introduction

'My mother's principal memories of the Emergency are of shortages, particularly of tea, sugar and flour, of trains on the Schull and Skibereen light railway ... running so slowly on inferior fuel that one could climb on and off them as they went uphill.'[1] Few accounts of life in Emergency Ireland are complete without such an anecdote about unreliable trains as locomotives struggled with inadequate fuel. This book is an attempt to explain this aspect of the history of the Emergency. In today's oil, gas and nuclear powered economies it is difficult to imagine the importance of coal in 1939, when economic life depended on coal for rail transport, steelmaking, town gas manufacture and domestic heating. One of the motivations for the foundation of the European Economic Community in 1951 was to place coal and steel under common control and thus lessen the chance of future European wars. At trade negotiations with Sweden in 1943, coal was described by the German side as 'an exceptionally valuable commodity almost as valuable as gold'.[2]

During the First and Second World Wars, trade was the continuation of war by other means. Neutral countries had resources that belligerents wanted, and vice versa. The British wanted access to the naval bases at Cobh, Berehaven and Lough Swilly, ceded by them in 1938, and when the Irish side refused to oblige, sanctions were imposed, of which restrictions on coal exports were a major part. However, for Britain as for Germany, using coal as a bargaining tool with neutral countries had to be tempered with the need to ensure that neutral railway systems could deliver much-needed goods. Throughout Europe, coal shortages were exacerbated by petrol shortages which severely restricted road transport and restored to railways the near monopoly they had enjoyed before the First World War.

This book will deal mainly with the operation of the Great Southern Railways (GSR) during the Emergency years. It will examine the company as a quasi-monopoly transport operator, as a strategic national resource and as one of Ireland's largest employers. However, the book will deal with two themes – technology and relationships. The reason why the coal supplied by the British was unsuitable for their locomotives was a matter of technology – how a steam locomotive works – but it was also a matter of the relationship between the Irish railway companies and their Welsh suppliers which caused Irish railways to depend on premium fuel in a way that railways in other countries did not. The solution to these problems was technological, but achieved by the development of a close relationship between the GSR and the British Ministry of Fuel and Power. Relationships between the government and railway companies were also important. The British railway companies were relatively prosperous, and were taken over by the state on generous terms at the outbreak of war. The GSR, in contrast, was financially so weak that the government was reluctant to take it over for fear of the potential cost to the taxpayer. The mutual distrust between the government and the GSR frustrated the preparation of Emergency plans in 1938 and 1939. As the supply position worsened, the government found that they could not cope with emergency conditions using a private company over which they had no control, and in the end took control but not ownership of the company using emergency powers legislation. The parallels with the banking sector in contemporary Ireland are intriguing.

The book examines other key relationships – of which one of the most important is Anglo-Irish trade. This book will examine the operation of the British sanctions policy and will show that, in operating this policy, the British administration was not a monolithic force but, in Sir Humphrey's immortal phrase, 'a loose confederation of warring tribes'. The British ministries of Mines, of Food and of Agriculture had a very different view of Britain's strategic interests than that held by the ministries of Economic Warfare and Shipping. On the Irish side, far from pursuing a policy of strict neutrality, the government offered to put the Irish manufacturing capacity at the disposal of the Allies in spring 1942. At a micro level, GSR aided the British and Northern Ireland authorities, loaning buses, locomotives and coaches and repairing goods wagons destroyed in the Belfast blitz. From 1943 onwards the GSR acted as a fuel laboratory for the British Ministry of Fuel and Power, anxious to get information on how locomotives reacted to lower grade fuels.

Another key relationship is between men and machines. From January 1941 until the end of 1946 the staff of the GSR struggled with the effects of low-quality coal. The brunt of that struggle was borne by locomotive crews, engineers and maintenance tradesmen. One of the problems facing the historian is 'presentism'. We now know that the GSR operations never collapsed. However, the GSR staff trying to keep the system going at the time had no such certainty. The development of innovation to keep trains running showed considerable ingenuity and towards the end of the war led to a decision to convert to diesel locomotives. Examining this decision again shows the danger of presentism. Today the move to diesel traction seems inevitable, but the diesel locomotive was unproven technology in the Europe of 1944.

In dealing with relationships, the chapters are thematic. The first chapter deals with the predominance of coal on the GSR and the attempts to find alternatives. Chapter 2 deals with the breakdown of coal supply in early 1941 and the effects this had on the government–GSR relationship, while Chapter 3 puts these shortages in an international perspective. Chapter 4 deals with Anglo-Irish trade politics, while Chapter 5 examines the vital task of transporting turf to the urban areas. Chapter 6 looks at the extensive lorry fleet of the GSR and its role in the Emergency economy and Chapter 7 examines the railway company as an agent of civilian and military mobilisation. Chapter 8 deals with the normalisation of train running between 1942 and 1944, while Chapter 9 explores the disruption caused by D Day preparations, the postwar shortages and moves towards an alternative form of power.

The Great Southern Railways, which operated trains, buses and lorries throughout much of Éire, had a virtual monopoly on land transport. The Great Northern Railway (GNR) operated east of a line from Dublin to Cavan; Donegal was served by two narrow gauge companies, while the road transport needs of the capital were met by the Dublin United Transport Company (DUTC), which was in the process of replacing trams with buses. The restrictions on petrol supply pushed much road traffic to rail and meant that freight traffic increased during the Emergency years, which saw the railway system become much busier, as is seen in the table below.

Table 1 GSR freight carryings 1938–1946 (million tons)

Year	1938	1939	1940	1941	1942	1943	1944	1945	1946
tons	2.3	2.4	2.45	2.6	2.55	2.8	2.95	3	2.63

Source: C Ó Gráda, *The Rocky Road*, pp. 14–15

The GSR was a child of Saorstát Éireann, and a sickly child at that. The privately owned Irish railway companies were taken over by the government in December 1916, ostensibly to aid the war effort. Sir Eric Geddes, the minister for transport (and himself an ex-railway manager), later told the Irish companies that the takeover was not for war needs but

The GSR route network in 1925

Figure 1: Map of the GSR System
(courtesy of Michael McMahon, Jeremy Clements and Colourpoint Books).

for financial reasons.[3] The cessation of compensation payments when the companies were handed back to their proprietors in August 1922 caused an immediate financial crisis.

This crisis was one of the first problems facing the Provisional Government and in response they established a commission – despite the fact that railways were envisaged as a function for the proposed Council of Ireland. The majority report of the commission recommended the amalgamation, and acts of 1924 and 1925 saw all companies lying wholly within the Free State amalgamating to form the Great Southern Railways. Amalgamation did not solve the financial problems of the railway companies. Further legislation in the early 1930s restricting road transport and allowing railway companies to compulsorily acquire their road competitors did not succeed in stabilising railway company finances, and by 1938 the GSR was facing bankruptcy. On 7 December 1938 a motion was put before the Dáil to establish a tribunal which would *inter alia* enquire into 'the circumstances which have led... to the present unfavourable financial position of the Great Southern Railways and of the other railway companies', and would make recommendations on 'changes in the ownership or in the methods of administration... of existing transport undertakings'.[4] The tribunal commenced its work with some urgency. The warrant for the tribunal was issued on 22 December, and it held its first meeting the following day, examining witnesses between 27 January and 15 May 1939. The GSR proposed a much slimmed down rail network much resembling today's. The majority report was dated 11 August 1939.[5]

The deliberations of the tribunal and the drafting of its report coincided almost exactly with the last nine months of peacetime. This caused a hiatus in relationships between the GSR and the government which in turn prevented the development of an effective Emergency plan in the last few months of peace. Just as the work of the tribunal prevented preparation for war, the outbreak of war precluded there being sufficient time and space at a policy-making level to implement the tribunal's recommendations, which included rejection of the railway companies' demand for further restriction on the use of private lorries and radical changes in the governance structures of the GSR with the number of directors being reduced to two, to be joined by an executive chairman and two controllers appointed by the government. The report of the tribunal lay unpublished for over a year, thus increasing the air of uncertainty.

The book does not deal in detail with the operations of the GNR in Éire. There are a number of reasons for this, not least of which is space. To deal solely with the GNR in Éire would unnaturally divide an institution which

criss-crossed the border and which since partition operated as an international entity. The alternative would have been to include the railways of
Northern Ireland, which would have made the project impractical in terms
of size and the sources available. Additionally, my use of their records
would lead me to believe that GNR management was economical with
what they committed to paper, and that many of the key files may not have
survived. One file which does not survive is entitled 'Jim crow rule –
request by American forces for special trains for black soldiers'. The
reader should keep in mind that the circumstances described in the book
were not as severe in the area served by the GNR – basically the
Dublin–Belfast mainline and the counties of Louth, Meath, Cavan,
Monaghan and Donegal.

My interest in this subject was aroused when the files of the general
manager of the GSR arrived in the Irish Railway Record Society (IRRS)
archives in Heuston station in the year 2000. This accession of over 200
boxes records every detail of the running of the railway company between
1937 and 1950. In addition to matters of high policy, they also detail
seemingly minor incidents which shine a light into other areas, be they the
lighting of Ennistymon station for the round-the-clock loading of
phosphates mined in Clare or the claims for expenses by locomotive
drivers away from home for long periods. These files made it possible to
write the PhD thesis on which this book is based, and compensated for the
dearth of surviving records of the Department of Industry and Commerce
dealing with railway companies or the Department of Supplies dealing
with coal imports.

One author describes the Emergency as one of the most under-
researched areas of modern Irish history.[6] And, it could be argued, the
economic aspect of the period is one of the most under-researched areas
within the Emergency. Most published work has concentrated on security
and high politics. The British official history of the Second World War, civil
series, written in the 1950s and '60s, contains sporadic references to Éire
and deals at length with food and fuel, but there is little written from the
Irish side. On the subject of railway operation, while there is an immense
literature on the steam locomotive, much of it is written for the enthusiast
market and contains little of use to the historian. However, the IRRS library
holds many contemporary technical works on the steam locomotive,
together with the *Railway Gazette*, the international journal of record of the
railway profession, which gave global coverage to railway operations.

One theme that emerges from the book is that Ireland's experience as a
neutral country was not unique. Anglo-Irish trade relations can be

compared with relations between Germany and Switzerland and between Germany and Sweden. In terms of railway operation we can see parallels between the contrasting experience of railway companies in Éire and Northern Ireland and those in neutral Argentina and belligerent Brazil.

Much of the narrative in this book may be set in a remote historical time, yet many of the issues raised have a current relevance. The problems facing the GSR in the 1930s were similar to those facing Iarnród Éireann in the 1990s: a network falling into decay, sporadic and patchy purchases of new equipment, an insufficiency of shareholder funds even for maintenance and ambivalence on the part of government as to what size of rail network was required. The Emergency years were the last period in the twentieth century when the Irish rail network suffered capacity constraints. The issue of capacity returned again for the company from about 2000 with all the challenges posed by rapid growth in an organisation accustomed only to cutbacks.

The relevance of this work has only become fully apparent in the period after September 2008 when the Irish government was faced with a delinquent corporate sector in the form of the banks. Whatever the failings of the GSR, they surely pale into insignificance when compared to the recent behaviour of the Irish banks and those tasked with regulating them.

Notes:

1 Clair Wills, *That Neutral Island* (London, 2007), p.2.
2 W.N. Medlicott, *The Economic Blockade, Vol. 1* (London, 1959), p.185.
3 CIÉ Arch MGWR Book 39, Minute of meeting 1 February 1921. For a brief biography of Geddes see Michael R. Bonavia, *The Organisation of British Railways* (London, 1971), p.119.
4 *Dáil Debates*, vol. 73, cols 1401, 1402, 7 December 1938.
5 *Tribunal of Enquiry into Public Transport Report, 1939* (Dublin, 1939, p4866), p.118.
6 R.M. Douglas, *Architects of the Resurrection* (Manchester, 2009), p.3.

1

Fuel Supply and Crew Skill

To the casual observer the first reaction to a cutting off of coal supplies might be to ask: 'Why didn't they use turf or Irish coal?' This chapter describes the close relationships between the Welsh coalfields and the Irish railway companies. This relationship made sense from a cost and efficiency perspective. Just as low oil prices have deterred investment in alternative energy technology since the first oil shock of the 1970s, the low cost and high quality of Welsh steam coal deterred experiments with alternatives. Welsh coal was part of the corporate culture of the GSR. It was a low-cost premium fuel and attempts with experimentation would have met resistance throughout the organisation, not least from loco-motive crew whose skill is a key, if neglected, element of the efficient operation of the steam locomotive.

From the foundation of the state, the railway companies were encouraged to use Irish fuels, and these pressures intensified after the accession of Fianna Fáil to power in 1932. One of the first battlefronts in the Anglo-Irish economic war was the coal trade but experiments with German, Polish and Irish coal by the Irish railway companies proved unsuccessful. The Emergency saw a re-run of some of the economic war experiments. It also witnessed the use of turf as locomotive fuel, which had been tried sporadically since the middle of the nineteenth century. This chapter argues that the experience of the GSR during the Emergency can only be fully understood in the context of its experience during the economic war. The chapter also examines one of the most important aspects of the operation of the steam locomotive – the skill of the crew.

The railway companies were Ireland's largest single coal importers, accounting for about 10 per cent of consumption.[1] The fuel was bought from coalfields on the west coast of Britain. The Belfast and County Down Railway (BCDR) purchased from Cumberland, while the GNR purchased from west Scotland (mainly Ayrshire) and South Wales.[2] The Great Southern and Western Railway (GS&WR) imported exclusively from South Wales and based an engineer in Newport to liaise with the coal producers.[3] Coal ranges in quality from lignite at the lower end, through bituminous coals to anthracite. The valleys of South Wales became renowned for their high-quality steam coal which fuelled railway locomotives and steamships.

Welsh steam coal was so rich in energy and low in ash that it outsold, even in Virginia, the product of America's great Pennsylvania field. It made the valleys north of Cardiff and Swansea the equivalent of today's Saudi Arabia with locomotives and 15 ton trucks standing in for pipelines.[4]

Coal was a key commodity in Anglo-Irish trade and in Irish economic discourse, as is illustrated by Dean Swift's comment that one should burn everything English except their coal. Sir Robert Kane's *Industrial Resources of Ireland*, published in 1845, gave a view of the coal resources of Ireland described by Cormac Ó Gráda[5] as 'over sanguine'. Laurence Kettle, home rule activist and engineer, in his evidence before the Coal Industry Committee of 1919 stated that 'the system of government under which this country has been labouring for the last century has been responsible for the failure to develop the Irish coalfields.'[6] Arthur Griffith asserted that coal deposits in Counties Antrim and Down remained unexploited because the Londonderrys were safeguarding their Durham coal interests.[7] The Irish coalfields that were exploited consisted of the Leinster coalfield, which produced anthracite, and the Connaught coalfield, centred on Arigna, which produced low-grade bituminous coal. These deposits were developed during the First World War when new railways were constructed at public expense to Arigna, County Roscommon, Castlecomer, County Kilkenny and Wolfhill, County Laois.[8]

Irish coal was seen through rose-tinted spectacles by its advocates. In 1908 an article in the *Journal of the Statistical and Social Inquiry Society* asserted that the Cavan and Leitrim Railway burned Arigna coal and achieved results equal to that of the best Welsh steam coal.[9] No statistical evidence was given for this statement and its veracity is open to question, as is seen by the company's experience during the First World War[10] when it reported to the Department of Transport that 'in comparison with the 77 lbs per mile used... working with Arigna coal, the same engine using Welsh on the same line is 47.5 lbs per mile.'[11]

At the 1919 enquiry into the Irish coal industry the railway companies were criticised for their reluctance to use Irish coal. A representative of the Castlecomer Colliery Company and a member of the committee said that the GS&WR had indicated in 1913 that it would adapt locomotives to burn anthracite if guaranteed a sufficient supply, but had failed to honour this commitment.[12] E.A. Watson responded on behalf of the company that 'Irish coal has been tried on this railway by practically all engineers since the line opened.'[13] Irish railway companies found Irish coal either unsuitable, in the case of anthracite, or of too low a quality, in the case of Arigna coal. The Irish coal industry prospered best in the disrupted trade of wartime, an experience it shared with Sweden, whose coalfields 'flourished during three short periods when there have been blockades: the Napoleonic war... the First World War... and the Second World War'[14] and of Switzerland, whose Riedhof mine was closed in 1921, to be reopened between 1942 and 1947.[15]

Steam coal has a 'high calorific power... [which enables the] rapid generation of steam'.[16] It is therefore ideal for a narrow locomotive firebox constrained by the width between the wheels. Boilers found in factories or ships are free from this constraint and can therefore burn lower grades of coal. Locomotives were designed around the coal that was to be consumed. In 1901, the New Zealand railways sought a locomotive capable of burning low-grade lignite. Their order went to the US builder Baldwin because the use of low-quality coal 'was far better understood in Philadelphia than it was in Glasgow – or in Lille or Berlin for that matter'.[17] At the other end of the quality scale, anthracite was used by a number of US railroads in purposely designed locomotives.[18] However, as the US anthracite mining industry was wholly owned by railway companies these locomotives were a testament to the integration of mining and railway companies rather than to the suitability of anthracite as a locomotive fuel. GSR locomotives were designed to burn Welsh coal, which was both cheap and plentiful in the buyers' market of the 1920s and 30s, and especially after the rout of the miners' union in the 1926 general strike.

Table 2 GS & WR and GSR contract price per ton of steam coal

1915	1921	1922	1923	1924	1925	1926	1927	1928
23/-	53/-	25/-	27/6	27/-	24/6	20/-	19/-	17/6

Source: GSWR Sec 3288a 'Steam Coal Supplies'

The global reach of Welsh steam coal is attested to by the statement of the chairman of the Central Argentine Railway that while 'they had co-operated with government efforts to burn maize... from the company's point of view coal from South Wales was pre eminent.'[19]

The Saorstát government strongly urged the railway companies to use Arigna coal, and the GNR carried out some tests in 1923.[20] When Welsh coal was substituted for Arigna coal on the Cavan and Leitrim Railway on its absorption into the GSR in 1924, coal consumption dropped by 20 per cent.[21] The district superintendent observed that 'Arigna steam coal is not able to impart sufficient heat to maintain a uniform supply of steam.'[22] In 1925 J.R. Bazin, the chief mechanical engineer of the GSR, urged that tests be progressed, as 'the general manager is being strongly pressed by the Ministry on the subject.'[23] In 1928 the GSR board decided against resuming use of Arigna coal despite a mine owner's threat to stop using rail transport.[24] The locomotive foreman in Ballinamore wrote: 'I could continue for a month renouncing (sic) the unsuitability of Arigna coal for locomotive steaming purposes . . . I sincerely hope that it will not again be seen on this section.'[25]

Total coal costs were a combination of the pithead price, the transport cost and the amount of coal burned to do a given amount of work. The cost advantage inherent in Arigna's proximity to the railway was negated by poor quality. In 1926 when Arigna coal was delivered to the railway it was 40 per cent cheaper than Welsh coal.[26]

When Fianna Fáil came to power in 1932 one of the first battlefronts in the Anglo-Irish economic war was the coal trade. A five shilling per ton duty was imposed on British coal, new suppliers were sought in Germany and Poland, and Irish mines were encouraged to increase production. Seán Lemass, minister for industry and commerce, told the Dáil that 'the [railway] company has estimated that the additional cost involved, if duty were paid on the whole of its requirements of coal, would be approximately £52,000 per annum. I have, however, no reason to believe that the company cannot obtain adequate supplies of suitable coal from new sources such as Germany and Poland.'[27] The new government was attempting to change longstanding trading arrangements and this upset both Irish railway companies and UK coal producers.

Measures to promote the use of indigenous coal were unexceptional in inter-war Europe. Coal was a globalised product in the years before the First World War but ceased to be so as countries developed their own mining industries in the face of wartime shortages. Received wisdom that native coal deposits were not viable was sometimes proved fallacious, as in the case of Brazil in 1938.[28] Britain lost market share both globally and in Europe. As the Dutch sought to reduce their reliance on imported coal, 'output rose from a mere 1.9 million tons in 1913 to 10.9 million tons in 1938'.[29] In 1927, the Spanish government restricted the importation of coal; the use of Spanish coal was made obligatory in companies assisted by the state through protective laws or concessions. Selected Spanish industries were allowed to import a proportion of their needs, with railway companies allowed to import 10 per cent of their requirements or 15 per cent if express trains were run.[30]

The economic war affected the Irish railway companies in a number of ways. The decline in Anglo-Irish trade caused an immediate reduction in railway traffic. The lucrative cattle traffic to ports such as Dublin, Rosslare and Greenore plummeted. By August 1933 GSR merchandise receipts had fallen by 17.98 per cent and livestock receipts by 31.15 per cent compared with the same period the previous year, January to August 1932.[31] The transport tribunal considered that 'depression in trade from 1930 and the late dispute with Great Britain have adversely affected the traffic of the company . . . their effect on goods traffic and in particular in livestock was serious.'[32] Faced with this fall in receipts, the GSR and GNR, unenthusiastic about fuel experiments at the best of times, were particularly unmoved by the enforced use of German or Polish coal. While the GNR was ostensibly more co-operative with government policy, in February 1934, W.H. Morton, general manager of the GSR, wrote: 'While the company is most anxious to facilitate the wishes of the minister as far as possible, it is a matter for regret that the products of the Saorstát coalfields cannot be used without serious detriment to our locomotives and . . . punctuality.' He hoped that the department would not press a course that would 'merely accentuate the heavy disabilities which we already endure from the enforced use of German coal'.[33]

Another effect of the economic war was renewed government pressure on the railway companies to use Arigna coal,[34] and both companies again tested Arigna coal in these years. The GSR tests were conducted in July and August 1933 and March 1934 on special test trains accompanied by a government inspector. The results showed increased fuel consumption, poor locomotive performance and a failure to adhere to specification, the ash content of 16 per cent being twice the maximum specified.[35] In September 1933, the government indicated that it would allow the companies to purchase 85 per cent of their requirements duty free, provided they bought the balance from Arigna.[36] The GNR undertook more exhaustive tests in November 1933 on pairs of scheduled service trains using the same locomotive. One train was fuelled with a blend of 15 per cent Arigna combined with 85 per cent Welsh, while the other was allocated Welsh coal for comparison. The GNR chief mechanical engineer reported that, balancing the lower quality of Arigna coal with the duties payable on British coal, 'by using 15 per cent Arigna coal the company would be in no worse position than they are at present.' He suggested that a figure of 10 per cent should be used in negotiations with the government, noting that it would be impossible for Arigna to supply 15 per cent of the requirements of the two big railway companies. The contradictory results of tests undertaken by the companies must have been obvious to the government, with the GSR claiming the coal was unsuitable while the GNR accepting that Arigna coal could be blended with British coal. On 20 November, the GSR passed to the GNR their draft letter to the government declining their offer. However, the following day Morton rang the GNR and indicated that the GSR policy might change, as 'last week they had several serious delays on the line owing to the use of German coal and if this continued it may necessitate their being driven to take advantage of the minister's offer much as they disliked the scheme.'[37]

A similar episode occurred in 1938, when the Portuguese railways placed a large coal order in Germany. The chagrin of the Cardiff coal exporters at this intrusion on their traditional market got little sympathy from the British embassy in Lisbon, which reported that:

> [The Railway Company]... is the largest single importer with requirements of 250,000 tons per annum, and the order of 127,000 tons was the largest ever given to a German firm... the Cardiff exporters were incensed at the idea that the [Portuguese railways] should place an order in Germany and... showed such resentment and were so unaccommodating that the mines dept of the Board of Trade agreed with me that the matter was not well handled. The only reason the Portuguese Railway bought German coal was that it was two shillings per ton cheaper than Cardiff coal. It proved to be of satisfactory quality and deliveries were per agreement.[38]

The substitution of German for British coal was therefore possible, but seemingly not for the GSR. More than two decades later, John Reihill, a coal importer, wrote to C.S. Andrews, then chairman of CIÉ:

> As far back as 1932 I played a certain part in bringing over to Ireland the Head Engineer of the Westphalian coal syndicate in order successfully to prove to the Southern Railways Engineers... that their assertion that the old Great Southern Engines, having been constructed to consume medium volatile Welsh steam coal [could not burn any other type]... it was quite a problem for us to give any satisfactory explanation... as to how it was the locomotives of the Irish Railways were the only ones in existence where no satisfactory results whatever could be achieved [with German coal].[39]

Reihill was not a naive enthusiast for native coal, but a businessman experienced in the coal business with a knowledge of coal similar to that possessed by railway managers.

On 16 March 1934 an agreement was reached which allowed the railway companies to import 75 per cent of their total requirements duty free from Britain provided they ordered 5 per cent of their requirements from Arigna. The Department of Industry and Commerce accepted that 'inability [by Arigna] to supply substantially to sample would be regarded as inability to supply for the purpose of the offer.' Germany and Poland were confined to 20 per cent of the market and the original government objective of weaning the railway companies onto a diet of German and Polish coal was shelved. George Howden of the GNR wrote: 'The use of Arigna coal...was agreed to merely as a means whereby the company could obtain as much coal as possible free of the emergency duty.'[40]

Deirdre McMahon has written: 'On 19 December [1934] J.H. Thomas, Dominions Secretary, reported to the cabinet that the...Great Southern Railway had cancelled its German coal contract as had the Board of Works ...Thomas wrote that this was the most gratifying behind the scenes gesture yet made.'[41] In January 1935 *The Economist* reported: 'The Irish Free State agrees to take all its coal from the UK in future,' and added that an increase in exports from South Wales was anticipated due to the agreement.[42] This agreement was referred to as the coal–cattle pact and was facilitated by John Dulanty, Irish high commissioner in London, who played on the British fear that the Irish would instead conclude a pact with Germany. The agreement of March 1934 between the government and the two railway companies was a precursor to the coal–cattle pact which in turn is regarded as a precursor to the Anglo-Irish trade agreement of 1938 which ended the economic war. These agreements confirmed the supremacy of British coal in Ireland and of Welsh coal on the GSR.

This was a victory for the railway companies, at least in the short term. It remained so as long as supplies of British coal remained available in the quantity and quality required. Greater perseverance with German coal might have left the GSR more adaptable in the face of the decline in coal quality that occurred from 1941. The reluctance of the GSR to conform to government wishes and use German, Polish or Irish coal did not endear them to a government waging a trade war. This attitude was clearly conveyed in September 1936 when the Department of Industry and Commerce wrote to the GSR – again on the issue of Arigna coal: 'The present request, which involves the employment of several hundred men in a rural area, is one which [can be reasonably pressed] on your company

... particularly on the grounds that various steps have been taken by the government which have tended to promote the interests of your company.'[43]

Only in the 1860s did steam coal become available at a price that made other options uneconomic as locomotive fuel. Up to that point locomotives used coal, coke or timber. Turf was tried in Ireland as early as August 1848, when the Midland Great Western Railway ordered 'a boatload of black turf for the new engine'.[44] In 1862 the Belfast and Northern Counties Railway carried out an experiment burning turf, with seemingly impressive results. According to the *Newry Telegraph*, the engine performed well 'with superior turf'. The GS&WR also carried out experiments with turf between 1873 and about 1877, establishing an experimental turf works at Mountrath, County Laois. The locomotive engineer Alexander McDonnell corresponded with his counterpart in the Bavarian railways on the use of turf in locomotives.[45] Many of these reports refer to the need for superior quality turf, readily available in experimental quantities but less so in quantities sufficient for widespread daily use. As Ó Gráda points out, the issue of heat per cubic metre as well as variability must be taken into account when comparing turf with coal, giving a ratio of between 4 and 5 tons of turf to 1 ton of coal.[46] In 1950 the *Journal of the Irish Railway Record Society* commented: 'From time to time over the last hundred years . . . a number of experiments have been made though it seems that in the majority of cases all that was done was to fill the tender with turf and hope for the best.'[47]

As a steam locomotive increases speed it produces increased exhaust and, in a process known as the Stephenson cycle, draws a greater amount of air through the fire, thus increasing its heat and producing more steam. This can become a vicious cycle with turf. Being much lighter than coal, turf can be drawn unburned through the boiler tubes as the draught increases, with consequent high risk of fire.[48] However, between 1940 and '41, a number of highly publicised turf-burning experiments were carried out by the GNR. These faltered on the issue of a sufficient supply of quality turf, and also demonstrated that turf was not feasible as a locomotive fuel without adapting locomotives in a way that made it impossible to burn coal. These experiments originated in 1938 when the Turf Development Board (TDB) sought to alert the railway companies to the possibilities of turf as locomotive fuel. They secured the interest of the GNR, whose general manager, G.B. Howden, sought a grant no greater than £1,000 to pursue experiments and wrote:

I do not think the use of peat in crude form is economically possible . . . difficulties, but nevertheless I think the matter could and should be disposed of once and for all by means of a simple experiment at a cost not exceeding £20 ... the use of peat ... is only economically ... possible ... when producing gas which would be used in the locomotive boiler.[49]

In a memo to the Department of Finance, C.S. Andrews succinctly stated the problem: 'Is there any form of apparatus suitable for use on a rail locomotive that would eliminate the carrying of huge quantities of turf in the bunkers and also cut out the stoking which turf involves?' While unenthusiastic about Howden's proposal, the department felt that, given the commitment of the GNR, 'it is doubtful if we would be in a strong position if we were to refuse sanction for the experiment.'[50] The grant was sanctioned in July 1939 and the GNR recruited a scientist named T. Bratt, who had worked in the Lullymore briquette factory.[51] Bratt's remit expanded beyond turf and he established a laboratory in Dundalk works which became particularly useful as Emergency shortages became more critical.[52]

In July 1940 a locomotive was modified to burn turf; experiments proceeded in an erratic manner and were suspended later in the year due to a shortage of suitable turf.[53] Resuming in February 1941 before coal shortages became severe, they were described as successful by the *Irish Press*, which quoted Bratt as saying:

If we could get compressed turf you might say that you have a perfectly adequate substitute for coal ... its water content is 10% compared with 3 to 4% in the case of coal and 30–35% in the case of machine cut unpressed turf ... Given plenty of compressed turf I can visualise the Irish railways run on it.[54]

This statement was ambiguous – perhaps deliberately so. The compressed turf referred to was high-quality machine-harvested turf available only from one or two bogs. Procuring turf of this quality in sufficient quantities to run a railway would prove impossible. The reporting of the GNR tests fostered the common misconception that ordinary sod turf was a usable locomotive fuel. The problem was exacerbated by de Valera telling the Dáil: 'We have the trains. The trains want coal, but they can be adapted ... it has been done in the North for the use of turf if we have it in sufficient quantities.'[55] De Valera mistakenly stated that the GNR tests were carried out in Northern Ireland; they were conducted in Dundalk with a view to the use of turf in Éire.

These positive reports from the GNR placed the GSR in a bad light by comparison. On 10 February 1941 Edgar Bredin, chief mechanical engineer of the GSR,[56] addressed the Engineering and Scientific Association of Ireland on the subject of 'The steam propelled locomotive and other forms of railway traction'.[57] Bredin was then at the height of his professional reputation, his 800 class locomotives having been introduced to critical acclaim. The *Railway Gazette* described the 'striking perform-ance of the new Irish locomotives' and wrote: 'Mr Bredin is to be congratulated on the exceptional competence which is being displayed in the performance of his new design.'[58] In the course of his address, Bredin made a number of points which, unbeknown to him, would give hostages to fortune in the hard times ahead. 'Under normal circumstances, Irish anthracite coal and peat could not in their unprocessed state compete economically with steam coal,' he said. 'We must also go further away for our oil fuel than for coal and the future of oil supplies at any time is by no means as secure as that of coal.' Bredin's speech was shortly afterwards described as 'unscientific anti-national blether' in *Irish Industry*, which drew attention to the different approaches of the GNR and GSR on the use of turf.[59] However, in reality the differences between the two companies were of emphasis rather than substance. For Bratt the glass was half full, as we have seen, while for Bredin it was half empty. However, this difference exposed the GSR to accusations of being out of sympathy with government policy at a crucial time.

By March 1941 the GNR experiments had come to a standstill due to a lack of the high-quality turf requested from bogs at Lyracrompane, County Kerry or Turraun, County Offaly. The Turf Development Board suggested that Donegal turf – available on a rail line served by the GNR – should be used,[60] and in July 1941 tests of Donegal turf were carried out. The locomotive inspector reported on 3 July that turf was mixed with slack coal, with 'excellent steaming results'. On 14 July he reported: 'The rate of firing is still high … I doubt it would be possible for a fireman to deal with the amount of work required … if turf had to be adopted as a fuel, substantial extension in timing would be necessary and loads kept within reasonable limits … using a mixture of coal and turf appears to be a more feasible proposition.'[61]

The GSR started to use turf in autumn 1941 as an emergency measure. In late September station masters were instructed to seek out sellers, as 'It might be desirable in view of the low prices to purchase substantial quantities of turf … for future use, including locomotives if necessary.' In October 1941 instructions were issued that turf was to be used on all branch line trains, in the ratio of two-thirds turf to one-third coal. In January 1942, Andrews wrote to Bredin requesting information on the quantity of turf used in GSR locomotives which he had promised some time previously to Hugo Flinn, parliamentary secretary to the minister for finance with responsibility for turf supply. Bredin was embarrassed by this delay and wrote to M.J. Ginnety, the running superintendent: 'Since October last I have been pressing you to make the fullest possible use of turf in locomotives... Please let me know what instructions you issued to your district superintendents, foremen etc. regarding the use of turf in locomotives, and as to whether or not such instructions were carried out.' Ginnety replied that 'Turf is not being used exclusively but has been used to a substantial extent augmented by coal.' Using turf in combination with coal alleviated some of the day-to-day train-running problems, but it did not facilitate the widespread import substitution desired by the government.

In January 1942 the stores superintendent informed Bredin that it had been impossible to procure turf for four west Cork branch lines 'as the only offers received were for a comparatively small quantity at a very high price'. Despite these emerging shortages, on 19 February Andrews offered the GSR up to 4,000 tons of turf per week for locomotive use. A plan to increase consumption from 300 to 3,849 tons per week was drawn up and submitted by Bredin on 10 March.[62] Transporting this amount of turf from the bogs to the locomotive depots would use turf for locomotive fuel and wagons, thus denying these scarce resources to other traffics such as the transport of turf for domestic consumption. This issue was in Flinn's mind as early as October 1941, enunciated in a conversation with Bratt: 'His primary consideration was the movement of the largest possible quantity of turf... to the centres of population in the south.'[63]

In March 1942 the GSR sought turf briquettes from the TDB and received 50 tons. Tests were carried out on 11 June on a Cork goods train. The results showed a fuel consumption of 107 lbs per mile (compared to around 40 lbs for good steam coal).[64] A second tender was needed to cater for the increased volume of fuel, which in everyday use would have required a second fireman. The result of the test was inconclusive and the remaining briquettes were mixed with low-grade coal. However, shortly afterwards the exercise became academic when the government allocated the entire output of briquettes to 'the poorer classes of Dublin'.

In summer 1942 the government intensified efforts to persuade the GSR to use more turf. In June, Hugo Flinn sent a report to de Valera outlining the lack of progress on the issue. The report was written by J.V. Candy, a

senior engineer in the OPW in charge of turf transport, and Flinn
commented: 'I have no evidence that any progress...has been made by
the Great Southern Railway in relation to the use of turf for locomotives.'[65]
Candy's report described a visit to Dundalk by himself and Bredin where
they...

> ...discussed mechanical stoking apparatus and problem of open
> firedoors. Travelled on footplate of special train with six coaches
> from Dundalk to Drogheda. [Locomotive] running wholly on turf.
> Hand stoking was continuous, got 30 mph average speed.[66]

This speed compared to an average of 45 mph with normal coal, which
meant using turf would require the slackening of timetables, as was done
in Sweden in the same period when timber was used as locomotive fuel.[67]
The use of a mechanical stoker might have alleviated the problems caused
by the need for continuous firing, but development work being undertaken
in Dundalk had to be abandoned due to lack of materials.[68] Candy's report
described a meeting with Reynolds: 'Progress [had been] slow in the last
year but since he had taken over he had been pressing his people [on] the
prime necessity of making the maximum possible use of other fuels.'
Bredin then joined the meeting and the three men discussed a range of
alternative fuels including turf, producer gas, oil and liquefied tar. Candy
reported that 'the briquetting of slack for the use of locomotives is being
pushed ahead by the GSR...107 tons of slack had been made into
briquettes the previous day.'[69] By June 1942 coal briquettes emerged as the
most promising alternative fuel as second-hand briquette plants (discussed
in Chapter 8) moved into production. Compared with turf, coal briquettes
had the advantage that the supply of raw material was non-seasonal, the
fuel could be stored outdoors with less danger of rain damage and no
modifications were required to locomotives.

By November 1942 the government realised that turf could not
simultaneously be a mass domestic fuel and a locomotive fuel. On 20
November Flinn reported to de Valera that 'a new buyer had come into the
market in the person of the GSR [who] were demanding an amount of turf
which, while small, was sufficient to disturb the market.' A TDB memo
showing that GSR purchases had raised prices by between 8 and 25 per cent
recommended that matters should be allowed to run their course for the 1942
season but that the company should be asked to review its policy in the 1943
season.[70] On 15 December 1942 a meeting was held involving the GSR, fuel
importers and the Special Employment Schemes office with a view to

'devising some method of eliminating competition', and on 18 January Bredin told those responsible for the purchase of turf to inform sellers that from 1 February the GSR would not pay more than fuel importers' rates.[71] The GSR's average weekly consumption of turf fell from 2,000 to 400 tons between the last week in December 1942 and the first week in February 1943. During the same period fuel consumption per mile fell by 27 per cent while fuel costs per mile fell by 17 per cent.[72] In November 1943 the sale of some reserve stocks was considered, but abandoned when a stocktake revealed a shortfall of 5,000 tons or 40 per cent of total stock. The deficiency was attributed to natural shrinkage, deficiencies in stock control and 'the disposition on the part of unscrupulous traders to supply turf with a high water content'.[73] These discrepancies may be due to the desperate situation of late 1941, when 'the locomotive fuel position made the physical possession of the turf the first consideration if services were to be maintained',[74] and to the fact that no procedures existed for managing the purchase or issue of turf before late August 1942, and then only at the insistence of the chairman.[75] Turf was adopted by the GSR in summer 1941 as a desperate measure, but in late 1942 C.S. Andrews, who had initiated the turf-burning experiments in 1938, wrote the memorandum which caused the virtual end of turf as a locomotive fuel.

In late February 1944 the Department of Supplies requested that the GSR should test turf briquettes in locomotives. A test was conducted, and Bredin reported to the department that while satisfactory for lighting fires, the costs and limited stocks available would not warrant depleting stocks. This changed when the Electricity Supply Board (ESB) coal allocation was cut to nil in late April. The dry spring of 1944 caused Shannon water levels to fall, which placed increased demands on Dublin's Pigeon House power station. Both railway companies received the entire output of Lullymore factory and transferred 4 tons of coal to the ESB in exchange for each 5 tons of briquettes received.[76] The GNR sought the approval of the British Ministry of Fuel and Power for the proposal, and it was approved, subject to 'the maintenance of railway services for cattle and various products for export to GB or NI'.[77] The exchange programme operated between June and October, and initially the turf briquettes were used to supplement locomotive coal. In July the TDB requested the railway companies to test the performance of turf briquettes used alone as a locomotive fuel.[78] The result of both sets of tests was similar. The GNR inspector reported that:

> The test engine steamed well and that while fuel consumption increased by 32.8% compared to the inferior coal then in use. The

steaming qualities of briquettes were much better and would involve less labour in its use. I have no hesitation in recommending this fuel.[79]

Such favourable comments were edited out of the final reports submitted to the TDB by senior management and problems with briquettes were stressed.[80] This can be seen in a draft of a report to the TDB, edited in Bredin's hand (see Figure 1).

Any positive aspects of the use of turf were, as can be seen, either toned down or edited out. Such responses were probably based on a fear that excessively optimistic reports would result in the enforced use of turf briquettes, on the lines of experience with Arigna coal during the economic war. As the GNR locomotive inspector noted in 1941: 'Using a mixture of coal and turf seems to be the most feasible proposition.'[81]

In the Dáil on 20 April 1944 Seán Lemass demonstrated the evolution of public policy on the use of turf as locomotive fuel:

Most of our railway engines are not designed to make the best use of turf. Nevertheless they could be operated with turf but it is a completely false idea that we are likely to have a surplus of turf and could divert it to railway use ... In fact the railway company some time ago proposed to purchase a very substantial quantity of turf ... we had to stop them from doing it because what they were proposing to purchase was required ... for the domestic ration.[82]

While in 1941 turf was seen as a panacea for all the problems arising from the fuel emergency, after five years' experience it was clear that while turf was freely available, quality turf was a scarce resource which had to be allocated to priority users. In September 1946 the Department of Industry and Commerce ordered CIÉ not to resume the use of turf in locomotives as weather conditions had made harvesting difficult and 'the requirements of the domestic consumers have not been met.'[83]

Bredin reflected on the turf-burning experiment late in 1945 in correspondence with Laurence Kettle:

Early in the emergency we fitted up a locomotive for experimental purposes for burning turf, the only important alteration made was to open the exhaust orifice in the smokebox in order to reduce the draught on the fire ... The results show that the engine's capacity was very considerably reduced and it could only handle light loads, the

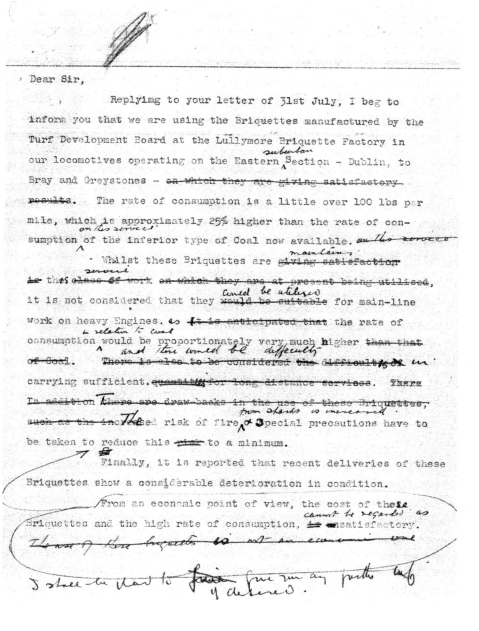

Figure 2: A report on the use of turf in locomotives from 1944, heavily edited by E.C. Bredin.

(courtesy of IRRS)

reasons for this are of course obvious. Locomotive boilers are designed to operate on good Welsh coal ... at maximum capacity the rate of firing is in the region of 90 lbs per square foot per hour. On the relative calorific value of turf the rate of firing ... would be 200 lbs per hour and in volume would mean at least five times as much turf as coal and it is simply an impossibility to handle such a volume of turf into the firebox and to burn it at this rate ... Special arrangements are necessary in the construction of turf-fired boilers ... to utilise the 'long flame' product of combustion. A practical illustration of this fact is that the paint on the smokeboxes of our locomotives using turf to any appreciable extent clearly indicating the high temperature of the gases leaving the boiler. The only other matter of interest to you is the use of Lullymore briquettes in locomotives. These briquettes gave very good results on suburban work as the frequent stops enabled the fire to be replenished. It was not practicable to adjust the locomotives in any way as due to the varying supplies of coal and briquettes the locomotive burning briquettes today might have to run on coal tomorrow. Of course the use of briquettes was far from economic as a large proportion of the heat generated passed up the chimney.[84]

In 1946 CIÉ reported to the World Fuel Congress that turf had:

A very high moisture content (varying between 28 and 40 per cent) and its bulk density made it difficult to carry sufficient for a journey: [varying] between 70 and 120 cubic feet per ton compared with coal at approximately 40 cubic feet per ton ... the calorific value varied over a wide range, 7,000 to 14,000 British Thermal Units. The exhaust blast had to be reduced very considerably or a large proportion [of the fire] was drawn through the chimney as sparks. In one experiment the fire was entirely eliminated.[85]

Trials with turf-burning locomotives undertaken by CIÉ between 1951 and '56 showed that the successful resolution of these problems would require a radical redesign of the conventional steam locomotive.

The skill of the crew is almost as critical to the efficient operation of a steam locomotive as the quality of the fuel. However, crew skill was rarely examined in the professional railway press. Two papers on this theme appeared in the *Journal of the Institution of Locomotive Engineers* during the 1930s and 40s. A manager on the Central Argentine Railway wrote 'The handling and consumption of coal' in 1938, while 'Low grade fuel in Indian locomotive practice' appeared in 1942.[86] These are the only two contributions on low-quality fuel to be found in the major locomotive engineering professional journal and they both come from the periphery rather than the centre of British locomotive practice. Notably, low-grade coal was not used in mainstream British or Irish locomotive practice, although it was used in the broader colonial sphere of influence (which included the British-owned railways of South America). This theoretical vacuum was addressed by C. Case, who wrote regarding the firing of locomotives that:

> In no branch of railway work are such vast sums expended under conditions of use so difficult to control... due to the nature of their work the men concerned are working without supervision... Everybody in the business knows how a locomotive should be fired and handled... but just how to impart that knowledge to the engine-men and what is more to see that they apply it is a different matter.[87]

In Britain and Ireland there was no formal period of apprenticeship for locomotive drivers. Young men were recruited as cleaners and were, in time, promoted to firemen and then drivers. While acting promotions could be made after a year's service, the time needed for a cleaner to become a proficient driver of passenger trains was estimated at five years – equivalent to a normal apprenticeship.[88] As early as 1877, self-help works were offering advice to aspiring drivers and firemen as to how to carry out their work in an efficient and safe manner.[89] Such publications abounded until the end of steam traction in the 1960s. Multiple copies of such works survive in the library of the Irish Railway Record Society. Some bear the signatures of individual drivers, others the stamp of company libraries in Inchicore or Cork, or the London-based Locomotive College.

This system of informal training contrasted with that of continental Europe where the driver was often a time-served engineering worker and the fireman was classified as semi-skilled, who rarely progressed to driving.[90] Some French drivers had previously been skilled fitters,[91] and in Germany most vacancies for locomotive drivers were filled from the skilled trades.[92] This allowed German railways to issue precise locomotive handling instructions.[93] In the 1930s, the Argentine government regulated training for locomotive crews[94] in partnership with the companies and the locomotive crew union, La Fradernidade.[95] The informal training systems of British and Irish railway companies made it more difficult for these companies to develop a high-skilled locomotive workforce and to promote good practice among locomotive crews. The payment of coal consumption bonuses promoted fuel economy, but these disappeared in Britain and Ireland with the national agreement of 1919,[96] as did the practice of each driver having his own locomotive. This latter practice 'caused drivers and their firemen [to take] a personal interest in their locomotives. When the system was abandoned this resulted in a loss of interest on the part of the running staff in the condition of the locomotives.'[97] During the 1920s and '30s, the GNR made efforts to encourage higher driving and firing standards. The company fitted out a mobile training centre in a converted coach which contained instructional models of locomotives and key components,[98] and also posted illustrated material on correct methods of driving and firing in locomotive sheds.[99] It also issued a textbook to each cleaner as he was passed for firing duties.[100] By contrast, GSR cleaners had to buy the book themselves, or borrow a copy from the company library.

Mutual improvement classes originated in Britain during 1920s, involving the attendance of enginemen at after-work classes where the tutors were their more senior colleagues, and by the 1940s a national federation of mutual improvement classes existed.[101] In 1943 the *Railway Gazette* described how savings of 10 per cent in coal consumption had been made through training programmes, which were 'a function of the mutual improvement class movement for which facilities were provided by the companies although the classes were managed by the men themselves'.[102] The London Midland and Scottish Railway (LMSR), in response to a complaint by the Associated Society of Locomotive Engineers and Firemen (ASLEF) on difficulties caused by bad coal, reported in early 1944 that 'The number of firing instructors has been increased in order to carry out a more extensive educational campaign... and this campaign is having a good effect.'[103]

Mutual improvement classes did not commence in Ireland until 1941. The first one was established in Dublin at the instigation of the National Union of Railwaymen, whose journal, the *Railway Review*, reported that 'it will come as a surprise... that mutual improvement classes are almost unknown... this has long been recognised by the Irish Office... [which] has paid for the construction of a wooden model of a locomotive valve gear.'[104] When the first Irish-based ASLEF organiser was appointed in 1942 he was struck by the relatively low level of technical skills in Ireland, and requested the establishment of the classes.[105] Val Horan describes how in Athlone, at the request of ASLEF, 'in 1943 lectures were started with a view to improving the mechanical knowledge of the footplate men; they were given... on one evening a week. The men were expected to attend in their own time.'[106] In both of these cases a newly arrived British union organiser was crucial in having classes established. While these classes raised skill standards, their voluntary nature would have weakened their effect compared to what could have been achieved in a systematic training programme. In addition, most research on the take-up of training shows that higher-skilled and higher-motivated workers will tend to take up training opportunities available, to the exclusion of their lower-skilled and less-motivated colleagues.

French railways made use of briquettes made from coal screenings from South Wales. Some good coal was used for passenger trains, with freight and shunting locomotives using varying mixtures of slack and low-grade coal.[107] A French locomotive driver referred to '*le prestigieux* Cardiff' as being reserved for express passenger locomotives.[108] In contrast, on railways within the British sphere of influence, all locomotives were fuelled with the same coal. Case describes how 'For many years the coal selected for use on the central Argentine railway was entirely of first grade locomotive Welsh... Some seven years ago a slightly cheaper [coal] was adopted and recently through [i.e. lower-quality] coal was added to the [purchasing] list.' Case went on to compare British and American practice as Argentine railways also used American-built locomotives, which unlike their British counterparts were not designed for high-grade coal. In the discussion on the paper one speaker said: 'With regard to design... the British designed locomotive looked as if designed for bad firing... with regard to the continental type... they had to be fired very light or they would not steam.' Another speaker said: 'In the United States most of the fuel was burnt with a thin fire, almost rubbish,' and that when they introduced through coal 'the firemen... had to carry a thinner fire.'[109] These discussions referred to the design of the firebox – narrow and between the frames as on a typical British or Irish locomotive or wide and carried on a set of trailing wheels as on a typical American-designed locomotive. The wider the firebox the greater the tolerance for low-grade coal. The papers by Case and da Costa[110] contain rare discussions on low-grade fuels with regard to British-designed locomotives, and of locomotive engineers in one area of locomotive practice discussing the practices in another area. They show the extent to which the British school of locomotive design relied on high quality and the absence of consideration of the challenges of inferior coal.

Comparing railway practices in Ireland with those in the other neutral countries poses some difficulties. We know that Portuguese railways used

both British and German coal from at least 1938, but there is no evidence
as to how this worked out in day-to-day operation. During the war Turkey
achieved a high level of import substitution in the area of coal. Sir Hugh
Knatchbull, the British ambassador, wrote that coal production in the
Zonguldak basin in central Turkey had been raised eightfold between 1942
and 1943, accounting for 77 per cent of Turkey's coal needs.[111] British
locomotives were exported to Turkey in 1942 accompanied by a
commissioning engineer, whose reports to headquarters give us a rare
glimpse of the use of low-grade coal in British locomotives as well as
showing a railway system where British and German practice co-existed.
In March 1942, Chacksfield wrote:

> Our first problems arose from the poor coal, which is practically all
> slack, of low calorific value, and the engines behaved most
> unsatisfactorily. I have carried out a large number of tests and found
> to my disappointment that no simple expedient exists...Now I have
> a shock for you...we were endeavouring to find just the right
> blastpipe diameter when we were summoned to Ankara...On our
> return we found that the [local] people had fitted the engine with...a
> permanent 'jimmy' of 12mm width. The works manager had already
> made a trip with this and reported very satisfactorily [on the results
> achieved] with this rather fearsome device. Incidentally we find that
> all the Turkish engines have permanent 'jimmies' – it is the standard!
> The Germans are up against the same thing on all the standard
> Prussian state and Reichsbahn types and the same measures had to be
> adopted. There is now no complaint of steaming and the Turkish
> people are well satisfied. So my feeling is that the best political
> outlook is to be satisfied too.[112]

This report shows that Turkish railways were accustomed to adapting
imported locomotives to cope with inferior-quality coal and highlights the
capacity of a railway in a country with inferior coal to successfully adapt
imported locomotives. The engineer also reports with evident surprise at
the everyday adoption of a jimmy, a device to modify the exhaust, which
improved locomotive performance at the price of higher fuel
consumption. This was considered a heinous crime in British practice, as
can be seen from a letter to ASLEF's *Locomotive Journal* of January 1941:
'Forty years ago there were many drivers who performed wonders...
aided by the use of that forbidden instrument known as james, jemmy or
jimmy. If any of my younger readers do not know what this is let him ask

one of the old brigade.'[113] One can well understand the surprise of a British engineer in finding this practice officially sanctioned.

Nationalist commentators denounced the predominance of British coal on Irish railways and deprecated the seemingly inconclusive experiments with Irish coal and turf. The fact remained that the high quality of Welsh coal made it cheaper to use than any Irish fuel. Any moves to substitute lower-quality coals were resisted by management on the grounds of cost and by locomotive crews on the grounds of ease of use. In 1911 the GS&WR bought Scottish and English coal during a dock strike,[114] and their chief mechanical engineer later wrote to his counterpart in the GNR that 'it is, as I am sure you found when you first started using Scotch coal, very difficult to convince the men that it is possible to use anything but Welsh.'[115] Using Welsh coal made financial sense for the GSR in the depressed inter-war coal market. The dependence of the GSR on Welsh coal, confirmed by the agreement of March 1934 and the Anglo-Irish trade agreement of 1938, meant that it had little experience of using lower-quality coal – unlike the GNR, which had been using Scotch coal for two decades, or the Argentine railways, who started to use low-grade coal in the 1930s.

The cases of Portugal and Turkey show that railway companies and their locomotive crews could adapt to the challenges of poorer coal. While no amount of technical knowledge or adaptability could have countered the sudden change in fuel quality which befell the GSR in 1941, a better training culture and experience of different coal types might have lessened the scale and duration of rail disruption experienced during the period. The GSR had been 'off message' on a key aspect of government policy during the economic war, in marked contrast to the GNR. The management of the GSR doubtlessly considered that they, as railway engineers (for they were mainly engineers), knew more about the efficient running of the railway than outsiders, no matter how well meaning their motives. The fact remained that the financial weakness of the GSR meant that it relied heavily on government goodwill. Such goodwill was rapidly draining away as 1941 drew to a close.

Notes

1   L.J. Kettle, 'Ireland's sources of power supply', *Studies*, no. 41 (1922), pp.61–75.
2   Great Northern Railway General Manager (hereafter GNRGM) 33/1113, 'Arigna coal', memorandum, 12 September 1933.
3   GS&WR Sec 3288a, 'Steam coal supplies', memorandum, 10 February 1921.
4   C. Harvie, *A Floating Commonwealth: Politics, Technology and Culture on Britain's Atlantic Coast, 1860–1930* (Oxford, 2008), p.69.

5   C. Ó Gráda, *Ireland: A New Economic History* (Oxford, 1994), p.319.
6   Irish Coal Industry Committee (hereafter ICIC), q.229.
7   P. Maume, *The Long Gestation: Irish Nationalist Life, 1891–1918* (Dublin, 1999), p.57.
8   S. Johnson, *Johnson's Atlas & Gazetteer of the Railways of Ireland* (Leicester, 1997), pp.98, 22, 120.
9   H.C. Geoghegan, 'A plea for Irish mines and minerals', *Journal of the Statistical and Social Inquiry Society of Ireland (JSSISI)*, 12, 83 (1908), p.155.
10 Irish Railway Record Society (hereafter IRRS) Cavan and Leitrim Railway (hereafter C&L) papers, circular letter, O'Brien to companies, 12 February 1920.
11 IRRS C&L papers, Shanks to Stewart, 11 May 1920.
12 ICIC q.1550, evidence of J.J Parkinson, colliery proprietor.
13 GS&WR Sec. 3288c, CME (chief mechanical engineer) to GSRGM, 1 March 1920.
14 S. Ollson, *German Coal and Swedish Fuel 1939–1945* (Goteborg, 1975), pp.66–7.
15 http://www.showcaves.com/english/ch/mines/Riedhof.html
16 R. H. Walters, *The Economic and Business History of the South Wales Steam Coal Industry* (New York, 1977), pp.3–4.
17 D. Ross, *The Willing Servant: A History of the Steam Locomotive* (Stroud, 2004), p.157.
18 C. McShane, *The Locomotive Up to Date* (Chicago, 1900), pp.428–9.
19 *Railway Gazette*, 28 November 1941, p.569.
20 GNRGM, 33/1113 'Arigna coal', report.
21 GSR unnumbered file, 'Arigna Coal', return of coal consumption, Cavan and Leitrim section, January to June 1924 and January to June 1925.
22 'Arigna Coal', running superintendent Athlone to Harty, 5 August 1924.
23 'Arigna Coal', Bazin to Harty, 8 November 1925.
24 GSWR Sec. 3288c Loco, Permanent Way and Works Committee minute, 21 December 1928.
25 'Arigna Coal', foreman Ballinamore to running superintendent Athlone, 11 November 1928.
26 'Arigna Coal', Bazin to Harty, 25 March, 26 May 1926.
27 *Dáil Debates*, vol. 44, col. 537, 27 October 1932.
28 F.D. McCann, *The Brazilian–American Alliance* (Princeton, 1973), p.194.
29 N. Buxton, *The Economic Development of the British Coal Industry* (London, 1978), p.168.
30 BNA, POWE 26/296, memo re. the Spanish coal trade, 15 November 1934.
31 Irish Railway Society, *Bulletin*, no. 1 (1933), p.198.
32 *Tribunal of Enquiry into Public Transport Report, 1939* (Dublin, 1939, p4866), pp.27, 32.
33 GNRGM 33/1113, Morton to Industry and Commerce, 9 February 1934.
34 P. Rigney, 'Report on Arigna coal mines 1942', *Breifne*, 10 (2002), p.513.
35 'Arigna Coal', report to board, 8 August 1933.
36 GNRGM 33/1113, Industry and Commerce to Howden, 12 Sept. 1933.
37 GNRGM 33/1113, CME report, 21 November 1933, draft GSR letter 20 November, note of phone message, 21 November 1933.
38 BNA, FO 371 22600, Arthur H. King, Lisbon to Anthony Eden, 12 January 1938.
39 CIÉGM 72839/44, Reihill to Andrews, 23 January 1960.
40 GNRGM 33/1113B, Howden to Stephens, 13 October 1936.
41 D. McMahon, *Republicans and Imperialists* (London, 1984), p.84.
42 *Economist*, 5 January 1935, p.7, 14 January 1935, p.119.
43 GNRGM 33/1113B, Maguire to Morton, 29 September 1936.
44 R.N. Clements, 'Turf-burning locomotives', *Journal of the Irish Railway Record Society (JIRRS)*, no. 7 (1950), p.64.
45 Ibid., pp.64–6.

46 Ó Gráda, *Economic History*, p.322.
47 *JIRRS*, news section, 7 (1950), p.60.
48 Ross, *Willing Servant*, pp.225–30. For warning on danger of sparks see GSR 1942 weekly circulars, passim.
49 National Archives (hereafter NA) Department of Finance (hereafter DF) 99/13/39, Howden to Andrews, 31 December 1938.
50 NA DF 99/13/39, Department of Finance memo, 27 March 1939.
51 Information re. Bratt from Jim Martin, BEng, retired Bórd na Móna engineer.
52 GNRGM 103/64, 'Salary T. Bratt, chemist, Dundalk', Bratt to Howden, 20 May 1943.
53 GNRGM 124/2, 'Turf for locomotive purposes', Bratt to McIntosh, 1 July 1940.
54 *Irish Press*, 5 February 1941.
55 *Dáil Debates*, vol. 82, col. 764, 14 March 1941.
56 E.C. Bredin, CME 1937–1942, general manager 1942–1945.
57 GSRGM file 48999 contains a copy of this paper.
58 *Railway Gazette*, 10 January 1941, p.42.
59 *Irish Industry*, 20 February 1941.
60 GNRGM 124/2, McIntosh to Lawlor, 22 March 1941.
61 Clements, 'Turf-burning locomotives', p.66.
62 GSRGM 50715/2, 'Use of turf in locomotives' contains this correspondence.
63 GNRGM 124/2, Bratt to McIntosh, 29 October 1941, Andrews to Howden, 11 November 1941.
64 GSRGM 50715/7, 'Use of Lullymore briquettes in locomotives', test report, 13 June 1941, Lawlor, TDB, to Bredin, 24 July 1942.
65 NA DT S12476, Flinn to Taoiseach, 11 June 1942.
66 NA DT S12476, Candy to Bredin, 22 May 1942.
67 *Railway Gazette*, 9 January 1942, p.43.
68 GSRGM 50715/7, 'Mechanical firing'.
69 NADT S12476, Candy to Flinn, 18 May 1942.
70 NA DT S12417B, Flinn to Taoiseach, 20 November 1942.
71 GSRGM 50715/2, minutes of meetings, 15 December 1942, 18 January 1943.
72 Figures extracted from weekly fuel returns in GSRGM 50715/2 and 50802.
73 GSRGM 50715/2, Hartnell Smith to Bredin, 17 November 1943.
74 Ibid.
75 GSRGM 50715/2, Bredin to Hartnell Smith, 20 August 1942, circular 21 August 1942.
76 GSRGM 50715/7, Bredin to Supplies, 3 March 1944, Murphy to Bredin, 1 July 1944.
77 GNRGM 114/15, 'Turf briquettes in Éire loco coal in lieu of', Howden to Supplies, 12 May 1944, Forsyth to Howden, 17 May 1944.
78 GSRGM 50715/7, Lawlor to Bredin, 31 July 1941.
79 GNRGM 114/15, McIntosh to Howden, 6 July 1944.
80 Ibid., Howden to TDB, 9 September 1944.
81 Ibid., Green to McIntosh, 14 July 1941.
82 *Dáil Debates*, vol. 93, col. 1347, 20 April 1944.
83 GSRGM 50715/2, Beere to Bredin, 25 September 1946.
84 GSRGM 65225, 'Use of turf in locomotives', Bredin to Kettle, 19 December 1945.
85 GSRGM 53960/10 'Briquetting: miscellaneous' contains this report.
86 C. Case, 'Handling and consumption of coal', *Journal of the Institution of Locomotive Engineers*, 143 (1938), pp.249–312, paper read before the South American Centre; J. da Costa, 'Low-grade fuel in Indian locomotive practice', *Journal of the Institute of Locomotive Engineers* (*JILE*), no. 166 (1942), pp.64–92, paper read before Indian and eastern centre.

87 Case, 'Handling', pp.265–6.
88 C. More, *Skill and the English Working Class, 1870–1914* (London, 1980), pp.143–4.
89 M. Reynolds, *Engine Driving Life* (London, 1877).
90 J. Tonnaire, *La Vapeur: Souvenirs d'un Mecano de Locomotive* (Paris, 1982), pp.23–4.
91 Ross, *Willing Servant*, p.13.
92 Dr -Ing. B. Schwarze, 'On the question of the methods followed in the training of staff, professional, technical and ordinary working grades', *Bulletin of the International Railway Congress Association*, XII, 4 (1930), p.1205.
93 D. Wardale, *The Red Devil and Other Tales from the Age of Steam* (Inverness, 1998), p.491.
94 Case, 'Handling', p.266.
95 *Railway Gazette*, 27 July 1945, p.99.
96 National Union of Railwaymen, *Irish Railway Agreements, 1919 to 1925* (London, 1925), pp.39–53.
97 South African Railways memo in Wardale, *Red Devil*, p.53. For this practice in Ireland see P.J. Currivan, 'Engineman's Son', *JIRRS*, 65 (1974), pp.263, 277. For France see E. Sauvage, *La Machine Locomotive* (Paris, 1918), pp.326, 328.
98 *Railway Gazette*, 16 September 1921, pp.434–5.
99 Information from P. McKeown, retired fitter GNR/ CIÉ / Iarnród Éireann (IÉ), 1945–1999.
100 IRRS Archives, GNR enginemens' record book, 1920–1960 recording transfers and promotions.
101 *Locomotive Journal* (January 1940), p.26.
102 *Railway Gazette*, 3 December 1943, p.559.
103 BNA RAIL 1172/2371, Royle, London Midland and Scottish Railway (hereafter LMSR) to Railway executive, 3 March 1944.
104 *Railway Review*, 7 February 1941.
105 Information from discussion with Val Horan.
106 V. Horan, 'Memories', *JIRRS*, 87 (1982), p.336.
107 W.H.B. Court, *History of the Second World War Coal* (London, 1951), p.83.
108 Tonnaire, *La Vapeur*, p.87.
109 Case, 'Handling'.
110 Da Costa, 'Low-grade fuel', p.67.
111 BNA FO 922/463B, Report by Hugh Knatchbull, 10 February 1943.
112 Chacksfield (Sivas, Turkey) to Sir William Stanier (Watford) 4 March 1942. Copy correspondence in possession of author. I am grateful to Tony Renehan of Iarnród Éireann for this reference.
113 *Locomotive Journal* (January 1941), p.12.
114 GSWR Sec. 971, 'Supply of steam coal seamen's strike', memo to board, 25 July 1911.
115 R.N. Clements, 'The locomotive exchange of 1911', *JIRRS*, 71 (1976), p.298.

2

Government Takeover

This chapter deals with the reorganisation of the relationship between government and the GSR. Although this reorganisation was ostensibly caused by the operational crisis due to bad coal, the situation was more complex. While the government priority was the movement of strategic goods such as turf and grain, the priority of the GSR seemed to be the more lucrative transport of passengers to race meetings and GAA matches. Compounding the bad relationship was the perceived abuse of the GSR monopoly as a result of petrol shortages, together with a dispute between the government and the GSR over an increase in bus fares. Faced with multiple crises and powerless under the Railway Acts to compel the GSR in the running of its business, the government dusted off the report of the transport tribunal which had been shelved since 1939, and used Emergency Powers legislation to partially implement it, taking control but not ownership of the GSR in the process. The GSR behaved – perhaps naively – as if peacetime rules still applied and in the ensuing power struggle proved no match for the state.

In Britain, the control of the railways in time of war was a given, and a shadow railway executive committee along the lines of that which had functioned between 1914 and 1918 was established in September 1938.[1] The British railway companies were brought under government control on 2 September 1939, and the government guaranteed to pay them a minimum sum of £40 million per annum. This arrangement was later criticised for its generosity by the Churchill government.[2]

War preparations took place later and on a much smaller scale in Ireland than in the UK. It was not until June 1939 that the supplies branch of the Irish Department of Industry and Commerce sought information from major firms on their stocks of essential supplies.[3] The Irish Banks Standing Committee was requested by the Department of Finance to consider low-interest loans to firms to accumulate supplies. The banks agreed to consider such requests sympathetically but declined to offer any reduction in interest rates. After the war the Department of Industry and Commerce observed caustically that 'it would have been no more difficult to organise credit in the years 1938 to 1940 than it was to organise shipping space in the years 1941 to 1944.'[4] In fact in July 1939 it was ordered that coal stocks should be run down 'as a matter of urgency to relieve the cash position' and stocks which stood at 3.45 weeks on 8 July fell to 2.5 weeks on 30 September. Just before the outbreak of war, the GSR sought the views of the Bank of Ireland on a government proposal that a year's supply of coal should be bought on overdraft at a cost of £3.6m. The bank replied three days later that the matter should be reconsidered in the light of control of supplies by the government.[5] Any large purchases by the GSR would have needed an overdraft. The overdraft required for a year's supply of coal was more than ten times the size of the overdraft eventually granted to the GSR.[6]

The GSR and GNR had widely diverging experiences of coal supply during the first year of the war. The GNR bought much of its coal in Scotland, where 'heavy demands for Scottish navigation coals for the bunkering of ships have created a shortage of these qualities for railway purchasers.'[7] On 26 June 1940 the GNR was advised that 20,000 tons of Welsh coal was available within a month, and decided to purchase the largest amount possible. In the period that followed, the GNR, the BCDR and the Northern Counties Committee (NCC) made a sustained and unsuccessful attempt to further build up their coal supplies. The vulnerability of the port of Belfast to bombing was advanced as a reason to build up stocks.[8] This argument did not get a sympathetic hearing from the Mines Department, which noted that the stock held by the GNR at that time was eight weeks, three weeks more than the stocks held by the British railway companies.

Bizarrely, during the first fifteen months of the war, the GNR which operated two thirds of its network in the UK, had more problems with its coal supply than the GSR, which operated exclusively in neutral territory. On 25 August 1939 the GNR indicated that attempts to obtain additional stocks were being frustrated by the British government commandeering vessels engaged in the Welsh coal trade and diverting coal for domestic use to areas scheduled to receive refugees.[9] The peculiar position of the GNR is reflected in its file on coal supplies. This contains correspondence between the company and the relevant departments in Dublin and Belfast together with Basil Brooke, Northern Ireland prime minister, and the general officer commanding (GOC) of British troops in Northern Ireland. When John Leydon (assistant secretary of the supplies branch of the Department of Industry and Commerce and later secretary of the

Department of Supplies) was informed of the GNR difficulties he expressed the opinion that no difficulties would arise, and advised against taking any action that would suggest difficulty. The GNR held three weeks' supply on 5 September 1939 but attempts to increase that stock level were restricted by difficulties in concluding a twelve-month contract 'owing to the coal arrangements between the British and Éire governments which also covered supplies for Northern Ireland'.

The GSR bought its coal on an annual contract which ran from June to May and continued to receive normal deliveries of coal until the expiry of its contract at the end of May 1941. After that date, as the price increased, low-quality coal constituted an increasing part of the GSR allocation. Much of this was termed 'duff' – dust and fine screenings which was shipped to continental Europe where it was used to manufacture coal briquettes for locomotives. The fall of France in June 1940 meant that Welsh coal destined for the continental market suddenly became available. The sheer volume of coal caused problems when 'in consequence of the capitulation of France a considerable number of wagons ... accumulated in the sidings and docks of South Wales. Some of the coal (2,920 wagons) consisted of duff which is not used in Great Britain in sufficient quantities to permit of supplies being disposed of through normal commercial channels. The remainder (approx. 24,000 wagons) could have been sold if sufficient transport was available.'[10] In February 1940 the GNR looked enviously at the coal supply of its southern neighbour. George Howden, the general manager, wrote:

> Mr Morton, GSR, phoned to say that their contract was for ... 20,000 tons per month. This contract does not expire until May of next year and up to the present deliveries have been carried out absolutely as stipulated. Mr Morton said that there were still 50,000 tons due to them and they had no reason to think that they would not be able to obtain delivery within the contract time. They had had no interference with supplies. Their present stock is equivalent to four weeks' consumption.

On 6 June 1940, Howden wrote to the Northern minister for finance that 'The Great Southern Railways obtain the whole of their supplies from South Wales and are experiencing no difficulties and it seems inexplicable that this company should be placed in the serious position in which it now finds itself.'[11] In the period immediately after Dunkirk, a large amount of coal suddenly became available on the spot market, and the GNR bought some of this through their agent, Kelly's. Both the GSR and the government were the subject of criticism later in the war, especially during the 1943 election, for not having stocked up in this period.[12] The directors of the Portuguese railways came in for similar criticism from their shareholders in 1943.[13] Two points arise in this context. Coal is a bulky material and its long-term storage presents difficulties from the point of view of deterioration in quality and spontaneous combustion. The GNR bought as much coal as it could store – to the point where storage became a problem[14] – yet they still needed to supplement their Éire allocation by removing coal from northern-based locomotives in southern depots. Secondly, in June 1940 the continuity of GSR coal supplies was assured through the company's regular contract with its Welsh suppliers. Foreseeing the problems which later arose would have required a level of foresight that was generally absent in the early years of the war.[15]

Under the terms of the 1938 Anglo-Irish trade agreement the coal trade between the two countries was negotiated centrally by a joint committee representative of the major Irish purchasers and the British producers. The stores superintendent of the GSR, J.P. Meadows, was a member of this committee, which gave the GSR access to British coal merchants at the highest level.[16] The Irish side of the committee was transformed into Coal Importers Limited on the outbreak of war. Negotiations on coal supplies for the Irish market for the 1940/1 coal year took place in Liverpool on 27 and 28 March 1940. J.P. Meadows reported on these discussions to the GSR board, and stated that the British government had taken complete control of the coal trade. Control was exercised through coal supplies officers in all districts and at all ports, who had the final say on the loading of each ship. Coal was allocated to the best advantage of the war effort, and coal producers had no jurisdiction over disposal of their product. Under the Anglo-French economic agreement of 1938, supplies to France and her colonies would be charged at the domestic rate, entailing an increased in price to the GSR from 22/- to 27/-. Meadows warned:

> The British Government will endeavour to maintain coal supplies to Éire, but . . . they cannot guarantee that coal in normal quantity will be available for our country . . . Britain is experiencing a very serious shortage of industrial coals and while our company has so far been fortunate in obtaining cargoes . . . it may happen at any time that no coal will be available for our ships when they arrive at Newport. Such an event will entail using up some of our small stock, now only four weeks' requirements unless consumption can be reduced by

curtailing train services on unremunerative branch lines or in some other way. The position ... already very serious, may become acute at any moment and I cannot too strongly recommend that all possible measures be adopted to conserve our existing stocks of coal.[17]

This warning to GSR management was discussed inconclusively at successive GSR chief officers' meetings. However, political and commercial forces combined to prevent the necessary decisions being taken. Cutting coal consumption meant curtailing operations. A general cutback was commercially unattractive, as petrol shortages had restored to the GSR the role of monopoly transport provider, lost in the decades after the First World War with the spread of road transport. The preferred option of the company was the politically sensitive one of closing branch lines in accordance with proposals made to the transport tribunal. The minutes of the chief officers' conferences of the GSR show the failure of the company to agree a method of conserving coal. The matter was discussed in April 1940 with the suggestion that some operating practices were leading to higher coal consumption, but no concrete decisions were taken.[18] At a meeting with Industry and Commerce on 25 June the company reported that coal stocks, which stood at six weeks, could be extended to eighteen weeks if the government imposed travel and transport priorities. The company sought suspension of its legal obligation to accept all freight traffic, the imposition of restrictions on its competitors and the suspension of union agreements that would lead to short time for train-operating staff and the layoff or dismissal of substantial numbers of maintenance and ancillary staff.[19] These proposals would have caused political difficulties for the government and some could have provoked strikes if adopted. In June 1940 the opportunity for an agreed approach between the GSR and the government to the conservation of coal slipped from the grasp of the parties. The matter was not discussed at the October chief officers' meeting, and by November the issue between the company and the government had shifted back to the closure of branch lines, a proposal being submitted for the closure of the entire west Cork system.[20] The government did not have power under the Railways Act 1924 to compel the GSR to act in the public interest. Such powers would require the use of emergency legislation – a matter that was contemplated by the government with reluctance. Thus in the last months of 1940, while there was still a possibility of building up coal stocks, the deadlock between company and government prevented any decision being taken.

In January 1941, eight months after Meadows' warning about potential coal shortages, a decision was taken to double the stock of coal to eight weeks' supply.[21] Implementing this decision was now impossible due to the British sanctions policy. In January 1941 the stock level was 6.75 weeks, but monthly deliveries were 6,000 tons less than the amount issued to locomotives. While such a shortfall might be sustainable in the short term due to shipping delays or strikes, a discrepancy of this magnitude was not sustainable in the long term.[22] Meadows reported to the February board meeting that increasing stocks to 40,000 tons would be a slow process.

> All boats entering the Bristol Channel are subject to Admiralty restrictions which... forbid them entering port after sunset. Mine sweeping... causes delays and [the] Channel is closed today to all shipping and a cargo loaded for us for Cork is held up there. Prior to the last few months each boat was able to deliver three cargos a fortnight but two cargos a fortnight is the usual working for each boat ... [a boat] will load 1,000 tons of briquettes which will be a valuable addition to our stock. A quantity of these briquettes is now available as they cannot be shipped to their usual markets in South America and other foreign countries.[23]

During February it was reported that 'the mixture of coals has had an effect on the timekeeping of trains the weights of which have considerably increased. Enginemen generally are handling their trains very creditably having regard to the various difficulties with which they have now to contend.'[24] Stocks had fallen to six weeks and were continuing to fall, due to the closing of the Bristol Channel for a week and disruption of rail traffic in South Wales. While some of these shipping delays were real, others would have served as a screen for the British sanctions policy.

In March 1941 the situation continued to deteriorate, with a report that 'with the various classes of coal now being supplied there is a considerable increase in the consumption by locomotives and under existing emergency conditions this cannot be avoided.' With any interruption to the quick turnaround of coal ships adversely affecting coal stocks, bad weather and the sinking of the SS *Castlehill* were blamed for the deficiencies.[25] In May it was simply reported that 'The quantity of coal supplied is not improving and this is reflected in time being lost with important trains.' Stocks of coal stood at five weeks.[26] After the termination of their 1940 coal contract, the situation deteriorated rapidly and by 17 July 1941 the stock level had fallen to 2.5 weeks, with a shortfall of between 4,000 and 6,000 tons a week. Meadows explained that the Northern Ireland railway companies, denied their normal Scottish coal, were being supplied from Wales, which would reduce the amount available to the GSR. He continued: 'Our supplies are rationed on a weekly basis [at] 3,600 tons per week. Efforts are being continued to have this figure increased, but owing to the uncertainty of the coal position in Britain . . . it may well happen that our weekly allocation will be reduced.'[27] The British policy of keeping their sanctions policy a secret, described in Chapter 4, was evidently successful.

The dwindling of coal stocks increased tensions between the GSR and the government. On 18 April 1941 John O'Brien, a principal officer in the Department of Industry and Commerce, wrote to Morton urging a reduction in (profitable) excursion traffic. Morton gave an undertaking that excursion trains would be discontinued.[28] However, on 25 September Leydon wrote to Morton advising him of discussions on continuity of supply with Norman Smith of the British Ministry of Mines. Leydon wrote:

> We do not feel satisfied that the position is fully appreciated by your company. The provision of special trains for Listowel races gave us a very bad shock. Having regard to your precarious position in the matter of coal supplies such an arrangement appears to us to have been utterly reckless and irresponsible. This particular incident . . . gives rise to a very uneasy feeling that the gravity of the position is not fully appreciated by your organisation.[29]

An annoyed Morton wrote to P.J. Floyd, the traffic manager, advising him of the undertaking given and asking him for an assurance in writing that 'the Gaelic Athletic Association and all other promoters who apply for special trains in future will be refused the facilities'.[30] Floyd naturally had close relationships with organisations that promoted mass travel, and was described by the racing correspondent of the *Irish Press* as a staunch friend of the industry.[31] However his provision of special trains for Listowel racegoers came at the cost of the GSR's credibility in government circles. The episode also demonstrated a weakness in managerial control with difficulty in securing the compliance of senior GSR management with policy directives.

The *Irish Press* and *Irish Independent* of 11 June carried the first reports that services would have to be cut in the face of dwindling supplies.[32] On 23 June the *Irish Press* reported that the export of coal from Britain had been suspended, save for gas and electricity undertakings. The *Cork Examiner* of the same day reported discontent in GAA circles over the lack of special trains to inter-county fixtures in the hurling and football championships. In the first week of July 1941 serious service cuts were announced with the withdrawal of the special trains for newspaper deliveries. On 23 July a further round of cuts was introduced, which *inter alia* reduced Dublin suburban trains to a peak hour service. On 30 July the *Irish Press* reported that turf had been tried and had been found reasonably satisfactory when mixed with coal. On 1 August Hartnell Smith, the GSR accountant, told the Irish Railway Wages Board that the company's stocks of coal had been running down since the previous November and that deliveries had been cut from 4,600 tons per week to 3,600 tons per week and surmised that the passenger train service would have to be reduced to one daily train each way between major centres.[33]

On 28 August Morton met Seán Lemass and John Leydon to discuss the worsening crisis and described how coal supplies had deteriorated in July and how ...

> ... during August, from the commencement of which deliveries have consisted mainly of 'smalls' and 'duff'... Engines stoked with... 'duff' are unable to maintain steam and frequently have to stop and relight fires on the road... due to the fact that [the coals]... fall through the ... firebars and choke the ashpan beneath, thus cutting off the draft... the suction of the blastpipe sucks the small pieces through the tubes... and considerable quantities are ejected through the chimney and scattered in red hot condition throughout the countryside... Efforts have been made to overcome these difficulties by mixing with turf... but the available supply of turf is very limited, and even when it can be obtained it does not prevent the small coal being sucked over it into the smokebox or percolating through the grates into the ashpans... We have endeavoured to [use coal] briquettes but find that the few briquette making plants in the country are almost fully engaged in making briquettes for domestic use.[34]

Morton reported to the September board meeting that Lemass had agreed to facilitate the company's requests for Castlecomer anthracite. It shows the desperation of railway management, as Castlecomer anthracite had been deemed by successive railway company representatives as unsuitable for locomotive use. However,

The minister intimated that he would require a further list of train reductions which would help to conserve the supply of coal for more essential services, that is grain harvest, turf transport and the beet season. It was the desire of the government that all unnecessary travel should be discouraged as far as possible.[35]

The government was prioritising the transport of goods while the GSR seemed to be prioritising the transport of passengers for leisure purposes. The phrase 'desire of the government' shows that those in power could advise or cajole but could not compel or direct a private company.

The coal supplied to the GSR would not burn, mainly because the draft in the firebox – estimated to have a speed of up to 260 mph, carried the fuel over the fire and out the chimney.[36] Additionally, the low quality of coal supplied caused locomotives to steam badly and significantly increased coal consumption. Tests carried out in Britain in the 1950s showed that a 20 per cent decrease in the calorific value of coal led to a 150 per cent increase in coal consumption.[37] The difficulties facing the GSR were described by Norman Smith in August 1941 when he reported on a visit to Inchicore. His visit...

... was not stage managed being arranged at less than one half hour's notice, and I saw one of the company's largest and most up to date locomotives return to the sheds after completion of a journey from Cork. I am no engineer but I think it would have made one of our express locomotive drivers weep if he had to run his engine on this type of coal... Many stories are circulating of the difficulties to which the use of this coal is giving rise. It is said that on the Friday previous to my visit five trains had left Dublin for the west to bring back turf. On Saturday they had not reached their destination and no one knew of their whereabouts!... In any case it seems rather anomalous that the Great Northern Railway which operates both in Northern Ireland and in Éire can obtain good coal for its trains running into Dublin whilst the Great Southern Railway has to make the best of poorer quality coal and duff. The Southern Railway officials were careful not to draw attention to this distinction but had they done so, I think I would have found difficulty in arguing that the Southern Railway's position was due to our shortage of supplies![38]

On 19 September the *Railway Gazette* outlined the latest round of cutbacks in the Dublin suburban services. Bray's fifty-four peacetime daily departures from Westland Row station were reduced to twenty-three.[39] The low point came in early October, as Bredin outlined to the Irish Railway Wages Board:

> When the board met on 1 August last the company had two weeks' supply of coal in reserve. This had on 6 October fallen to one day's supply, and were it not for the fact that the company received a supply of coal from Irish sources the rail services would have ceased to function. The company's coal reserves today represent approximately eight days' supply ... This figure I regret to say is the worst we have had since our complete collapse on 6 October ... Our difficulty today is not so much to get coal but to get ships. We have no ships to carry our coal at the moment and we are steadily losing ground.[40]

The people with the most intimate knowledge of locomotives are members of the locomotive crew. Martin White worked suburban trains to Bray during this period. He later described to the Irish Railway Record Society how:

> For the next few years the lot of the footplate staff was truly unenviable ... 'Baling out' became part of the footplate man's vocabulary ... this meant cleaning the fire sometimes after only five miles and lighting up again by timber from any available source ... I remember seeing almost every engine from Canal Street and Bray depots at a standstill in Dun Laoghaire station ... On the same night the foreman at Canal Street got the loan of two engines from the Great Northern ... to work the remaining trains and haul home the stranded locos and coaches from Dun Laoghaire.[41]

In October 1941 GNR suburban trains began to run through to GSR stations such as Westland Row and Dalkey while GSR trains started running through to Malahide.[42] The GNR covertly agreed to give the GSR 36 tons of coal per week. Bredin instructed Floyd that 'the Great Northern people are anxious that no comment whatsoever should be made to the press in regard to the question of coal supplies.'[43] The GNR coal came mainly from Northern Ireland stocks, with seven out of eight invoices showing Belfast as the point of origin.[44] The inter-working of trains provided some relief for the GSR at a very difficult time. Martin White describes the response of GSR locomotives to even a small supply of coal obtained from GNR locomotives as 'like doping a racehorse, the way our engines responded after such a chance'.[45] The inter-working ceased in May 1942 when Howden claimed that it was due to the depletion of the coal stocks of the GNR.[46]

The real reason was the increased vigilance of the Northern Ireland authorities. In 1941 the GNR was allowed to export 300 tons of coal a quarter from Northern Ireland to Éire. Later in the year the export of loco coal to Éire was prohibited. The company was asked to provide particulars of coal supplies which passed through Éire in transit via depots in Northern Ireland. The GNR informed the County Donegal Railway that they could no longer help them with coal. Locomotives based in Clones and Dundalk were frequent visitors to depots such as Portadown, Belfast or Enniskillen. This facilitated a thriving export trade of uncertain legality in coal as northern-based locomotives had some of their coal removed at southern depots. As this practice became known, the passage of coal across the border was closely monitored, and in spring 1942 the northern customs authorities complained that coal was being illegally exported on engines working to Clones.[47] Later in the year the British Ministry of Fuel and Power demonstrated its continuing vigilance regarding exports of coal on locomotives when it informed the company of its view that all Éire and cross-border supplies should be met entirely from coal imported from Britain to Éire. This clampdown by the British side had the desired effect, as can be seen in the complaint of the foreman in Clones that he had to draw on emergency stock but had not received regular replenishment.[48] On 21 August 1942 the locomotive foreman in Dublin wrote to the running superintendent in Belfast complaining about coal exports on locomotives: 'The position... is gradually becoming worse due to tenders not being filled to capacity... The small consignments of coal received in Dundalk in steamers which is being used in Dublin is of such poor quality that it would be almost impossible to use it if not mixed with a small percentage of good coal which can only be obtained from the tenders of cross border engines. I trust therefore that you will endeavour to effect some improvement.'[49] By the end of 1942 the GNR received a permit to export 300 tons of coal to Clones and Dundalk from dumps at Tynan, Newtonbutler and Goraghwood; the fact that it needed a permit shows that control had been re-asserted and that the lax export controls of 1941 had been tightened up.[50]

The day-to-day operation of the GSR during this period can be seen in works of fiction. Myles na gCopaleen (Brian Ó Nualláin) published an ingenious plan to maintain fuel services in his *Irish Times* Cruiskeen Lawn column: 'My plan is that all lines would be relaid to traverse bogland only and that the locomotives could be fitted with a patent scoop apparatus which would dig into the bog...and provide an endless stream of turf to the furnace...The principle is at present recognised in taking up water when the train is at speed.' The author noted the differing responses of the GSR and GNR to his proposal, with humour reflecting reality. Myles' later proposal 'not to banish steam but to banish coal' through an electrically heated shunting locomotive was a reference to a conversion undertaken by Swiss railways and illustrated in the *Railway Gazette*.[51] In his fictional treatment of Erwin Schrodinger's life in Ireland, Neil Belton describes a trip from Galway to Dublin:

> By the time it reached Athlone the train was crawling. It stopped at the station, barely making steam. A guard slid the door of the compartment open and shouted something about fuel...After two hours the whistle blew and the carriages were pulled slowly on across the flat plain but their progress was so hesitant that the constant frustrated expectation of an increase in speed exhausted him. He imagined the stoker [sic] raking and raking trying to get air up through the burning red mass in his firebox. Sinéad drowsed against the window. 'Burning duff,' she said quietly.[52]

Additional tensions between the GSR and the government arose when the GSR decided to increase bus fares to the maximum extent permissible under law with effect from 19 March 1941.[53] This decision provoked a disagreement with the GNR, with whom the GSR operated a cartel for bus services in counties Louth, Meath and Cavan. George Howden wrote

> Shortly after the outbreak of war your company proposed the policy of abolishing all...return fares and we agreed somewhat reluctantly to follow suit. The consequence unfortunately proved so serious that the policy had to be revised...in order to offset the alarming fall in gross receipts...I am therefore most reluctant to consider any change. I still consider that fares would be still further improved by revision downwards rather than upwards.[54]

A disagreement between two members of a cartel had the potential to be extremely embarrassing and Griffith, the GSR road passenger manager, wrote to Morton that 'I would suggest you having a conversation with Howden...This course would keep the subject out of further correspondence.' While publicity for the disagreement between the two railway companies would have been highly embarrassing for the GSR, there was little hope that such matters could be kept secret, given the small size of Dublin and the close relationship between GNR chairman, Lord Glenavy, and the Dublin political elite. The development of a culture of secrecy in dealing with government was potentially very dangerous for the GSR as the evasiveness of the company in one area might trip it up in another. This is shown in a memo from the accountant which stated:

> It is undesirable that any alterations of the omnibus department's accounts should be made... it will involve the Company in the risk that if the minister asks for the separate accounts of the road freight department... the alteration in the omnibus accounts will be discovered and make the minister suspect the bona fides of the company.[55]

The reservations expressed by the GNR about the effect of higher fares were raised with the GSR a week later by the Department of Industry and Commerce when seeking financial information on the increase. On 16 June 1941 the department asked the company to reconsider 'the increases [which] went far beyond the limit which would be justified by increased operation costs or which judicious management might dictate'. Griffith reacted in a bellicose manner and urged that:

> Owing to the attitude of the minister and the general trend of this correspondence I recommend we stand firm for the policy... until the apparent attempt to interfere with the company's... operation of its road passenger transport within the law is defeated.

In a conciliatory reply Morton wrote that 'the company is always prepared to meet the reasonable wishes of the minister [but] the company alone is best able to say whether the policy of increased fares is justified.' On 22 September the department observed that since the GSR had increased bus fares the three bus companies that had frozen or moderately increased fares had seen their revenue increase by between 10.9 per cent and 54.4 per cent while GSR bus revenues had fallen by 8.61 per cent. The department concluded that 'these facts supported the minister's contention that the increases have been made in an arbitrary and indiscriminate manner... and the interests of the public and the company would have been better served by a more moderate and equitable system of increases.' The bus fares controversy was yet another irritant in the relationships between the railway company and the government. Combined with a failure to put fuel-saving measures in place, controversies about the running of special trains, and a collapse in timetables, it showed a management that was seemingly incapable of running a vital public utility.

In the midst of the bus fares controversy, the report of the transport tribunal was published on 19 July 1941.[56] The majority report recommended raising the road tax on lorries to be paid into a fund that could be available to the GSR for the development of its road freight business. The report recommended against the further restrictions on road freight operators demanded by the railway companies. While Morton put a brave face on the report, its critique of management can have given him little comfort. The tribunal stated that while it discounted much of the criticism in relation to accusations of faulty organisation and waste, there was room for considerable improvement and 'diversity of opinion between certain of the departments has been allowed to interfere unduly with…that co-ordination which is essential to efficiency.'[57] In a clear indictment of the governance of the company the tribunal recommended that for a period of five years, instead of the business being carried on by seven part-time directors operating through a general manager, the board should consist of three directors, two of whom would act in a part-time capacity and would be elected by the shareholders while the remaining director who would be chairman would act in a full-time capacity and be nominated by the government. They would be assisted by two controllers with specialist and financial knowledge, who together with the chairman would be primarily responsible for the day-to-day administration of the company.[58]

These recommendations had been drafted in August 1939, and the problems of the GSR had worsened in the interim. Petrol shortages had re-established the company's virtual monopoly on land transport, and it had responded by abusing its bus customers and using its scarce coal allocation for the most profitable services rather than focusing on strategic operations. The GSR appeared arrogant, badly managed and insensitive to key national objectives. In contrast, the GNR provided a better rail service with the same low-quality fuel and gave the impression of being in tune with national policy objectives. However, implementing the tribunal's recommendations would have been difficult and complex and could have conflicted with the right to property contained in the new Constitution. A minister proposing such legislation could anticipate trenchant opposition from the management and directors of the GSR and extravagant demands for compensation from its shareholders.

Morton expressed his desire to retire as early as possible to the July board meeting, 'if possible no later than 30 September'.[59] His retirement arrangements were finalised at the September meeting. He was retained as a consultant by the company for an annual fee of £900; E.C. Bredin was given the title deputy general manager while M.J. Ginnety was appointed deputy chief mechanical engineer.[60] These arrangements became public on 13 October in the *Irish Press*. At the October board meeting, requests for retirement were received from Griffith, the road passenger manager, Woodley, the Cork divisional engineer, H.W. Crosthwaite, the company's materials inspector in Britain, and Reid and McNamara – senior clerical staff in the General Manager's Office.[61] Some at least of these retirements had been planned for a number of months. Morton sought service details for Crosthwaite on 31 May 1941 and on 16 June wrote to him assuring him that 'I do not wish in any way to hurry your retirement from the service...but it is clear that in the present emergency...there are overwhelming circumstances that prevent the general coal position being materially altered by the efforts of a company's officer.'[62] Crosthwaite was then 61 years of age and he was replaced by the 33–year-old Charles Johnston. Whether this action was a culling of dead wood or an attempt by Morton to 'look after' certain senior people before he retired is uncertain. However, for those who did not go voluntarily, on 2 January 1942 the board decided that 'the retirement of all salaried [and waged] staff shall be compulsory and automatic at the age of 65...from June 1942.'[63] This order took immediate effect, as the *Irish Press* outlined on 7 February 1942, and among its first victims were the company secretary, Coe, and P.J. Floyd, the traffic manager. Floyd's position carried responsibility for the lack of punctuality and for the misuse of scarce fuel on unnecessary excursion traffic. The *Irish Press* report concluded that 'further administrative changes in the company are expected in the near future.'

The days of the GSR as constituted in 1925 were numbered. Since the establishment of the state, successive attempts to mend its finances had failed. In September 1941 Hugo Flinn, TD, in a memo to the taoiseach, analysed the problems existing between the company and the state.

Pre-war the railway system had ceased to be capable of maintaining itself in normal times against the competition of alternative services ...the position of the railway system has essential residual functions to perform and that it is incapable of discharging them under free competition has been recognised by the state by means of:

(i) open and disguised subsidies;

(ii) legislation authorising them to eliminate statutory services which were unprofitable;

(iii) handing over to it of the most profitable road services...by discouraging legitimate alternative traffic services; and

(iv) by further legislation of an extreme character in the same direction as recommended in the recent tribunal of enquiry into public transport.

Flinn stated that the justification for any help given to the GSR should be judged by the service it gave to the state in the Emergency. He recommended that a controller of railways should be appointed, as proposed by the transport tribunal.[64] Flinn's suggestion that the tribunal's recommendations be implemented, at least in part, received an unfavourable reaction from Finance, being described as...

> ... altogether superfluous as there is no evidence that the GSR ... is not trying in every way to meet the wishes of the government. Whatever confusion exists is, I think, due largely to overlapping by Government Departments and semi government bodies like Comhlacht Siuicre Éireann. The latter wants priority for beet, Agriculture for wheat, Office of Public Works for turf, Industry & Commerce for raw materials and all make their claims on the railway company without any attempt at prior co-ordination. The priority order will...help to clear up this muddle though...we must endeavour to get some space for revenue producing goods such as beer, spirits, tobacco etc., which have value also in keeping out the cold when no fuel is available and have according to the best authorities certain therapeutic properties not lightly to be overlooked! The appointment of a controller over what is private property would certainly furnish the railway with a reasonable case for compensation on grounds of interference with private property. No court would sustain any objection we might have on national grounds to such a claim.[65]

Although the response is tinged with sarcasm it is probably a realistic estimate of what could be done without having recourse to emergency powers. It is nevertheless a strange response from a department to a suggestion from its own parliamentary secretary. Finance's pronouncements are not noted for humour or levity, and this combined with the references to the calorific value of alcohol would indicate that Finance did not rate Flinn's suggestion as likely to succeed.

This memo was written just before Emergency Powers Order 504 came into effect, according priority to certain freight traffic. Increased demand on the railway caused by the turf harvest (described in Chapter 5) made it necessary to set priorities. This order forbade the GSR from increasing any service above the level provided in November 1941 without the authority of the minister for industry and commerce. It prevented the company from serving lucrative markets such as race meetings and GAA matches at the expense of strategic freight traffic such as turf. Having taken control of such a major aspect of the company's business, Industry and Commerce seemed unenthusiastic about making further major changes in the administrative arrangements of the GSR. In December 1941 R.C. Ferguson, assistant secretary in the Department of Industry and Commerce, wrote to J.J. McElligott, secretary of the Department of Finance, that 'our relations with the railway companies are sufficiently complicated, without putting a further strain on them by taking a step [decontrol of road haulage for grain] which would be...a reversal of the general policy of the government...Only a drastic necessity...would justify such a step.'[66] Despite this desire by the department to maintain the status quo, relationships between the government and the GSR were about to change radically.

On 3 January 1942 a memorandum for government was submitted containing the bones of Flinn's proposal. This was certified as an emergency item for the cabinet meeting of 6 January by Seán Lemass on the basis that 'the position of railway transport generally calls for immediate action.' The memorandum for government stated that the management of the GSR required attention due to problems that had arisen out of, or been accentuated by, the Emergency. Seán Lemass wanted to implement certain of the transport tribunal's recommendations, though not necessarily in the exact form in which they were made. The sense of frustration felt at the behaviour of the GSR is encapsulated in a paragraph on the issue of the bus fares increase:

The company have been relieved...of competition from private motor cars. Instead of using this opportunity to the best advantage the company handled it in a manner immediately prejudicial to the interests of the community at large and ultimately harmful to its own best interests. Gross receipts from some services have actually declined. Despite continuous pressure from the responsible department the company has wholly failed to justify its policy in the matter of fares...In the opinion of the Minister there is little

likelihood of any improvement in the operations of the company as at
present administered. The administration, which was weak at the best
of times, in the opinion of the transport tribunal would not appear to
be competent to cope with the ... problems of the emergency ... The
present time appears to be particularly opportune for introducing
administrative changes on the lines recommended by the transport
tribunal in that the position of the general manager of the company is
officially vacant, the previous general manager being temporarily
retained by the board.[67]

The Department of Finance opposed the proposal on the basis that the
move was a first step towards the nationalisation of the railways (a prediction
which eventually proved to be true), that the taking over of a business would
expose the government to compensation claims and that the existing board of
the company should be given a chance to rectify the matter to the
government's satisfaction. The fourth reason is of interest, in that Finance
claimed that the justification for the step was insufficient as it ...

... could not ... be expected to effect any improvement in the existing
occupants of key positions nor would it enable ... difficulties due to
lack of coal fuel and rolling stock to be overcome. These difficulties
are mainly accountable for the delays ... in the handling of turf. The
carriage of beet is understood to be reasonably efficient and as
regards both turf and beet the road transport department is understood
to be satisfactory.[68]

If we take Ferguson's December letter with Finance's opposition it is fair
to infer that on the balance of probability the proposal to take control of
the GSR emerged from a political rather than a civil service source and
was developed in some haste, possibly over the 1941 Christmas holidays.
    The proposal was approved by the cabinet at its meeting of 9 January,
'it being understood that the appointment of the new general manager will
be subject to the approval of the minister'.[69] The failure of the GSR board
to act decisively to fill the vacancy caused by Morton's resignation left a
vacuum which the government moved to fill. Prior to the 1932 Transport
Act, a report on the GSR had stated that:

The history of the chiefs of British and Irish railways had been that
of their general managers and not of the unknown chairmen of their
board. In the GSR the chief executive officer though described as a

general manager has practically no powers. The undertaking is actually managed by directors or by a section of them who ... cannot possess a fraction of the practical training and experience ... necessary for reasonably efficient management.[70]

Leaving the post of general manager vacant less than a decade later opened for government the 'appalling vista' that the GSR would revert to control by directors rather than by professional managers. This was unacceptable in peacetime and unthinkable in wartime.

The cabinet decision was communicated to the GSR on 19 January and Lemass met the board on 28 January. No record survives of this meeting in the archives of either party, but a memo for government recorded that 'the representatives of the board said that their reaction was one of keen resentment [and asked] if the scheme was open for discussion ... The minister indicated that the government had taken a decision ... but any observations which might be offered would be taken into consideration.'[71] In a move that surprised the stock market, the directors recommended payment of arrears on 4 per cent preference stock for the three years 1938 to 1940. According to *The Irish Times* the market and the shareholders expected only two years.[72] At a further meeting on 13 February the directors unsuccessfully requested some form of compensation for carrying low-value, high-priority traffics such as turf. They did not, however, leave the meeting empty handed as Lemass agreed to increase the number of shareholder directors from two to four.[73] The arrangements for a quorum made the number of directors irrelevant as the chairman alone constituted a board quorum and no board meeting could proceed in his absence. These proposals were approved at the cabinet meeting of 17 January, with Lemass indicating on the emergency certificate that 'owing to the transport situation it is necessary that the reorganisation of the management of the company be brought about immediately.'[74]

Emergency Powers (no. 152) Order was signed on 17 February and came into effect a week later. An *Irish Press* report of 19 February 1942 predicted that A.P. (Percy) Reynolds, managing director of the Dublin United Transport Company, would be appointed by the government as chairman of the GSR to be assisted by two controllers with special expertise in engineering and accountancy. Percy Reynolds took up office unaided by controllers on 24 February 1942 on a salary of £2,500 per annum.[75] Although the GSR had not been nationalised, private control of the company had ended and an era of hybrid control had begun. This restructuring of management could not improve the quality of coal but it would institute – perhaps for the first time since the foundation of the state – a railway management structure which the government fully trusted. *The Irish Times* reported on 20 February that Reynolds had become a 'transport dictator' and that the government had, after a strong case was made by the directors, agreed to the retention of four of their number, although their role would be largely advisory. The report stated that the challenges facing Reynolds would be to secure improved efficiency which would ensure the continuity of fuel to the cities.[76]

An *Irish Independent* editorial of 20 February stated that the one good aspect of the affair was the appointment of Reynolds. It criticised the use of emergency legislation, noting that 'not in the lean years but as prosperity had begun to return had the government chosen to seize the shareholders' assets.' The other Dublin papers dwelt more on the national interest and less on those of the shareholders. The *Irish Times* leader expressed some surprise at the appointment of Reynolds, given his lack of railway experience, but stated that 'he emerged from the quiet of an accountant's office to become an extremely capable, far sighted and ambitious organiser of the city's transport services . . . if he contrives to inject into the GSR even one half of the efficiency which he injected into the DUTC his appointment will have been a signal success'. The editorial continued: 'The GSR system . . . is antiquated. It can be brought into line with the country's needs by . . . the relentless sacrifice of branch lines . . . Unless the new directorate has the mandate to carry out this reform its appointment will be without purpose.' It concluded: 'Last night's announcement represents the first and very long step towards the nationalisation of Irish railways.'[77] The *Irish Press* editorial of 23 February best captures the low esteem in which GSR management was held. It described the events of 1941 when . . .

> . . . a breakdown in Irish transport at the greatest crisis in its history . . . at that very moment when it was vital that native fuel should be rushed into the cities . . . the supplies of steam coal were found to be completely inadequate . . . All who are concerned with the national economy . . . will be immensely relieved that a private concern which practically lived by state aid, state subsidies, even state coal and yet failed the public is at last to be controlled in the interests of that public.

The Dublin correspondent of the *Connacht Sentinel* wrote that:

> He [Reynolds] has made a big success of the Dublin transport services and has made a big reputation for himself in the process . . . I

am told he was not anxious to assume control of the railways but that Mr Lemass pressed him strongly . . . Mr Reynolds has gone in much as a commissioner would go in to take control of the affairs of a public body . . . I do not believe that a board of directors elected by 'shareholders' will ever again control the railways . . . I believe that before the Emergency has ended the government will put through the Dáil a bill . . . on the lines of the emergency machinery now being operated by Mr Reynolds.[78]

The analogy of a commissioner going into a local authority is apt. Twelve local authorities were suspended between 1922 and 1942, with the honours equally shared by Cumann na nGaedheal and Fianna Fáil ministers.[79] Commissioners were installed when authorities were found delinquent in some manner and dissolved. Emergency legislation allowed the government to provide for the Emergency while preparing for the post-Emergency world. According to Myles na gCopaleen, who as Brian Ó Nualláin was an assistant principal officer in the Department of Local Government, the state could 'do anything from frying onions to squirting chocolate on a fly boy's yellow shirt under the emergency powers act'.[80]

While Reynolds' term of office was to expire at the termination of the Emergency, his appointment was at least in part motivated by longer-term strategic interests and aimed at resolving another emergency which had arisen in 1938, the prospect of a receiver being appointed to the GSR. The relationship between Percy Reynolds and Seán Lemass was a matter of speculation. At one point it was rumoured that Lemass kept a string of racehorses at the Curragh under Reynolds' name.[81] Reynolds lived in Abbeville, Kinsealy, and owned the Derby winner of 1941. Uinseann Mac Eoin (chronicler of the IRA in the 1930s) described Reynolds as 'head of a successful bus company – which was amalgamated to form the Dublin United Tramways which then became part of CIÉ. He was appointed head of CIÉ by Seán Lemass who was a racing buddy.'[82]

Percy Reynolds was also the son of John Reynolds, who was Seán Mac Diarmada's accountant and treasurer of the Irish Volunteers.[83] Bureau of Military History material shows that Percy Reynolds was active in the pre-1916 physical force nationalist movement, being adjutant of the youth movement Fianna Éireann until 1915.[84] He was also a member of the IRB circle within the Fianna which numbered Con Colbert, Seán Heuston and Liam Mellowes among its members.[85] He was active during Easter Week 1916[86] and was afterwards deported to Frongoch.[87] On his return he disappeared from sight in the nationalist movement, and did not figure in

the reorganisation of Fianna Éireann in 1917.[88] Given his political
background and his business experience Percy Reynolds seemed an
obvious choice to steer the GSR out of its crisis. Apart from his political
affinity with most of the members of the cabinet, he was a transport
manager with an established professional and national record. He was
relatively young by the standards of railway managers and the DUTC had
the reputation of being an efficient, well-run and profitable company, in
the process of converting from tram to bus operation. Reynolds was
appointed general manager of the DUTC in 1936 and co-opted to the
board of the company and appointed its managing director in April 1941.[89]
He was also, together with Morton, a member of the board of Aer Lingus.

Any change in ownership of the railway system exposed the taxpayer to
possible claims by Irish railway shareholders who enviously eyed the
generous arrangements made with the British railway companies in 1939.
At the shareholders' meeting of March 1942 Col. the O'Callaghan said:
'That in a sister isle...where government had taken control...a sum
[had] been put aside for shareholders.'[90] A cartoon from Myles na
gCopaleen's topical Cruiskeen Lawn column shows GSR shareholders
washing the company's dirty linen in public and comments as follows on
the capacity of railway shareholders for rent seeking: 'Same old boring
story as if anybody but themselves could be interested in their dividends.'[91]

The shareholders' protection association of the GNR demanded that the
state take control of Northern Ireland's railways on the same basis as in the
rest of the UK on the grounds that their shareholders 'were entitled to the
same consideration'.[92] By 1941 Irish railway shareholders on both sides of
the border were seeking government control of their enterprises on a basis
similar to that applying in Britain. A parallel case in Britain is the coal
industry. Both British coal and Irish railways had been in a dire financial
state since the 1920s following wartime control. Nationalisation of both
industries had long been a controversial aspect of politics. In both cases a
form of government control without ownership was instituted in 1942, and
nationalisation was undertaken by both states after the war.

The style of board meetings changed upon Reynolds' arrival.
Attendance at board meetings was confined to the directors and to the
company secretary, unlike in the previous dispensation where the heads of
function (locomotive, traffic stores, etc.) attended. Accounts of board
meeting became briefer, with ninety-three pages of minutes in the year
until February 1942, fifty-two pages in the year after and forty-two pages
in the year ended February 1944. The appointment of Reynolds was
swiftly followed by a number of appointments at middle management

level. These moves away from seniority-based promotion provoked protests from the Railway Clerks' Association about the passing over 'of clerks of long and unblemished service and experience by clerks with little more than half their service'.[93] Moving from seniority-based to merit-based promotion was a culture change that may in fact have been welcomed by younger and possibly better-educated RCA members. The transport tribunal had recommended that a means be found to recruit clerical staff at promotional level as well as at entry level, as was the case for engineers.[94]

Percy Reynolds took up his new tasks with a considerable store of public goodwill. He also took office at a time when initiatives that predated his arrival were just beginning to bear fruit. Foremost of these was the commissioning of the briquette machines which enabled the GSR to manufacture acceptable fuel from low-quality coal. Within months of his appointment the crisis in train punctuality ended, and further improvements came in the summer timetable. The retirements that followed Morton's departure gave him the ability to make key senior management appointments and he actively sought out new talent. Bredin's vacancy as chief mechanical engineer was filled on an acting basis by M.J. Ginnety. In April 1942 W.A. Smyth, a Broadstone-trained engineer working in the British aircraft industry, received a letter from Bredin inviting him to Dublin. On arrival Smyth was taken to see Reynolds, who asked him to return to Inchicore in a new post of deputy chief mechanical engineer and then to immediately begin a major reorganisation of the works, with a promise that he would succeed M.J. Ginnety when the latter retired in September 1943.[95] Smyth did not take up the offer and no-one else was recruited. The episode highlights Bredin's low opinion of Ginnety at a time when Emergency shortages were placing increasing demands on engineering capacity as well as showing Reynolds' involvement in the resolution of this problem.

In early 1942 the government took control of one of the largest commercial undertakings in the state through emergency legislation. Was it necessary to take this step in order to resolve the operational crisis of the GSR? The answer from an engineering point of view is probably not. It is difficult to distinguish measures taken as a result of Reynolds' arrival from experiments under way (such as briquetting of coal) that would have been undertaken in any event. However, organisations are about people as well as machines and large organisations need leadership if they are to function well. The failure by the board to act decisively to fill the vacancy caused by Morton's resignation left a leadership vacuum which after some months the government moved to fill. Apart from the operational considerations, the likely successor in normal times would have come from a British or colonial railway, which might have proved difficult in the circumstances of the Emergency.

Reynolds seems to have enjoyed a good relationship with Bredin, who retained most of the functions associated with the post of general manager. As well as preparing plans for a financial restructuring of the company, Reynolds took an active role in certain key areas such as the use of turf in locomotives, relations with the British Ministry of Fuel and Power, and the procurement of Irish coal. Reynolds' role as chairman was threefold: the first task was a tactical one – to bring an outside mind to the running of the company; the second was to manage relationships between the government and the main transport company in Emergency Ireland; while the third was to reorganise the GSR and bring a solution to the financial problems that had dogged the company since its foundation. This was a key strategic task and one attended with considerable urgency as the enabling legislation would lapse with the end of the Emergency. According to one commentator, '[Fianna Fáil] found it difficult to get people to believe in these projects or to find the right people to carry out the projects.'[96] The government needed a safe pair of hands to bring the GSR out of its operational crisis and lay the basis of a post-war transport policy. Percy Reynolds was just such a person and the emergency powers legislation the only way of imposing the managing director of one publicly quoted company as executive of another without the permission of either board of directors.

Notes

1   K. Hancock, Inland Transport (London, 1952), p.52.
2   Ibid., pp.124–9.
3   GNRGM 1023/19, 'Coal supplies', circular signed John Leydon.
4   National Archives (hereafter NA), 'Emergency Historical Record' (hereafter EHR), 2/3 p.3.
5   GSRGM 37917, 'Supplies of materials in the event of emergency' GSR–bank correspondence, 5, 8 September 1939.
6   GSRGM 37917, Johnston to Morton, 19 October 1939.
7   GNRGM 1023/19, Mines Department to War Office, 13 March 1941.
8   GNRGM 1023/19, Minnis (BCDR) to Pope (NCC), 4 April 1941.
9   GNRGM 1023/19, Irish Bank Standing Committee (hereafter IBSC) decision circular from Leydon 14 August 1939; Howden to Leydon, 25 August 1939.
10 BNA T160/1041, N. Smith to Biggs, 8 August 1941.
11 GNRGM 1023/19 contains this correspondence.
12 Dáil Debates, vol. 90, cols 500–4, 20 May 1943.

13 *Railway Gazette*, 17 September 1943, p.280.
14 GNR Adelaide file 40/2238, 'Banbridge: danger from ashes near emergency coal dump', district civil engineer to McIntosh, 2 December 1940.
15 See Note 11 above.
16 See Note 17 below.
17 GSRM 43737/2, 'European war supplies' contains a copy of this minute.
18 GSRM 43436, 'Chief Officers' Conference', meeting of 23/4 April 1940.
19 GSRM 43436, meeting of 26 June 1941.
20 GSRM 43436, minutes of October and November meetings.
21 Board minute 4796, 7 January 1941.
22 GSRM 47354, officers' report for December 1940 board meeting, p.4.
23 GSRM 47918, officers' report for January 1941 board meeting, p.6.
24 GSRM 48401, officers' report for February 1941 board meeting, pp.4–5.
25 GSRM 48802, officers' report for April 1941 board meeting, pp.3–4.
26 GSRM 49143, officers' report for May 1941 board meeting, pp.3–4.
27 GSRM 50163, officers' report for August 1941 board meeting, p.5.
28 GSRM 41876, 'Restrictions on excursion traffic', O'Brien to Morton, 18 April 1941, Morton to O'Brien, 23 April 1941.
29 GSRM 41876, Leydon to Morton, 25 September 1941.
30 GSRM 41876, Morton to Floyd, 26 September 1941.
31 *Irish Press*, 7 January 1941.
32 *Irish Press*, *Irish Independent*, 11 June, *Cork Examiner*, 12 June 1941.
33 Irish Railway Wages Board, *Proceedings*, 1 August 1941, pp.21–2.
34 GSRM 53960/10, 'Briquetting miscellaneous', Bredin to Morton, 26 August 1940.
35 GSRM 50349, officers' report for September 1941 board meeting, p.2.
36 *Railway Gazette*, 4 September 1942, p.216.
37 Wardale, *Red Devil*, p.503.
38 BNA T161/1402, minute of meeting 11 September 1941 contains this report.
39 *Railway Gazette*, 19 September 1941, p.295.
40 Irish Railway Wages Board, *Proceedings*, 14 November 1941, p.16.
41 M. White, 'Fifty years of a locoman's life', *JIRRS*, no. 32 (1966) p.266.
42 Prior to this all trains of both companies terminated in Amiens Street (Connolly).
43 GSRM 45932, 'Suburban service interworking with the GNR', Bredin to Ginnety, 21 October 1941, Bredin to Floyd, 24 October 1941.
44 GNRM 72/3, 'Through working GSR', copy invoices GNR to GSR, October 1941 to June 1942.
45 White, 'Locoman's life', p.267.
46 GSRM 45932, Howden to Bredin, 21 May 1942.
47 Louth County Archives, Mallon Collection, GNR mechanical engineer's letter index, 1941, p.63, file 41/259, p.65, file 41/260.
48 Mallon collection, letter index 1942, p.65, file 42/749, p.64, file 40/755.
49 GNR Adelaide files, 42/1868, Greene to Morrison, 12 August 1942.
50 GNR Adelaide files, 42/2236 'Loco coal', secretary to running superintendent, Dundalk, 24 December 1942.
51 K. O'Nolan (ed.), *The Best of Myles: A Selection from Cruiskeen Lawn* (Dublin, 1968), pp.114–16, 173; *Railway Gazette*, 4 June 1943, p.565.
52 N. Belton, *A Game with Sharpened Knives* (London, 2006), pp.253–4.
53 GSR Road transport committee, minute 735.
54 GSRM 48473/2, 'Pool area', Howden to Morton, 14 March 1941.
55 GSRM 48473/2, 'Increase in bus fares' contains this correspondence.

56 *Irish Independent*, 21 July 1941.
57 *Reports of the Tribunal of Enquiry on Public Transport, 1939* (Dublin, 1941, p.7634), p.61.
58 Ibid., p.83.
59 GSR board minute 4937, July 1940.
60 GSR board minute 4974, September 1940.
61 GSR board minute 4993, October 1940.
62 GSRM 50541, 'Retirement of HW Crosthwaite, material inspector', Hartnell Smith to Morton, 31 May 1941, Morton to Crosthwaite, 16 June 1941.
63 GSR board minute 5038, 2 January 1942.
64 NA, Department of An Taoiseach (hereafter DT) 12641, Flinn to de Valera, 7 November 1941.
65 NA, Department of Finance (hereafter FIN) s/99/64/41, minute sheet, 8 November 1941.
66 NA FIN 099/0019/41, Ferguson to McElligott, 1 December 1941.
67 NA DT S12684, memo for government, 3 January 1942.
68 NA DT S12684, finance memorandum, 5 January 1942.
69 NA DT S12684, cabinet minute, 9 January 1942.
70 D. Delaney, 'English and Irish railways', *JIRRS*, 112 (1990), p.240.
71 NA DT S12684, memo for government, 16 February 1942.
72 *Irish Times*, 7 February 1942.
73 NA DT S12684, memo, 16 February 1942.
74 NA DT S12684, teastas práinneach (Emergency certificate), 17 February 1942.
75 NA DT S12684, cabinet minute, 19 February 1942.
76 *Irish Times*, 20 February 1942.
77 Ibid.
78 *Connacht Sentinel*, 24 February 1942.
79 M. Daly, *The Buffer State: The Historical Roots of the Department of the Environment* (Dublin, 1997), p.297.
80 O'Nolan, *The Best of Myles*, p.322.
81 J. Horgan, *Seán Lemass: The Enigmatic Patriot* (Dublin, 1997), p.102.
82 http://ireland.archiseek.com/buildings_ireland/dublin/northcity/store_street/busaras/interview_maceoin.html
83 G. MacAtasney, *Seán Mac Diarmada: The Mind of the Revolution* (Manorhamilton, 2004), p.125.
84 BMH WS 191, Joseph Reynolds, WS 1377, Hugh McNeill, WS 646, William Christian.
85 BMH WS 8, Séamus McCaisin.
86 BMH WS 195, Molly Reynolds (sister).
87 *Sinn Féin Rebellion Handbook* (Dublin (*Irish Times*), 1917), p.79; S. O'Mahony, *Frongoch: University of Revolution* (Dublin, 1987), p.193.
88 My thanks are due to Eve Morrison for use of her database of BMH witness statements to identify statements of Dublin Fianna activists.
89 *Irish Times*, 26 April 1941.
90 *Irish Times*, 12 March 1942.
91 O'Nolan, *The Best of Myles*, p.135.
92 *Railway Gazette*, 30 January 1942, p.178.
93 *Irish Press*, 23 February 1942.
94 Such a recommendation was implemented in 2002.
95 W.A. Smyth, 'My service on Irish railways', JIRRS, 83 (1980), p.128.
96 Kevin O'Doherty, Centre for Contemporary History witness seminar, Trinity College Dublin, October 2003.

3

Coal Crisis: A Comparative Perspective

Slow trains and inferior coal are hallmarks of the collective memory of Ireland's Emergency experience. This collective memory appears to have been distorted in two ways. Firstly the experience of the period from summer 1941 to summer 1942 is applied to the Emergency period as a whole, when in fact what happened during that time was not representative. The second distortion is represented by the *Dublin Opinion* cartoon of a deserted railway station.[1] By contrast, the fact is that, in common with most wartime railways the Irish railway system was busier between 1939 and 1945 than in preceding or subsequent years. All across the world, wartime railway networks were saturated with freight traffic, while passenger trains were fewer in number, more crowded and less comfortable. Looking at GSR operations in a comparative framework gives a clearer view of how the railway actually performed and counteracts the myths that have been absorbed into the historical narrative.[2]

In March 1941, under the headline 'Unusual locomotive fuel substitutes', the *Railway Gazette* described how restrictions on coal distribution caused many countries to experiment with alternatives such as maize in Argentina, rushes in Astrakhan and turf in Ireland.[3] In 1943 the *Gazette* reported that 'one of the major wartime problems . . . throughout the world [was] the need to maintain essential services using native fuels.'[4] The experience of the GSR can best be understood by comparing it with the experiences of other railway companies, especially those in neutral countries such as Portugal, Argentina and Sweden.

In his work on Swedish–German wartime trade, Sven Ollson states that the countries of Europe could be divided into three categories: 'Surplus countries', which produced more coal than they consumed (Britain, Poland, Germany); 'deficit countries one', which needed imports for specialist purposes despite having a fairly large domestic production (France, Belgium, the Netherlands); and 'deficit countries two', which had a great need for imports and little or no domestic coal production (Italy,

Greece, the Scandinavian countries).[5] Applying this categorisation would place Ireland, Portugal and Switzerland in the deficit two category and Spain in deficit one. Britain exported locomotive coal to deficit one countries such as Spain and France and deficit two countries such as Ireland, Sweden and Portugal. Beyond Europe, Britain also supplied Argentina and Brazil as well as Egypt and Palestine. Ollson's categorisation needs to be treated with some caution as it measures coal rather than overall energy use, ignoring hydro-electricity in the case of Switzerland or indigenous timber in the case of Sweden. Ireland's proximity to Britain, the past political union between the two countries and the wide circulation of English newspapers in Ireland meant that Irish people tended to make comparisons with Britain rather than with mainland Europe where comparison would, in any event, have been impeded by language and censorship.

Compared to Ireland, coal quality was not a severe wartime problem for British railways. In 1944 ASLEF raised with the railway executive the difficulties being faced by their members in Britain. The most common complaint was the poor condition of locomotives rather than poor coal. The response from the Great Western Railway stated: 'This company in common with other users has had to accept a reduction of large coal and use in its place unscreened through coal and other substitute fuel [which we] will attempt to minimise by checking wagons.'[6] The LMSR replied that 'the quality of coal used on passenger services and important freight trains is of pre-war standard but it has been necessary to accept a certain proportion of coal of a lower grade quality for use on less important freight services.'[7] Coal supply was similarly unproblematic for the German railways until the very end of the war,[8] when in January 1945 it 'turned to using brown coal to power its locomotives. Brown coal fouled the fireboxes...and could ignite flammable cargo. Fuel consumption tripled, and this necessitated the use of a second fireman and a larger tender.'[9] This experience with lignite, which was superior to top-grade turf, gives an indication of how widespread turf burning might have been handled in Ireland.

The experience of the GSR can be placed in a broader context by analysing the *Railway Gazette* which was (and remains) the authoritative trade periodical for the rail industry. The *Gazette* was established in 1905 but its origins can be traced to the *Railway Magazine*, founded in 1835 at the dawn of the railway age. The *Gazette* prided itself as a journal of record, recording in 1945 that the Soviet authorities had in 1941 sent a forwarding address in the event of Moscow falling. From the account of its wartime activities published after censorship was lifted in 1945 and in its obituaries for prominent German railwaymen we can see how it valued its impartiality. In 1942, Fritz Todt was described as 'one of the most outstanding civil engineers produced by the Nazi regime and by reason of his transport achievements one of our most dangerous enemies'. In 1945 Julius Dorpmuller, head of the Reichsbahn since before 1933, was eulogised as 'the most outstanding railwayman on the European continent ... representative of the best features of the German character'.[10] Through a network of correspondents in neutral countries 'who ... continued to send us news by devious routes often at some risk to themselves' the *Railway Gazette* carried regular features on the operation of the railway system in areas under Axis control.[11] The scepticism that historians often apply to the wartime press due to censorship and planted stories may be discounted in the case of the *Gazette*, which was openly contemptuous of the Ministry of Economic Warfare. In October 1941 the *Gazette* wrote that:

> In these columns ... care has been taken to avoid a delusion fostered in some sections of the daily press that the enemy's transport system is unable to cope with the strain to which it is subjected ... the continental transport system is not creaking its way to breakdown as some would suggest.[12]

This contempt for the ministry was expressed more explicitly in June 1943 in a condemnation of the ...

> ... pitifully ill informed statements and ill judged deductions [which] continue to be made about enemy facilities. For nearly four years we have tried to explode [this] fallacy ... but the story continues to rear its head (usually with the assistance of the Ministry of Economic Warfare).[13]

The desire of the *Railway Gazette* to maintain a position as a journal of record makes it an authoritative source for historians.

Regarding alternatives to coal, generally speaking 'on the technical level, the Second World War started where the First World War left off.'[14] The continuity between 1919 and 1939 is most apparent in the continuing predominance of the coal-fired steam locomotive. Railway managers responded to coal shortages in the same way that they had during the 1914–18 war through discouragement of passenger travel, cuts in passenger train services, the withdrawal of dining and sleeping cars and the favouring of freight over passenger services. A significant difference between 1919 and 1939 was in the area of railway electrification, which had expanded in response to shortages of imported coal between 1914 and 1918. Countries that had undertaken extensive electrification in the inter-war period were best able to cope with shortages between 1939 and 1945. Both Italy and Switzerland had electrified some lines before 1914 using hydro-electricity but had deferred further electrification until technical issues including the choice of voltage and electrical standards were sorted out. The wartime coal shortages gave an incentive to resolve these issues. Between 1917 and 1918 the Italian railway system was almost paralysed due to coal shortages.[15] The *Railway Gazette* noted that train speeds had been reduced to as low as 10 mph due to low coal quality and that 'the dependence on foreign coal explains why the question of railway electrification had aroused such attention.'[16] In the immediate post-war years, companies that bordered on the Alps with their potential for hydro-electric power carried out electrification programmes. In Switzerland the Federal estimates for 1918 contained 20 million Swiss francs for electrification, which was widely demanded as 'one of the best measures of becoming independent of ... German coal',[17] where 'patriotic Swiss are pressing on with the electrification of their railways ... The Swiss would rather pay more and have the work done by their own workmen.'[18] A Swedish report, published in 1918,[19] recommended electrification to 'free the country from dependence on foreign supplies of fuel'.[20] In continental Europe, railway electrification was seen as a means of escape from dependence on imported fuel.

During the inter-war years, diesel-powered railcars were developed and became increasingly popular in Europe as an economical alternative to steam locomotives for light trains. In 1938 diesel railcars carried 17 per cent of the passenger traffic in France.[21] In Emergency Ireland diesel railcars allowed the County Donegal Railways – the cradle of diesel railcar development – to maintain a good level of service, while enabling the GNR to maintain its Dublin suburban schedules relatively unscathed. Alternatives to steam traction on the GSR focused on the development of battery-powered trains led by Professor Drumm of University College Dublin through a company bearing his name. This initiative came from a desire to develop to the full the potential of electricity from Ardnacrusha in County Clare, and was undertaken as an alternative to full electrification. With the benefit of hindsight it can be seen that battery traction was a technological dead end. When the French railways were considering the development of railcars in the 1930s 'accumulator operation was rejected . . . as 1 kg of battery weight provides 22 watt hours of power, a quantity which a diesel railcar produces by burning an almost imperceptible amount of fuel oil.'[22] Four battery trains (known as Drumm trains after their inventor) had been delivered in 1939. They allowed the GSR some certainty in assuring Dublin suburban services, but a fully electrified service or a fleet of diesel railcars similar to those of the GNR would have provided a more efficient solution.

Prior to 1939 railways were among the largest consumers of coal, typically accounting for about 15 per cent of national coal usage.[23] As consumption was cut under wartime conditions the proportion used by railways could increase to a level of 30 per cent as it did in Spain. Some countries restricted rail services as a precautionary measure at the outbreak of war while others awaited the emergence of actual shortages in 1941. War conditions led to shortages of shipping for coal transport, while the victories of 1940 left all of continental Europe, outside Iberia, dependant on German-controlled coal. Before the coal shortages of spring 1941 affected the GSR, reports of fuel shortages in European countries started to appear in the *Railway Gazette*. In February 1941 a 5 per cent cut in passenger services in Vichy was reported, together with a piece on the introduction of a 'crisis timetable' in Sweden with 'a heavy reduction in services to save fuel'.[24] Both of these countries were reliant on German coal, having previously received steam coal supplies from Britain.[25] The Deutsche Reichsbahn began to cut services in May 1941 due to 'shortages of rolling stock and coal',[26] but throughout the war the Reichsbahn 'gradually reduced the quality of its services by slowing trains, allowing overcrowding and restricting access to premium trains'.[27] Despite this, the number of passengers carried increased each year between 1939 and 1944.

The developing global shortage of coal was demonstrated by the experience of neutrals. In early June 1941 it was reported that cuts were expected in Swiss services due to shortages of coal, while a week later Portugal's railway company announced a drastic curtailment of rail services, with Lisbon to Oporto services reduced from two trains a day to four trains a week.[28] A fortnight later additional cuts were announced in Sweden, with passenger trains reduced to running three or four days a week.[29] On 4 July it was reported from Argentina that maize was being used as fuel for freight trains, in accordance with a government decree. This was not as a result of a fuel shortage per se but the need to find a use for stocks of maize that were no longer exportable due to shipping restrictions.

The first Irish difficulties were reported in the *Railway Gazette* of 18 July 1941 when news of the restricted GSR timetable shared the page with a report on a shortage of coal in Argentina, where 'the Central Railway is to use both wood and maize and... states that there can be no guarantee that trains will run on time.'[30] The following week's issue reported that in Egypt high-price coal was being displaced by oil.[31] Egypt would 'greatly reduce her need for coal by converting her railways to burn oil of which there was a plentiful supply near at hand'.[32] News of further train service reductions on the GSR on 5 August was followed immediately by a report on service cuts on Dutch railways, where services on steam-operated lines were down to between 10 and 30 per cent of pre-war levels while electric services were at 50 per cent of pre-war levels.[33] Continuing cuts on the GSR meant that within three months the service level had declined to what the *Railway Gazette* described as 'the minimum consistent with the maintenance of trade and commerce'.[34] Table 3 shows the spread of coal shortages across Europe and illustrates that the cuts in passenger service imposed by the GSR were part of a European pattern.

Table 3 Curtailment in passenger services

Country	First reported cuts	Principal trains per day	Operating days per week	Sleeping cars withdrawn
Sweden	February 1941	–	–	June 1941
Vichy France	February 1941	1	3 or4	–
Portugal	June 1941	–	3 or4	–
Ireland	July 1941	1		n/a
Holland	August 1941			–
Spain	January 1942		4	–
Denmark	March 1943	2		–

Source: Railway Gazette

In September 1941, the *Gazette* described the service cuts in Éire as being 'more serious than in belligerent and occupied countries',[35] while on November 28 it wrote that 'it is doubtful whether the entire history of railways has seen any parallel to the present position of the GSR. The... present meagre service has every prospect of staying in force for some considerable time in a country which is not even a belligerent.'[36] The central issue was that of an emerging global fuel shortage affecting all railway administrations.

The German conquests of September 1939 placed the mines of Poland at the disposal of the Reich. Shortages nevertheless emerged from spring 1941 onwards, but the service cuts that followed were less severe in areas where the rail network was electrified. This holds true regardless of whether the electricity was generated by hydro power, as in Switzerland or Italy, by coal, as in Holland, or by a mixture, as in Sweden or France. The view that the vulnerability of transmission and generating plant made electrified railways vulnerable in wartime was debunked in May 1941 by a *Railway Gazette* article which contended: 'So far as electrified railways being a danger in war it is an advantage to the countries which have undertaken it.'[37]

Switzerland maintained a stock of steam locomotives as a strategic reserve. In order to keep these locomotives occupied, a number of secondary lines were steam worked. When the Germans restricted coal exports to Switzerland, the Swiss responded by electrifying the lines in question, causing the *Gazette* to report: 'Electrification since has been so rapid that with the exception of a few unimportant branches the working is now entirely electric.'[38] The service curtailments in Switzerland were of an entirely different order to those applied elsewhere in Europe. In August 1942 the tram services in Zurich were described as being curtailed when the frequency was cut from one every six minutes to one every eight minutes![39] In January 1945 the *Gazette* observed that 'the one European country in which passenger services have shown little deterioration...and in some respects have improved is Switzerland.'[40]

In Sweden a pre-war committee had concluded that electrification was at its optimum level, given the price of coal needed for power generation. In 1943 this decision was reviewed and a number of electrification projects commenced which were scheduled for completion in 1944 and 1945. In France it was reported in October 1941 that 'the best services are on electric lines.'[41] Despite material shortages, the French expanded their electrified network during the war, linking Paris with the Mediterranean, albeit in a somewhat circuitous manner. The most striking case is that of Holland, whose electricity was all coal generated, and whose train services were described by the *Gazette* in 1944 as being 'up to recently the best in Europe'. The Dutch decided to completely electrify their network in 1945.[42] The ability to electrify railways in wartime as in Switzerland demonstrates an availability of supplies such as copper and aluminium which was beyond the capacity of the British war economy, where a number of electrification projects were shelved for the duration.[43]

The railways of Spain had become more self sufficient since the 1920s as a result of government policies on increasing the use of native coal. In 1938, Spain produced 7.4 million tons of coal and imported 1.1 million tons from Britain. In 1941 it produced 7.4 million tons of coal, 1.1 million tons of anthracite and 0.8 million tons of lignite and imported no coal. Spanish railways consumed 2.3 million tons of coal per annum in 1941 or approximately 30 per cent of national coal production.[44] Despite this, Spain began to encounter difficulties in January 1942 when the *Gazette* reported: 'The coal shortage is proving to be a serious handicap to rail traffic and moreover the available coal is of poor quality...so that timekeeping is bad. The services have been reduced by about a fourth and all ordinary fast trains have been discontinued.'[45] From the point of view of Allied strategy the pressure point on the Spanish authorities was oil rather than coal. Oil shortages impacted on the railways through shortages of lubricant and through 'the heavy burden thrown on the railways by the almost total cessation of road transport'.[46] Rail cuts in Spain went in tandem with the sanctions policy of the Allies, and were applied again in February 1944 when services were reduced to three days per week.[47] Railway service cuts commenced in Portugal in June 1941 and by November the *Gazette* reported that services had been curtailed drastically, with the Lisbon to Oporto service reduced from two trains per day to four per week. The *Gazette* concluded that 'many locomotives are said to be burning wood with which the country is well supplied.'[48] In January 1942 services dwindled to the point where 'only mails and a few passenger trains are now being run.'[49] Given the shortage of coal in Ireland, it is ironic that Portugal was sometimes supplied with coal by Irish ships sailing from Britain, such as the Arklow schooner *Cymric* which was lost in unexplained circumstances in February 1944 while sailing from Ardrossan to Lisbon.[50]

The US was one of the world's greatest coal-producing nations, and many of its western railroads used oil-burning locomotives since the turn of the twentieth century. The country was relatively unaffected by coal shortages. Production of bituminous coal increased by 78 per cent between 1938 and 1944 and the market preference for the higher grades of coal was curbed by the Solid Fuels Administration for War. In contrast, coal and shipping shortages were felt in Latin America from September 1939.[51] Problems with supply also developed in Canada, where experiments with lignite were undertaken in summer 1941 on the Northern Ontario Railway.[52] In October it was reported that the Canadian National Railway was buying US coal. 'Before the war Canadian coal was used as far west as Toronto but now American coal is used as far east as Mount Joli, Quebec and Edmonstown, New Brunswick.'[53] The fact that shortages developed before Pearl Harbor shows how the outbreak of war pushed the global coal market into shortage.

South American railways used oil and imported coal. Until 1940 Argentine railways imported more than 98 per cent of their coal from South Wales.[54] All the major Argentine railways were British owned, managed by British staff and from a technical point of view were in the British sphere of influence. During the First World War they had converted locomotives to burn oil. In 1939, 'the companies rearranged their time-tables, curtailing or abandoning non-essential services.'[55] A shortage of shipping made it impossible to export maize and it was used in factory and locomotive boilers. Maize has a calorific value near to timber and had been used in this manner during the First World War.[56] The use of a certain amount of maize as locomotive fuel became mandatory. There are parallels with the pressure brought on Irish companies to use Arigna coal during the 1930s and turf during the Emergency.

On the British side there were differing views as to what extent Argentina should be supplied with coal. The Mines Department wished to maintain coal exports, the Ministry of Food to maximise food imports, while the Ministry of Shipping wished to 'ship only whatever coal is sent in the shipping space required to bring back essential food'.[57] After the entry of the United States into the war all South American countries except Argentina expressed support for the US position at the Rio Conference of January 1942.[58] This isolation increased the political problems of Argentine neutrality and this in turn affected coal supply. The Foreign Office cabled: 'We agree not to supply to South America supplies which are being withheld for good reason by the US. Argentina is a special case ... we intend to cooperate with the US in bringing the Argentine government into line but this does not mean we should not argue with the Americans when we think they are wrong.'[59]

Despite the development of native coal resources, shortages of locomotive fuel remained a perennial problem for Argentina for the duration of the war years. Locomotive coal consumption fell by 70 per cent between 1940 and 1942.[60] By 1942 Brazilian coal was being successfully used mixed with Argentine coal.[61] At this time the Ministry of Economic Warfare proposed to supply Argentina with coal from South Africa but the proposal did not come to fruition.[62] Oil was also in short supply and in December 1942 drastic cuts in the Buenos Aires suburban services were averted only when the navy released some of its fuel oil reserve to the railway companies concerned.[63] In October 1944 the British embassy in Buenos Aires indicated that the railways had no difficulties other than with fuel and that coal represented 75 per cent of the problem.[64]

According to Norman Smith of the British Ministry of Mines, 'it was agreed [in 1941] that the US should look after the coal needs of Brazil and the UK after the coal needs of Argentina... the difficulties in supplying Brazil from the US [arose] not from a lack of supplies but from a lack of transport.'[65] Despite a 96 per cent increase in coal production between 1938 and 1941 Brazil was far from self-sufficient in coal and it was reported that many factory boilers would be converted to burn charcoal emulsion or cotton seed.[66] In early August 1942 a British civil servant wrote: 'There is an acute shortage of coal... the central railway has stopped railing ore. Unless something is done no [iron] ore will be shipped to the UK in six weeks.' Matters began to change when Brazil entered the war on the Allied side on 22 August 1942, but as late as October the British had to 'assist' the Brazilian navy in order to avoid requisitioning of bunker stocks.[67]

The use of native coal by the Brazilian Central Railway almost trebled to 35 per cent of the company's coal needs between 1937 and 1942. Even then, timber was used as fuel on flatter sections of line and coal was only used on hilly sections where greater tractive effort was needed. According to the *Railway Gazette*, 'no satisfactory substitute for Cardiff coal has yet been found.'[68] In 1943 it was largely due to national coal that the railways had been able to maintain their services.[69] In the following year, Brazilian coal production fell by 20 per cent but the shortfall was made up with supplies from South Africa and Mozambique.[70] The contrast between neutral Argentina and belligerent Brazil could not have been more apparent than in the area of railway fuel. While Argentine locomotives struggled on timber, maize and linseed oil, the Brazilian railway was kept supplied with coal and even completed an electrification project during the war years. There is a parallel between this and the contrasting performances of the GSR and GNR on either side of the Irish border.

South American native coal and timber were generally unsatisfactory as alternative fuels. Brazil coped best, especially after it joined the Allies, supplying them with iron ore and with base facilities and earning itself supplies of coal from Africa. In Uruguay the predominant locomotive fuel was oil and in June 1941 the Central Railway was warned that cuts in deliveries of up to 25 per cent were imminent, while in Chile service cuts due to coal shortages were made in 1943.[71] The overall experience of the railways of this sub-continent which was almost untouched by war shows the global nature of energy shortages.

Egyptian railways began to convert locomotives to oil burning in 1941, having unsuccessfully experimented with cotton seed cake as locomotive fuel when the export of cotton seed became difficult and 'coal of sufficient quality was almost unprocurable'.[72] This was similar to the experiments with burning maize in Argentina. In Palestine coal was supplied from Britain, but when deliveries dropped by 40 per cent during 1940, large stocks of wood fuel were acquired and alternative coal supplies were sought from India.[73] When coal shortages developed in India in 1942 the conversion of Palestinian locomotives to burn oil was accelerated.[74] Oil was supplemented by low-grade coal mined by British forces in north-eastern Iraq but it was reported that 'consumption of this stuff on locomotives...would be higher if quality had been more suitable.'[75] Oil was the chief substitute for imported coal in this region. When the British took over the Iranian railways in 1941 as a conduit for supplies to Russia, they first imported their own coal-burning locomotives and later adapted them to burn oil, the most plentiful fuel in the region. When the US army took over operation of the railway from the British they took the use of oil one step further by using diesel electric locomotives.[76]

The sheer size of the Indian sub-continent meant it consisted of a number of regional markets for coal. The railways of the south and east depended on Bengal coal while those of East Bengal and the North West Provinces relied on Middle East oil. Services were cut by 25 per cent in 1942 due to coal shortages, a fact not reported until June 1944, when additional service cuts were highlighted.[77] On the North West Railway (now in Pakistan), 'for many years most of the locomotives working in the Karachi area burned imported oil but in recent years in spite of the distance of the haul from the Bengal coalfields it has been found preferable to burn coal.'[78] Coal shortages developed in Ceylon in spring 1941 arising from shortages of shipping. These difficulties led to unsuccessful experiments with a coconut by-product as a locomotive fuel. These difficulties increased during the year and it was 'not possible to continue the service due in part to delays in getting coal. Firewood is being increasingly used and the sale of old sleepers has been prohibited.'[79]

Japan used indigenous coal for 86 per cent of its needs and imported the balance from China. This coal had an ash content of between 11 and 23 per cent, and would have been considered unusable in Britain and Ireland, as the correspondence on Arigna coal shows. This reflects the trend outlined in Chapter 1 whereby steam locomotives were built to suit the coal available and the crews accustomed themselves to the locomotive and fuel at hand.[80] In a move reminiscent of British policy in 1939, internal coal distribution in Japan was switched from sea to rail transport. As a result, passenger services were cut and sleeping and dining car services were withdrawn, a fuel conservation measure that had been widely adopted in Europe.[81]

The wartime period saw a global energy shortage with new types of railway fuel being used. The pattern of use depended on availability of fuel, availability of shipping to carry it and the political relationship between producer and consumer countries. Brazil's coal supplies improved markedly after it entered the war in August 1942. In the Middle East, oil replaced coal as a locomotive fuel in Egypt and Palestine, while coal replaced oil in north-western India.[82] Where timber was adopted as a substitute fuel, its use was limited to the flatter sections of line in Brazil and on the notorious Burma–Thailand railway.[83] The Irish experience was not unique but part of this global shortage, made to look worse by comparison with its nearby coal-rich neighbour, Britain. British railways suffered less from coal shortages than railways in Britain's export countries of Éire, Portugal and Argentina. A similar pattern can be observed on the networks of mainland Europe where the Reichsbahn and its associated Ostbahn network suffered less from coal shortages than did its export destinations of Vichy, Sweden and Switzerland. The record of the GSR compares well with that of the railway systems of other neutral countries. The most appropriate comparator countries are Portugal and Argentina, where the wartime experience of railway operation was very similar to Ireland, whether in restricted running, such as in Portugal, or government encouragement to use unsuitable alternative fuel – turf in Ireland and maize in Argentina. However, Irish citizens viewed the world based on Irish and British newspapers and on information from returning migrants, not from the trade press. Even if that was possible, it would have been a cold comfort for the Irish public in the twelve months wait from summer 1941 for an alternative locomotive fuel to emerge.

Notes

1   J.T. Carroll, *Ireland in the War Years* (Newton Abbot, 1975), p.86.

2   See Girvin, *Emergency*, p.226; T. Grey, *The Lost Years* (Dublin, 1997), pp.142–4.

3   *Railway Gazette*, 7 March 1941, p.245.

4   *Railway Gazette*, 3 December 1943, p.568, dealing with Victoria railways, Australia.

5   S.O. Ollson, *German Coal and Swedish Fuel, 1939–1945* (Goteborg, 1975), pp.21–2.

6   British National Archives (hereafter BNA), RAIL 1172 2371, GWR to railway executive, 25 March 1944.

7   RAIL 1172 2371, LMSR to railway executive, 3 March 1944.

8   A.C. Mierzejewski, *The Collapse of the German War Economy: Allied Air Power and the German National Railway* (Chapel Hill, 1988), pp.45, 138, 154.

9 Ibid., p.154.
10 *Railway Gazette*, 13 February 1942, p.217 (Todt), 31 August 1945, p.211 (Dorpmuller).
11 *Railway Gazette*, 31 August 1945, p.226.
12 *Railway Gazette*, 10 October 1941, p.374.
13 *Railway Gazette*, 25 June 1943, p.630.
14 W.G. Jensen, 'The importance of energy in the First and Second World Wars', *Historical Journal*, vol. XI (1968), p.545.
15 *Railway Gazette*, 30 November 1917, p.607.
16 *Railway Gazette*, 14 June 1918, p.679.
17 *Railway Gazette*, 1 February 1918, p.124.
18 *Railway Gazette*, 16 August 1918, p.174.
19 *Railway Gazette*, 1 November 1918, p.479.
20 *Railway Gazette*, 19 March 1920, p.468.
21 *Railway Gazette*, 4 February 1944, p.122.
22 *Railway Gazette*, 4 February 1944, p.122.
23 T. Wright, *Coal Mining in China's Economy and Society* (Cambridge, 1994), p.75.
24 *Railway Gazette*, 7 February 1941, p.138 (Sweden), p.152 (Vichy).
25 *Railway Gazette*, 27 June 1941, p.713.
26 *Railway Gazette*, 30 May 1941, p.609.
27 A.C. Mierzejewski, *Hitler's Trains: The German National Railway and the Reich* (Stroud, 2005), pp.157–9.
28 *Railway Gazette*, 6 June 1941, p.635 (Switzerland); *Railway Gazette*, 13 June 1941, p 663 (Portugal).
29 *Railway Gazette*, 27 June 1941, p.713.
30 *Railway Gazette*, 18 July 1941, p.67.
31 *Railway Gazette*, 25 July 1941, p.106.
32 C.B.A. Behrens, *Merchant Shipping and the Demands of War* (London, 1955), p.231.
33 *Railway Gazette*, 6 August 1941, p.146.
34 *Railway Gazette*, 19 October 1941, p.392.
35 *Railway Gazette*, 19 September 1941, p.295.
36 *Railway Gazette*, 28 November 1941, p.547.
37 *Railway Gazette*, 30 May 1941, p.609.
38 *Railway Gazette*, 15 January 1943, p.61.
39 *Railway Gazette*, 21 August 1942, p.186.
40 *Railway Gazette*, 9 February 1945, p.126.
41 *Railway Gazette*, 3 October 1941, p.343.
42 *Railway Gazette*, 22 June 1945, p.629.
43 M. Bonavia, *A History of the LNER, 1939–1948* (London, 1983), pp.60–1.
44 *Railway Gazette*, 17 July 1942, p.54.
45 *Railway Gazette*, 2 January 1942, p.7.
46 *Railway Gazette*, 24 April 1942, p.503.
47 *Railway Gazette*, 17 March 1944, p.285.
48 *Railway Gazette*, 7 Nov 1941, p.483.
49 *Railway Gazette*, 6 February 1942, p.211.
50 F. Forde, *The Long Watch* (Dublin, 1981), pp.19–20.
51 R.M. Weidenhammer, 'A national fuel policy III: Bituminous coal, postwar prospects', *Journal of Land and Public Utility Economics*, 21, 3 (1945), p.232.
52 *Railway Gazette*, 12 September 1941, p.258.
53 *Railway Gazette*, 3 October 1941, p.343.
54 *Railway Gazette*, 7 January 1944, p.25.

55 *Railway Gazette*, 26 September 1941, p.310.
56 *Railway Gazette*, 24 October 1919, p.525.
57 BNA, Ministry of Agriculture and Food (hereafter MAF) 83/215, J. Frank to Whalley, 19 March 1941.
58 F.D. McCann, *The Brazilian–American Alliance* (Princeton, 1973), p.250.
59 BNA MAF 83/1114, Foreign Office to Washington, 6 June 1942.
60 *Railway Gazette*, 11 September 1942, p.260.
61 *Railway Gazette*, 20 February 1942, p.258.
62 BNA MAF 83/1114, Frazer, War Transport to Eggers MEW, 12 December 1942.
63 *Railway Gazette*, 12 March 1943, p.264.
64 BNA MAF 83/1114, Embassy, Buenos Aires to Ministry of Food, 6 October 1944.
65 BNA MAF 83/1114, Smith to Mather Jackson (MAF), 27 July 1942.
66 *Railway Gazette*, 5 June 1942, p.631.
67 BNA MAF 83/1114, Smith to Jackson, 8 August 1942, Ferguson to O'Rourke, 2 October 1942.
68 *Railway Gazette*, 5 June 1942, p.631.
69 *Railway Gazette*, 21 January 1944, p.61.
70 *Railway Gazette*, 10 August 1944, p.141.
71 *Railway Gazette*, 17 December 1943, p.621.
72 *Railway Gazette*, 1 August 1941, p.106.
73 *Railway Gazette*, 26 September 1941, p.310.
74 *Railway Gazette*, 9 April 1943, p.374.
75 BNA FO [Foreign Office] 922 333, A/D [assistant director] Industrial Production to Middle East supply centre, 23 March 1944.
76 *Railway Gazette*, 16 February 1945, pp.159–60.
77 *Railway Gazette*, 2 June 1944, p.568.
78 *Railway Gazette*, 16 July 1943, p.65.
79 *Railway Gazette*, 23 May 1942, p.598.
80 *Railway Gazette*, 11 September 1942, p.234.
81 *Railway Gazette*, 13 November 1942, p.474.
82 *Railway Gazette*, 16 July 1943, p.65.
83 R. Beattie, *The Death Railway* (Bangkok, 2006), p.60.

4

The Politics of Trade, 1940–1942

Wartime governments take control of international trade and regulate it through bilateral agreements, trade sanctions or outright blockade. Wars cause scarcity, and services, facilities and commodities controlled by neutrals come into the trading equation. Most neutrals fell into the exclusive trading orbit of one of the belligerents. Ireland and Argentina were part of the Allied orbit while Switzerland and Sweden were part of the Axis orbit. Spain and Portugal were exceptional in that they traded with both sides. The case of the Irish Treaty ports was mirrored by the case of the Azores bases for Portugal, by Norway–Finland troop transit for Sweden and by transalpine railways for Switzerland. Commodities played a central role in trade between neutrals and belligerents as in the case of Swedish iron ore, Portuguese[1] and Spanish wolfram, Turkish chrome and Swiss electricity. Coal assumed a critical role for all the neutral countries as Britain and Germany were Europe's only coal-exporting countries. Coal figures prominently in trade relationships between Ireland and Britain, between Germany and Switzerland and between Germany and Sweden.[2]

In December 1940 the British cabinet imposed a sanctions policy on Éire in retaliation for the refusal to grant access to the Treaty ports. This policy did not succeed in its stated aim, and by late 1941 it had become apparent to observers on the British side that the ports would not be returned. In spring 1942 a new policy emerged, more in tune with the needs of the British war economy. This change coincided with the assumption of responsibilities for Irish matters by the dominions secretary and deputy prime minister, Clement Attlee. A new pragmatic approach brought about an increase of some supplies to Ireland, and was based on the value of the commodities and services the Irish had to offer Britain.

During 1940, negotiations on a renewed trade agreement between Ireland and Britain continued at a slow pace, and in November became entwined in the issue of the Treaty ports.[3] Both Churchill and Cranborne, the then dominions secretary, had decided to take a policy initiative on

Ireland, but were unsure as to what shape such an initiative might take. Cranborne, 'a deeply traditional Conservative...devoted to monarchy, church, country and empire [which was] intrinsic to his notion of British identity' had been brought into cabinet by Churchill in October 1940. The basis of an Irish policy was provided by Sir Wilfrid Spender, a Stormont civil servant who urged a boycott and/or price cuts on Irish agricultural exports, combined with severe restrictions on the sailing of British ships to Ireland. Cranborne prepared a memorandum for cabinet describing the situation in Ireland as one where...

> ...the ordinary life of peace is still carried on...People still hunt and shoot and race, dine out and go to the theatres and cinemas in the evening. Rationing has indeed been instituted but it is of a very mild kind, and all reports that reach this country speak of abundant food, lashings of cream and practically unlimited petrol.[4]

Cranborne's statement reflected the sentiments of the GSR road passenger manager, who said in January 1940 that 'the neutrality of the country, combined with the lack of blackout regulations and of food rationing, should make the country especially attractive as a holiday destination.'[5]

In autumn 1940 there were no intimations of shortages to come, and the main Irish concern was with the price rather than the quantity of coal available. In September John Reihill, a prominent coal importer, wrote to the Department of Supplies that he had learned confidentially that 'the advice to coal shipping firms was not to estrange the Irishmen these days.'[6] On 8 November, John Leydon wrote to Norman Smith complaining of the increased prices being charged.[7] Smith played a key role in coal exports and was regarded as an expert in the matter by the Ministry of Economic Warfare.[8] Ireland's favourable position as regards coal supply was shortly to change as Churchill took a lead role in the question of trade relations with Ireland. John Colville, Churchill's private secretary, describes the role of this small circle who...

> ...conspired with Cranborne, Rob Hudson, Kingsley Wood and Oliver Lyttelton about the means of bringing pressure on Ireland. Refusal to buy her food to lend her our shipping or to pay her our present subsidies seem calculated to bring de Valera to his knees in a very short time. On the other hand the Irish are an explosive race, and economic coercion might mean trouble. But the issues at stake justify the risk.[9]

On 5 December Churchill instructed Kingsley Wood, chancellor of the exchequer, to convene a meeting to discuss the measures necessary to reduce the burden on shipping consequent on the sinkings off the Irish coast:

> A general plan should be made for acting as soon as possible, together with a timetable … It is not necessary to consider either the Foreign Affairs or Defence aspect at this stage. These will be dealt with later. The first essential step is to have a good workable scheme, with as much in it as possible that does not hit us worse than it does the others.[10]

On 27 December, Churchill asked Kingsley Wood:

> Have you held your meeting on the Irish business? I propose to tell them we cannot carry the 400,000 tons for them in 1941 … Let me know exactly how this process is being put into operation, who gives notice and of what interval between the notice being given and imports coming to an end … the timing of this action must be fitted in with President Roosevelt's financial performance and the Congress decision thereupon.[11]

A memorandum outlining measures to be taken was brought to the British cabinet on 2 January 1941. It stated: 'The Éire Government would feel difficulties because they would see their supplies of feeding stuffs, food and coal endangered.' The inclusion of coal was initially uncertain, showing the influence the weak state of the Welsh coal industry had on British policy makers. The memorandum continued: 'The only serious effect on us would be felt by the South Wales coal miners.' Prior to the finalisation of the cabinet memo it was by no means certain that coal would be included in the programme of trade sanctions. A further memo from Kingsley Wood to Churchill stated: 'Éire takes 3m tons from South Wales which employs 10,000 men and as in the case of [other industries] where there is an export drive we shall not have the same ground for starving Éire', while a Treasury minute stated: 'It seems undesirable to include coal in view of the existing under-employment and its complication by the recruitment question.'[12] For goods other than coal a system of exports licences was introduced limiting 1941 exports to half of 1940 levels and 1942 exports to one third of 1940 levels. This initial package of measures, termed 'stage one', included restrictions on the sale of coal, phosphates, oil and wheat to Ireland together with a restriction on the supply of shipping to transport Irish goods and a scaling down of remaining exports.

Stage two was not elaborated on, being mentioned in a single paragraph at the end of the document, where the policy was described as being 'in effect economic war', and would involve the Ministry of Shipping withholding war risk shipping insurance, meaning that the Irish would get no ships. Administrators and politicians on the British side were at pains to stress to each other that stage two should be avoided. These sanctions were imposed at a time when Ireland's bargaining position was at its weakest. Since the time of the Napoleonic war, Ireland's contribution to British war efforts had been food and manpower. In spring 1941 the British economy was not yet on a full war footing, so the need for Irish labour was not yet fully appreciated.[13] In the area of food, Ireland's position was weakened by an outbreak of foot-and-mouth disease first reported on 24 January 1941. This meant a suspension of all cattle exports.

During the First World War coal was the most important commodity in discussions between Germany and Holland.[14]

> For every ton of coal, steel or timber... the Dutch had to supply one ton of food. It became a question of priorities: food or coal. Both were absolute essentials and there were not enough sources of coal or other fuels to meet Dutch consumption needs.[15]

In December 1916, in response to the perceived failure of the Norwegians to exercise more controls on German U-boats, the British government imposed a ban on coal exports. This had a devastating effect on the Norwegian merchant marine, causing 'a terrible energy crisis that lasted for three months'.[16]

Coal was the most important commodity in Anglo-Irish trade diplomacy during the Emergency period. The Irish side sought priority for public utilities such as gas undertakings, the ESB and the GSR. Gas undertakings used Durham coal, and the employment sensitivities applying to the South Wales coalfield did not apply in Durham. The gas industry was of crucial importance in urban areas but it could be substituted by electricity or solid fuel cookers. Most of Ireland's demand for electricity could be met by Ardnacrusha power station, supplemented by the coal-fired Pigeon House power station, which had just undergone an extensive refurbishment in 1940, part of which had adapted it to burn anthracite duff.[17]

At the British Coal Control Committee meeting of 20 May 1941, the chairman of the Great Western Railway urged the other British railway companies to use more Welsh large steam coal as 'at present a substantial amount of this type of coal was being shipped to Éire because it could not be disposed of in the home market.'[18] This demonstrates why cuts in steam coal deliveries to Ireland were opposed by the Ministry of Mines. In early 1941 a debate was also under way between the ministries of Mines and Food regarding exports of steam coal to South America. A Mines Department representative said: 'Argentina and Uruguay were practically the only markets for large coal left and a reduction in exports could not be made up in other directions. It was now very difficult to get as much as 500,000 tons a month (already below the 750,000 needed to keep the South Wales miners at work). Of this 125/150,000 tons went to the River Plate and to reduce the last figure to 50,000 tons would put about 24,000 men out of work.'[19]

The existence of a trade sanctions policy was consistently denied by the British side. In the absence of records it is difficult to state with accuracy when the Irish side recognised such a policy was in place. On 23 January 1941 Leydon spoke to Norman Smith advising him of many complaints from the ESB and the Dublin Gas Company regarding the new licence regime. Smith assured him that Ireland was not suffering any more than the British were themselves.[20] Within a week the true nature of the supply problems was conveyed to Leydon by W.J. Grey, manager of the Dublin Gas Company, who said that 'his supplier could not understand the refusal of a licence as there was adequate coal and wagons to carry it.' When Grey pressed for a reason he was told 'it was political and the decision had come from the very highest quarters.'[21] The British side made every effort to keep secret the existence of an informal committee chaired by Kingsley Wood, which first met on 7 February 1941. The desire for secrecy caused the committee to have an uncertain status, being described as 'a committee under the chairmanship of the Chancellor' rather than a cabinet sub-committee.[22] The uncertain nature of the committee can be seen in this letter from the Ministry of Food to the Treasury.

I am told that you act as secretary of the meetings held from time to time by the Chancellor of the Exchequer on exports to Éire. It must be extraordinarily difficult to produce orderly minutes of these meetings, particularly in view of the lack of any papers circulated beforehand, and I write to enquire whether you would not like us and the other departments concerned to put in some sort of paper in advance for future meetings.

The Treasury replied: 'I do not think that the character of the meetings really requires that papers should be circulated.'[23]

As early as February 1941 concerns were expressed at 'one or two recent observations by Éire Ministers which seemed to suggest that the shortage of supplies was as a result of deliberate actions on our part'. A Treasury minute of 21 March advised that 'the Prime Minister is particularly tender about the secrecy of our present policy towards Éire.'[24] In July John Dulanty, the Irish high commissioner in London, had established the source of the decision when he wrote to Leydon that 'not only on coal but on anything involving a cabinet decision he is certain that any request we make at present will be turned down.'[25] Dulanty had worked in the Ministry of Munitions during the First World War and understood the workings of a war economy.[26] He had also been Churchill's private secretary at the ministry and had a good insight into the prime minister's temperament and outlook. On 28 October the chancellor's committee discussed with alarm Dulanty's mention of a British cabinet committee in the course of a meeting on fertiliser supplies and recorded that 'it would be very dangerous if further enquiries from Éire received the answer that there was a cabinet committee responsible for policy.' The following day, Kingsley Wood wrote to Geoffrey Lloyd, minister for petroleum that 'we have been particularly careful to keep confidential the fact of these periodic reviews by ministers of supplies going into Éire.'[27] The objective of this secrecy was to avoid uniting the Irish electorate behind de Valera.

Initial evaluations of the sanctions policy were optimistic. On 20 February Kingsley Wood reported to Churchill that the policy 'is making Éire daily more uncomfortable with daily accelerating effect, and Éire will very possibly come to us in the next three or four weeks'.[28] The capacity of the Irish to hold out until harvest time was a key indicator of the success of the policy. On 11 March Oliver Lyttelton, president of the Board of Trade, said that 'he had in mind to give the screw another turn' and that 'in March Éire would be feeling the effects of his policy quite considerably ... the Éire Government have sent a representative to the USA ostensibly to buy arms but in effect to buy ships and wheat. The Government has stated officially that Éire can hold out until her next harvest is available but another view is that they may have no wheat by June.'[29] The Irish grain position was raised ten days later with Lord Woolton by the prominent miller J.V. Rank, who wrote:

I am egotistical enough to think I know a bit about their point of view which, I am afraid is only possessed by a small percentage of the citizens of this country...their flour mills will stop by the middle of July...the flour they have will be consumed by mid August; they cannot be certain about their harvest until mid September. All they require is 9,000 tons of wheat a week, 3,000 of which they can produce for themselves...an opinion is strongly gaining ground in this country that we think we are going to get the ports or anything else by doing it. Well, I should imagine knowing the people over there as I do, they would sooner starve.[30]

Between Lyttelton's memo and Rank's letter the critical date for Irish wheat supplies imports had moved from mid-June to mid-July – nearer to harvest time. Rank's letter shows how the policy went against longstanding trading relationships that had survived the Belfast boycott, Irish independence and the economic war.

On 26 April *The Economist* observed that 'Éire is at present experiencing the reality of self sufficiency...and it is generally accepted that the advantages of this condition are not unmixed.' At the meeting of 22 May, Cranborne stated: 'The façade of the policy of self-sufficiency is crumbling, but...there is no general bitterness against the [British] policy.' He went on to say that the policy was 'not likely to give quick results'.[31] This acceptance that the Treaty ports would not be made available in the foreseeable future brought a changed emphasis in British policy as British ministries approached the Treasury seeking authority for commodity exchanges with Ireland. The Ministry of Food when requesting authority to exchange rennet for cheese and cocoa for chocolate crumb also sought a general sanction to issue export licences 'where the object of the export is to a correspondingly desirable import'.[32] Such applications show the increased pressure for exemptions from British ministries doing war-related business in Ireland.

The sanctions policy did not command unanimous support on the British side. The meeting of 29 August was attended by Sir John Maffey, who stated:

The strength of de Valera's position rested on the general approval... of the policy of neutrality [which] made it impossible for our friends to make an effective opposition...There is a strong danger that Éire is being drawn further towards self-sufficiency and to the status of a foreign country.

Notwithstanding Maffey's warning, the consensus view remained that the policy should be continued. This meeting decided that 'the supply of good quality coal to Ireland should be gradually restricted, as existing supply levels were not consistent with the full application of stage one policy.'[33]

A decision was deferred until 'Lord Cranborne had had time to discuss with Sir John Maffey certain advantages (other than the return of the ports which Sir John thought could never be secured by this policy) which might be obtained in return for tempering these proposals.' Cranborne was beginning to doubt the effectiveness of the policy towards Ireland. As a Conservative party grandee his reservations are all the more telling. In a memorandum to Kingsley Wood on the matter of tea, he wrote:

> I have never been in favour of treating the Irish too gently. On the contrary, it was a memo which I sent to the cabinet which started the policy of restriction... But the essence of the policy has always been that it should be so manipulated that the Éire Government should never be given the chance of accusing us of imposing an economic blockade. It seems to me essential that we should keep this consideration uppermost in our minds. Otherwise we shall have de Valera rallying his people behind him, which is the last thing we want.[34]

Churchill continued to demand results, asking Kingsley Wood: 'What has happened about our measures to make southern Ireland feel the weight of the war? Have you enforced all the steps decided upon by the cabinet? It does not seem to have produced any effect. Please let me have another report.'[35] A report was presented to the September meeting of the chancellor's committee which concluded: 'Whilst it might be said that the policy has not made Éire surrender the ports, the policy has shown Éire how dependent she is on us.'[36] Nine months after the introduction of the sanctions policy an acceptance began to dawn that the policy would not achieve its intended result.

It is difficult for governments to retreat gracefully from a policy impasse, and shortages of coal in Ireland provided a highly visible retaliatory effect, becoming almost an end in themselves. The September committee meeting considered the report of Norman Smith, who in response to a request from Maffey visited Dublin on 29 and 30 August. Smith's brief was solely to explain the policy on coal. He reported a seemingly cordial meeting with Leydon, who stated that he appreciated the British difficulties but expressed the hope that:

> We might see our way, if our supplies position improved, to release more and better coal for Éire... coal for public utility undertakings

... [The Irish are] very anxious about the winter months ... He asked whether we would make it possible for them to build up stocks equal to two or three weeks consumption ... their inability to maintain adequate supplies of suitable coal had created a very serious difficulty for the Great Southern Railway ... delays of several hours to passenger trains were the rule rather than the exception.

On Saturday 30 August, Smith met Seán Lemass and reported that ...

... during the course of the conversation there was no attempt to press me for supplies, but it was abundantly clear that if we could see our way to improve ... quality and ... quantity our action would be highly appreciated.

In an addendum to his report Smith wrote:

I learned from Sir John Maffey that the question of cutting down supplies of gas coal ... had been discussed at the latest meeting of the Chancellor's committee and I was disturbed to hear that action in this sense was likely. My instructions on leaving London were to make no concessions: these I followed but I did say that it was our intention, subject to exceptional circumstances, to keep the gas undertakings going, and I feel it would be most important and would create a painful impression if we were to restrict supplies.[37]

Smith outlined his discussion of supplies to industries such as creameries and dairies in which the Ministry of Food had a special interest. Leydon refused to countenance any special arrangements save in the context of an increased fuel allowance. Smith warned of the possibility that the Irish government would take control of coal imports and institute a barter system of coal for dairy products.[38]

The sensitivities surrounding the sanctions policy can be seen in the August meeting of the committee, when the purchase of ships by the Irish was being discussed. Lord Leathers, the minister for shipping, was recorded as saying he hoped 'to prevent any further purchases'. A civil servant asked the Treasury that the minute be re-drafted, as Leathers 'thinks it important that he was not suggesting any action which might in fact land us in stage two'.[39] Another report prepared for the meeting noted that:

Ministers decided that shipments of coal to Éire should not exceed
about 25,000 tons a week but authority was subsequently given for an
additional tonnage of such poor qualities as slurries and low-volatile
duffs unmarketable in this country to be exported... The only coal of
any use to this country now being exported is coal for gas making
amounting to some 3,000 tons per week of second-grade quality
which is being sent to Dublin gasworks to supplement the allowance
of Durham gas coal (which is insufficient to meet requirements) and
some low-grade Welsh coal for the railways. The gas works have
been kept on a hand-to-mouth basis and have not been allowed to
accumulate stocks.

It was hoped that new restrictions might lead to a situation where 'Mr de
Valera came to us with a piteous appeal for more coal.'[40] Leydon's candour
with Smith was probably used against Irish interests, as the chancellor's
committee decided to reduce further the gas coal allowance from 3,000 to
1,500 tons per week.[41] This severe cut in coal may have been a final
attempt to secure concessions on the issue of the ports. At this point even
Churchill seemed to question the efficacy of the approach when he
annotated a memo on the Irish policy with 'Yes, but is the medicine
working?'[42] Coal sanctions had become an end rather than a means.

From an Irish point of view summer 1941 was a milestone. Dr Jim
Ryan, minister for agriculture, announced that the wheat crop was the
biggest since 1847 and the general harvest was the best ever. On 31 August
the *Irish Elm* arrived in Dublin from Halifax with 6,000 tons of Canadian
wheat, the first Irish Shipping vessel to complete a commercial voyage.[43]
Cereal supplies to Ireland were off the agenda as a pressure point for
another year. Although this estimate of the harvest was later proven to be
over-optimistic, the harvest of 1941 was a key psychological milestone in
demonstrating that Ireland had the capacity to either grow or import its
own cereals.[44]

Norman Smith visited Dublin on 10 October 1941 and met Leydon. He
had just arrived from Belfast where he had been attempting to impress the
need for economy in the use of coal on the Northern Ireland authorities,
where he 'had the greatest difficulty in getting them to accept
restrictions'.[45] As there was no screening plant in Northern Ireland, Smith
suggested that coal bound for there would be routed through Dublin,
where it would be screened before being railed to Belfast. The coal
screenings would be retained for use in Dublin. Leydon declined this offer
because of the adverse impression it would create. Some days later

Leydon offered 200,000 tons of Donegal turf for Northern Ireland in exchange for 110,000 tons of coal delivered to Dublin. Smith declined, saying that 'the attitude in Northern Ireland is that they cannot use anything but the best quality domestic coal.'[46]

Between September and October 1941, British policy changed. At the September committee meeting Woolton stated that as the Irish had no option but to sell their agricultural produce to Britain he was not greatly moved to grant them any concessions. However, in October Leathers sought permission to export steel to the Liffey dockyard in Dublin for repairs to the *Irish Hazel*:

> While he was very reluctant to send steel for this, he nevertheless advocated the sending since the Éire facility had been very useful to us and had dealt with 34 ships ... Lord Cranborne thought that this proposal did not raise political issues but should be treated on the footing that it was of benefit to ourselves. Lord Woolton would like to send steel since at the moment he wanted Éire goodwill more than they wanted his. The cattle situation had reached a turning point and he wanted to import a lot of fat cattle first and store cattle later.[47]

The cessation of the foot-and-mouth epidemic meant that Irish cattle were now again in demand and this increased the bargaining power of the Irish side.[48] When the October meeting declined an Irish request for slurry coal, Cranborne questioned whether it was right to refuse this request since he understood the material in question was available. Leathers opposed the request, and it was agreed that the refusal would be explained by the shortage of shipping. Churchill conveyed his gratitude to the committee for its work, concluding with the note: 'I am sorry for all this but it is only necessary and just.'[49]

Canning writes: 'After his defeat over extending conscription to Northern Ireland in May, Churchill, in June 1941, gave up trying to win his way over Ireland ... Although he remained a strong opponent of concessions to Ireland, his heart was no longer in it.'[50] While Churchill's direct interest may have ended by June, his communications with Kingsley Wood in September showed that he fully supported the continuing Irish sanctions policy. The committee which oversaw trade policy on Ireland was still that small tight group that had 'plotted with him' in December of the previous year, when they concluded that a sanctions policy would 'bring de Valera to his knees in a short time'.[51] The sanctions policy had failed to secure concessions on the ports but an

unintended consequence was the establishment of Irish Shipping, when
the Irish state established a deep sea merchant fleet.

By October 1941 the political position of de Valera was, if anything,
strengthened. The cross-party support for neutrality was underscored by
the visit of Fine Gael TD Maurice Dockrell to London on 5 November.
Carrying a letter of introduction from Maffey, Dockrell was described
as . . .

> . . . pro-British in outlook and always friendly disposed towards the
> UK Trade Commissioners office . . . Mr Dockrell was very careful . . .
> to display no partisan feelings of any sort. He did not criticise the
> policy of HMG [Her Majesty's government] in the UK, nor did he
> criticise Mr de Valera . . . [but] pointed out that the transport capacity
> of the Éire railways was diminishing . . . some of the traffic must
> disappear. Mr Dockrell said that he did not know what the Éire
> governments decision would be in a case of this sort but he could
> venture to guess that Mr de Valera would feel bound to see that
> during the winter Éire did not go short of fuel, and that it seemed
> probable at any rate that a great part of the export trade would have
> to be delayed . . . He asked me to clearly understand that he was not
> using this in any way as a threat, because he came purely as a
> businessman and not as a member of parliament and he did not know
> what was in the mind of the government of Éire.[52]

While Grey of the Dublin Gas Company informed the Irish government of
the situation in late January 1941, it was not until May that the Irish
authorities took counter-sanctions when they imposed a ban on the export
of timber pit props – timber baulks essential for the mining industry – on
the grounds that the timber was needed in Ireland as fuel. A further
counter-sanction followed in December 1941 when the export of cement
to Northern Ireland was forbidden. When the Mines Department made
representations on this issue Leydon told him that the Irish 'could not
defend a decision to allow substantial quantities of coal to be used in
maintaining an export trade in cement at a time when our coal consumers,
including . . . the GSR and the gas companies are not getting their
minimum requirements'.[53]

In tracing the Irish response to the British sanctions policy the historian
is almost totally reliant upon material in the files of the Department of
External Affairs. These include reports of meetings and conversations
between John Leydon and British officials and notes of meetings between

Dulanty and the British authorities.[54] What is lacking is a record of the deliberations of the Departments of Supplies or of Industry and Commerce. Coal Importers Limited was one of the companies established early in the war to control the imports of certain key commodities. However, in contrast to the companies importing tea or grain, the records of Coal Importers never reached the national archives. The absence of such significant records from the Emergency period is as perplexing as it is frustrating for the historian, especially in view of the writing up of the 'Emergency Historical Record' series after the conclusion of hostilities. John Leydon was conscious of his historic role. In a letter to F.H. Boland of External Affairs on the 1943 petrol allocation he wrote: 'I think it should not be left open to delving historians of the future to say that we accepted the terms of Attlee's letter.'[55] Historians are thus required to make use of British, External Affairs or company sources to compensate for the lack of records on coal imports from either of Leydon's two departments.

In March 1942, the oversight of British economic policy towards Ireland moved from the chancellor's informal committee to a cabinet sub-committee, chaired by Clement Attlee. The establishment of this committee represented the return of Dominions Office predominance in dealings with Ireland. In contrast to the monthly meetings of Kingsley Wood's com-mittee, the cabinet committee was less intense in its deliberations, meeting six times in 1942, twice in 1943 and once in 1944. Again in contrast with its predecessor, the cabinet sub-committee functioned in a conventional manner, with an agenda and papers circulated in advance. Another change occurred in June 1942 when the Ministry of Fuel and Power was established, centralising government control over fuel. This move reflected growing problems with fuel and in particular with coal supply.

The most significant change in coal supply policy towards Ireland was triggered by the arrival of American troops in Northern Ireland in January 1942.[56] This deployment provoked strong protests from the Irish govern-ment, but ironically opened the way for the Irish to secure additional supplies. Provisioning additional troops in Northern Ireland involved either importing supplies from Britain using scarce shipping or importing from Ireland. These increased needs allowed the Irish side to bargain from a greater position of strength. In March 1942 the Irish threatened to embargo the export of Guinness, a matter that was on the agenda of the first meeting of the cabinet sub-committee on Éire. The committee noted 'the serious problem which would arise especially in Northern Ireland if the Government of Éire placed a ban on beer exports'. While it was doubted that the Irish would maintain an export ban for long, the Ministry of Food was authorised to offer 30,000 tons of wheat in exchange for one million barrels of beer.[57] The agreement subsequently reached was described by Kingsley Wood as 'reassuring both from the point of view of revenue and morale. We have undertaken to arrange for Éire the purchase and shipment of 20,000 tons of American wheat on condition that their exports of beer to us are maintained at 650,000 standard barrels.[58] This is not seriously below the figure for the first two years of the war.'[59] David Grey, US minister in Dublin, was unenthusiastic and told Dulanty that he believed 'the transaction will have unfavourable repercussions in the US on the grounds that shipping is being sent to a country not contributing to war effort and that the commodity obtained in exchange is at best a luxury and at worst poison.'[60] However, the requirements of US troops remained a priority for British civil servants, one of whom wrote to a colleague that he was 'negotiating for the production of more beer in Éire in connection with American troops'.[61]

At its first meeting the cabinet committee defused a potentially difficult situation while in addition considering a proposal from the Irish side that had the potential to put Anglo-Irish wartime trade on a different footing. This proposal submitted by Dulanty had been drafted by Erskine Childers, secretary of the Federation of Irish Manufacturers. It involved certain Irish factories being allocated raw materials and in exchange exporting the majority of the goods manufactured to Britain. This saved on British labour and transport and was the antithesis of the retreat into self-sufficiency feared by Maffey and Cranborne in 1941. In a sense it represented a partial retreat from neutrality. It was an unintended consequence of the British sanctions policy although it fell far short of the objective of access to the ports. The committee agreed that this matter had to be scrutinised with care as 'hitherto our policy had been to maintain economic pressure on Éire except when our own essential requirements were involved.' The Ministry of Agriculture and the Board of Trade were instructed to consider the matter further in discussions with Maffey.[62] This signifies a movement towards a less adversarial form of bargaining, with both sides focusing on mutual gains. The Irish proposal to put production capacity at the disposal of the British war economy was a move towards integrative bargaining. The earlier Irish counter-measures had been ineffective, as neither pit props nor cement were sufficiently important to the British authorities.

At a meeting of 1 May 1942 the cabinet committee on Éire approved the release of steel to Pierces of Wexford for the manufacture of agricultural machinery, while declining a request for additional coal.[63] A

Mines Department paper advised of the possibility that 'the GSR and the Dublin Gas company would shut down . . . the greatest part of our present shipments to Éire were slurry and duff which were not capable of being consumed in this country without adaptation.'[64] Lord Leathers responded that he would continue to ship at present levels, but not large coal for railways. The action of a transport minister in deciding the nature of the goods to be transported seems strange. However, Leathers was a recognised authority on coal and shipping, having been an advisor to the Ministry of Shipping in the First World War.

At the cabinet sub-committee meeting of 29 May the sanctions policy of December 1940 was abandoned. In accordance with the cabinet decision of December 1940 export levels were due for a further reduction to 33.3 per cent of 1940 levels. The committee concluded:

> If exports to Éire were reduced except on grounds of economic necessity it might provoke retaliation and we would revert to barter trade between the two countries . . . It was true that our exports of coal to Éire provided a powerful bargaining weapon. On the other hand we imported from Éire a considerable number of commodities.

The meeting decided that 'only such cuts were to be made as could be justified on the basis of scarcity . . . there should be no general scaling down of exports by a fixed percentage.' The extent of the change can be seen in Attlee's remark that 'Any policy of putting economic pressure on Éire with a view to securing political concessions was most unlikely to succeed. Our policy in this matter should be dictated solely by our economic interests.' The committee then approved an extra supply of coal for the Guinness brewery on the basis of continuation of beer exports to Northern Ireland, although noting the 'risk of opening the door on a series of other transactions of this kind: cement, creameries etc. . . . . It was for this reason that we had rejected proposals of this kind [pit props] which had been made in the past.'[65]

These policy changes on the Irish and British sides undermine Brian Girvin's assertion that 'Éire could have provided manufacturing facilities without endangering its neutrality.'[66] Éire did in fact offer manufacturing facilities in early 1942 while remaining neutral and provided commodities and manufactured goods to the British war economy. Given that by 1944 Éire was supplying 'cement, beer, rubber manufacture, creamery products, cattle, cattle feed, agricultural machinery, flax and jute yarn, binder twine and cordage, talc, glycerine',[67] it is clear that Irish trade policy was not shaped by an absolutist version of neutrality. The British side, in accordance with their general aversion to barter, expressed a concern as to the development of a barter trade with Ireland. In July 1942 the Foreign Office expressed concern about the Argentines who had 'only recently and on several occasions expressed their concern at the reductions in exports of coal [and] might well be tempted to insist on coal as a quid pro quo for canned meat'.[68] From the point of view of belligerents, the development of a barter culture was to be guarded against. In April 1944 the German industry commission based in Berne drew up a balance sheet of German–Swiss trade and analysed the likely effects of an all-out economic war between the two countries. The analysis concluded that 'The danger exists that Germany will require from Switzerland some urgent services or deliveries despite the economic war such as transit facilities or spare parts for Swiss-manufactured machines. Inevitably a compensation culture would then develop in which the Swiss would demand coal or iron ore from Germany.'[69]

This Guinness/wheat exchange was the culmination of pressures placed on British departments that had contracts with Irish suppliers. From as early as July 1941, the British Ministry of Food began to deal with increasingly frequent requests for coal from Irish food processing companies supplying British markets.[70] In a note of a phone call from October 1941, Leydon recorded that:

> Norman Smith phoned me last evening and . . . told me that he thought it might be possible to send us 5,000 tons of large coal and two cargoes of very good coal all large . . . I told him that one should go to the GSR and the balance . . . could go to the merchants . . . Norman Smith asked me could I make coal available from these cargoes to creameries who are continually pressing him for coal. I told him that of course I would be glad to relieve him of any difficulties if he would let me have particulars.[71]

Smith's request was totally at variance with his warnings to colleagues in other ministries that the Irish government would take control of the coal trade if they discovered special imports of coal, 'thus depriving the Mines Department of the small amount of influence they have'.[72] It demonstrates the centrality of Norman Smith in the Anglo-Irish coal trade. A Ministry of Food internal memo of October 1941 recorded that:

> Smith does his best to direct small consignments to food-producing concerns in which we have an interest [and] should continue to

further our interests surreptitiously and should not attempt to interfere in the question of coal distribution in Éire ... any attempt to do this systematically would almost certainly result in the Éire Government taking over control of coal imports.[73]

It seems clear that Smith's surreptitiousness was not intended to mislead the Irish authorities but rather other departments seeking to maintain a hard line on Ireland, contrary to what he saw as the overall strategic objectives of the war effort.

In April 1942 the Mines Department reported to the Éire committee that the GSR was in severe difficulties: 'In recent weeks no large coal has been released ... they are in imminent danger of having to suspend their service. It is not known whether it is desired that these utilities [GSR and Dublin Gas] should close down. With supply restrictions as at present it is difficult to see how they can continue to function.'[74] The challenge to the Irish side was to frame their requests for materials in a manner which appealed to British self-interest. This was not possible in the case of town gas, which served an exclusively domestic market. In the case of electricity, the merits of an electricity interconnector had been raised informally by the ESB with their Northern Ireland counterparts from 1938.[75] This would allow the ESB to sell surplus current from Ardnacrusha, thus reducing Northern Ireland's dependence on a single generating plant in Belfast harbour. The triangular nature of these discussions slowed progress on this venture, but the line was completed during 1942. From the time of the Dockrell visit in November 1941 the GSR sought to portray itself as an essential conduit in the export of food to Britain. A key player in crafting this image was Charles Johnston, who had been appointed as the materials inspector of the GSR in January 1942. Johnston reported directly to Bredin, who had encouraged his aging predecessor to go on pension. Bredin urged Johnston that 'if you have not yet met Mr Norman Smith of the British Ministry of Mines, you should endeavour as soon as possible to get the necessary introductions and thereafter keep in the closest possible touch with him.'[76]

In March 1942 the Ministry of Food proposed a joint initiative to the Mines Department aimed at improving the supply of coal to the GSR.[77] Norman Smith expressed a fear that when 'it will become known that these people have got a cargo of good coal the Éire authorities will ask how we found coal for them and not the Dublin Gas Company which is almost *in extremis* for supplies.' Smith warned again in June that 'we risk incurring curiosity (and possibly some action) on the part of the Éire authorities. However much we try and keep these things *sub rosa*, information always seems to leak out.'[78] However, by mid-July the proposal gained the support of the Ministry of Fuel and Power. Denis Browne of the import plans division of the Ministry of Food recorded:

> I have had a series of telephone conversations with Mr Norman Smith about the coal requirements of the Éire Southern [sic] Railway ... [they] receive an allowance of 4,000 tons a week, 75% of which is dust... They represent that the increase... in livestock traffic... will make it impossible for them to carry on without increased supplies of coal... the meat and livestock division ... are anxious that sufficient supplies of coal should be made available to enable this traffic to be handled... I suggested to Mr Smith that it was probably undesirable that the railway company should be left without an indication of our views since they would then approach their own government who would probably take advantage of the situation to ask for considerably more coal than was needed... [Smith] will then notify the company to approach him in the first place, and will pass on to us their request with his opinion on its reasonableness. The matter might then be dealt with if the Minister thought fit by his writing to the Minister for Fuel and Power without the necessity of an approach to the Éire Cabinet Committee.

On 18 July J.S. Townsend wrote to Denis Browne:

> The bulk of the supplies of livestock which we receive from Éire pass over the Southern [sic] railway at this time of year... In our view it would help us if the Ministry of Fuel could take a favourable line in regard to coal... Although we cannot vouch for the information we are told that the Southern railway is less favourably placed than the Northern railway. This may be due to the nearer position of the Northern railway to the coal supplies, however poor they may be, in Northern Ireland. At the same time there may be other reasons for this position of which we are not aware... I hope this will provide the information you want for Norman Smith.'[79]

This letter contains two significant references. It marks the point when British policy makers accepted that Irish cattle exports were linked with coal supplies for the GSR. Secondly, it refers to the superior coal available to the GNR in Éire and the indication that the information was intended for Norman Smith. Norman Smith was well aware of the superior coal available to the GNR in Éire as his report of October 1941 makes clear.[80] Who is the source feeding this information to the Ministry of Fuel and Power? The phrase 'although we cannot vouch for the information' indicates an Irish source, probably Charles Johnston, whose role was moving from the technical to the political.

On 7 August Browne suggested that a blanket authority be granted to manage special requests for coal by Irish suppliers at official level, as the Mines Department was 'bound by a rigid cabinet ruling which not only limits the total quantity of coal which may be sent to Éire, but also lays down that it must be of a quality which makes it unsuitable for use in this country'.[81] This was described as doubly inconvenient because ministerial sanction had to be sought for every derogation from the policy. Browne suggested that:

> The ideal arrangement would be for the Mines Department to be allowed a discretion to supply coal in such quantity or quantity as may be required to ensure that the Ministry of Food's essential requirements are met. For this arrangement to work...it will be necessary for this department to limit its demand strictly to essentials and for the Mines Department to take precautions to ensure that what is done attracts the least possible attention from the Éire government. Objections to such a proposal will presumably be primarily political. The answer is that in respect of other commodities it is recognised that arbitrary restrictions should be relaxed when such a course is in our interest.[82]

This minute shows how the sanctions policy was being seen as self-defeating and not in Britain's best interest by British administrators. The description of the possible objections as being 'primarily political' must be seen through the eyes of the writer. All trade decisions are 'primarily political' but if this phrase is read as meaning 'administratively unsound and self-defeating', subsequent developments will be more easily understandable. On 18 August 1942 Lord Woolton wrote to Gwyllim Lloyd George, Minister for Fuel and Power, indicating his concern at:

> The capacity of the Éire Southern [sic] Railway to carry the quantities of livestock which will be coming forward for shipment this autumn ...officials of our departments...are agreed in thinking that the railway's present allowance of fuel will be insufficient...While I

appreciate the political necessity for keeping our coal exports to Éire
at a minimum the rigidity of the ruling now in force seems
unnecessarily inconvenient... The absolute ban on sending any coal
to Éire unless it is unfit for use here may prove a false economy
unless exceptions can be made where necessary.[83]

At the Éire policy committee of 19 August 1942 Lord Portal, Minister
of Works and Planning, secured approval for export of low-quality coal in
exchange for a resumption of Irish cement exports to Northern Ireland.
Such exports had been banned since September 1941, but a year later
cement was needed for airfield construction in Northern Ireland.[84]
Coincidental with the lifting of the export ban, supplies of cement in the
Irish domestic market improved. In July a shortage of cement was
impeding employment relief schemes, and the matter was certified as
urgent for the Irish cabinet meeting of 3 September. By December the
situation had changed to such an extent that Industry and Commerce wrote
to Maurice Moynihan: 'The position in regard to supplies of cement is
reasonably good at the present time [and] there are no practical restrictions
on the sale of cement.'[85] The additional coal imported by the Drogheda
cement factory was used to alleviate a domestic shortage of cement in
addition to providing for exports to Northern Ireland.

The Éire policy sub-committee of 19 August was advised that a
proposal on the GSR coal supply would issue from Food and Fuel and
Power. The Ministry of Agriculture and Fisheries indicated its support for
the proposal, stating that 'our interest in the maintenance of adequate rail
transport in Éire fully coincides with yours.'[86] Lloyd George saw no
difficulty in increasing the amount allocated to Éire, provided the quality
was not increased.[87] In accordance with the strategy agreed between Smith
and Browne in July, Charles Johnston forwarded a letter from Bredin to
Norman Smith on the coal position. This letter highlighted the issue of
coal quality, pointing out that a decrease of 62 per cent in passenger miles
produced a decrease of 44 per cent in coal consumed, whereas an increase
of 14 per cent in freight mileage produced a 66 per cent increase of tons
consumed. Johnston confirmed that this letter had been well received and
reported to Bredin that he 'now required a further letter to be written and
would cross to Dublin next week with a suggested draft of this letter'.[88]
The letter that was drafted was signed by Reynolds. It was shorter than
Bredin's letter, focussed more on the carrying capacity of the GSR for
British food imports and concluded with the sentence: 'The present
position appears to be as serious from your point of view as it undoubtedly

is from ours.'[89] Norman Smith cannot have been surprised at the contents of the letter, as given the report of the phone conversation between Johnston and Bredin he probably had some part in drafting it. The GSR had succeeded in having its case put on the agenda of the British cabinet sub-committee.

The proposal for an additional 500 tons per week of low-grade coal for the GSR was circulated on 20 November. Attlee proposed that the matter would be taken as approved without a meeting, subject to periodic reports on the situation by Fuel and Power.[90] In a move to prepare the political ground, a Unionist MP was told in the Commons on 3 December, when he asked why the rails from the closed Clogher Valley Railway were sold to a neutral state, that 'The undertakings in Éire which are using these rails ... indirectly assist the war effort.'[91] Nevertheless Attlee's proposition drew immediate opposition from the Ministries of War Transport and Economic Warfare. Lord Selbourne considered that the cattle in Éire were a food reserve that could, if necessary, be walked across the border. The memo concluded: 'In relation to Éire, a policy of masterly inactivity seems appropriate.'[92] The proposal was further considered at the cabinet committee meeting of 9 December. The Ministries of Food and Fuel and Power were anxious that export of cattle remain unchecked. Fuel and Power noted that 'from the point of view of conserving supplies the present proposals were of little consequence. The greater part of the coal was in any case of a quality that would only be used here in the last resort.'[93] However, Lord Leathers stated that 'the proposals represented insuperable difficulties from the point of view of transport' and was supported by Selbourne from the Ministry of Economic Warfare (MEW).[94] In a defeat for Lord Woolton and Lloyd George, the matter was deferred for three months.

The reasons for this outcome were both political and administrative. At a political level, opponents of concessions to Ireland such as Selbourne and Leathers remained influential. At an administrative level the powers sought by the ministries of Food and Fuel and Power meant bypassing the cabinet committee, thus reducing the influence of the Ministry of War Shipping and rendering superfluous the role of the Ministry of Economic Warfare. This latter department saw itself as the keeper of the flame on Irish supplies, and seemed to regard the policy of January 1941 rather than that of May 1942 as being the guiding light on the issue of supplies to Ireland. In October 1943 Selbourne wrote to Cranborne: 'My Dear Bobbety ... the committee has thrust on my department the duty that Éire does not get an undue share of the world's goods.'[95] The Ministry of War

Shipping could also be expected to oppose a measure that would increase the demand for shipping.

However, the most significant feature of this episode was that the rejected proposal for additional coal supplies for Ireland was implemented almost immediately by civil servants. On 17 December Denis Browne wrote to his superior: 'In strictest confidence Smith proposes to ensure the Great Southern Railway does get certain additional supplies by manipulating shipments within existing quotas... should we tell the minister?' On 28 December the reply came: 'What a good man Norman Smith must be. I have mentioned the matter to the minister [Lloyd George] without showing him the papers and he seems well satisfied.'[96] It is impossible to conceive civil servants taking such actions, especially in wartime, without relying on the political support of their ministers. In the coalition government the Ministry of Fuel and Power and the Dominions Office were held by Liberal and Labour ministers. The civil servants could justify their actions as being fully in accordance with the position on Ireland adopted by the Economic Committee on Éire in March 1942. They had the previous August dismissed the objections to a change of policy on Irish supplies as 'primarily political. The answer is that... arbitrary restrictions should be relaxed when such a course is in our interest.'[97]

The urgency of the Irish coal supply position diminished after 1942, judging from the frequency of conversations between Leydon and Smith. On 19 March 1943, Robson, Norman Smith's deputy, wrote in an aside: 'Insofar as the GSR is concerned, I think we are keeping them going fairly well.'[98] The success of this initiative is attested to in a letter from Bredin to Leydon on 31 March 1943: 'Representations made to the British Government in August 1942 resulted in an improvement in the allocation of coal to the company for the operation of the existing restricted services connected with the conveyance of goods and livestock for export.'[99] In 1943 the GSR was urgently seeking additional supplies of lubricating oil. On this occasion, the Ministry of Food was not prepared to take the lead on presenting a memo to the war cabinet. In a number of memoranda, Denis Browne stressed that the coal initiative of 1942 had not been accepted and no additional supplies had been allocated. The vehemence with which this untruth was written into the file on a number of occasions suggests a desire by all concerned on the British side to cover their tracks.[100]

This strange episode demonstrates the capacity of the Guinness for wheat deal to trigger further demands from other ministries who dealt with Ireland. It also proves conclusively that for coal consumers the central issue was one of coal quality. Norman Smith was able to solve the coal problems of the GSR 'by manipulating existing quotas'. Given that the Ministry of War Transport controlled tonnages carried, it was only through directing higher quality coal that existing quotas could be manipulated. A hierarchy of ministries developed, with those like Economic Warfare and War Transport taking a secondary place to ministries that had actual control of the commodities in demand.

It is difficult to estimate how many extra cattle were carried as a result of the additional coal. As can be seen from Table 4, fewer cattle were transported in 1943 – when better British coal became available – than in 1942. During the peak livestock season (the last two quarters of the year), 1,906 special trains were programmed in 1943 compared to 1,795 trains in the same period of 1942, an increase of four trains per week. Based on a round trip of 300 miles and a consumption estimate of 80 lbs per mile, this gives a consumption of 42 tons of coal per week, a figure much less than the extra coal delivered.[101]

Table 4 Cattle carried on GSR rail services

1940	1941	1942	1943	1944
804,000	626,000	993,000	882,000	805.000

Source: GSR annual reports, 1941

The restriction of coal exports in January 1941 was approached with caution by the British side due to concerns with the economy of South Wales. These restrictions were unexpected in Ireland, and the Irish response was to seek priority for the GSR and the gas companies. By October 1941 it was clear that the return of the Treaty ports, which was the object of the sanctions policy, would not be achieved. While the sanctions policy no longer had clearly defined objectives, it could not be abandoned without loss of face. The only tangible benefit of restrictions on coal deliveries was that it inflicted visible retribution on the Irish. Severe cutbacks in coal deliveries took place in September 1941 when the Irish had acquired ships, harvested a bumper grain crop, and landed their first cargo of Canadian wheat in an Irish vessel. Further cutbacks took place in spring 1942, leading to chaos in rail transport, yet these were effectively reversed by administrators in the British ministries responsible for food and fuel.

As Irish administrators such as Leydon lost faith in their British counterparts and learned the skill of wartime trade diplomacy, they placed successive embargos on exports of pit props, cement and Guinness. The first two initiatives were unsuccessful, but the threat of a Guinness embargo paid dividends in the form of 20,000 tons of American wheat. When the control of Irish trade policy was regularised in March 1942 with the establishment of a cabinet committee, British policy was re-aligned to take account of the needs of the war economy. This resulted in the British side being drawn towards a system of barter. Despite Maffey's fears of a retreat into self-sufficiency, the Irish side offered its industrial capacity to the British war effort. In a parallel development the increase of appeals for fuel by Irish food processing companies caused the Ministry of Food to promote a more pragmatic policy towards Ireland. This process was aided by the move of Gwyllim Lloyd George from the Ministry of Food to be the first Minister for Fuel and Power, the two ministries that jointly proposed a relaxation of policy on Ireland as it applied to the GSR. Elements of these wartime transactions entered into the folklore of the Emergency, as can be seen in James Meenan's 1969 Thomas Davis lecture which runs together a number of incidents in Anglo-Irish trade: 'The good humour of British and American forces in the six counties depended on supplies of stout: and there was at least one occasion when an intimation that these supplies could not be guaranteed on account of lack of coal for the trains to convey them produced coal supplies with remarkable celerity.'[102] Meenan was relying on recollections rather than records, so the linking together of incidents is understandable. However, he accurately describes the forces at work.

The GSR was central to the functioning of the Irish economy. Whatever the desire of Churchill's immediate circle, the British Mines Department – later the Ministry of Fuel and Power – had no intention of allowing rail services to collapse. The Mines Departments had the capacity to prevent the granting of export licences for the briquette plants in the first half of 1942. It did not do so. The option of crippling the GSR through frustrating the export of the briquette machines or duff was not exercised. Instead the Mines Department facilitated a process whereby the GSR reorganised its fuel operation in the image of a French or Spanish railway, using coal briquettes.

In late 1942 the GSR successfully linked its coal supply with the needs of the British war economy by establishing a connection in the British official mind between Irish trains and British cattle imports. Johnston, its resident representative in Britain, was central to this process, which involved securing an extra allowance of 500 tons of coal per week to assist in livestock exports. In addition, from June 1942 the GSR received regular deliveries of Phurnacite, a premium fuel, the significance of which is discussed more extensively in Chapter 8.

The inter-departmental conflicts on the British side arose from the failure of the sanctions policy to achieve its objective. The ministries in charge of commodities had difficult mandates with tangible objectives and were prepared to co-operate in the evasion of a cabinet decision in order to achieve these objectives. Continuity of supply was of prime importance to the Ministries of Food and Agriculture and Fisheries, which were charged with putting food on British tables. The Ministry of Fuel and Power continued the mandate of the old Mines Department to maximise British coal exports. It had in addition a mandate of 'inducing industry to burn more duffs and slurries, coke breeze and opencast coal. It was not an easy task.'[103] This explains its strong interest in 'Keeping the GSR going'.[104] This mandate would have suffered a setback if GSR services had collapsed due to a failure in the coal supply.

Caruana and Rockoff, in their analysis of the wartime trade sanctions imposed on Spain, draw three general conclusions:

1. The outcomes of sanctions are hard to predict because the factors which influence the outcomes are so diverse.
2. The choice of goals that can be monitored effectively is an important determinant of whether goals can be achieved.
3. Co-operation among the countries imposing the sanctions is critical for success.[105]

The relevance of point one to the Irish situation can be seen in the way the Irish side partially counteracted the sanctions policy of December 1940 through the national turf campaign and the foundation of Irish Shipping. With regard to point two, it is clear that once the British side had acknowledged that the ports were unlikely to be returned, there was no alternative objective to the sanctions policy. A new British policy emerged in March 1942, developed in response to the Irish embargo on Guinness exports and the offer of Irish manufacturing capacity. Taken together, these initiatives allowed the British side to quietly abandon Churchill's December 1940 policy without loss of face. In offering manufacturing capacity the Irish side moved from an Iberian model of economic neutrality based on the supply of primary produce to an economic relationship with Britain equivalent to the economic relationship between Sweden, Switzerland and Germany where manufactured articles were supplied in addition to primary products.

Point three regarding co-operation among those imposing sanctions does not at first seem applicable to the Irish situation, as only one country was imposing sanctions. However, if 'interests' is substituted for 'countries', the relevance of point three becomes obvious. A unity of purpose in the maintenance of sanctions is vital to success. In the case of the GSR, a gap opened up between the ministries concerned with the administration of the British sanctions policy. This vacuum was filled by administrators in those departments responsible for food and fuel who applied their own view of the needs of the British war economy and in so doing subverted a cabinet decision. They also reflected the needs of 1942 rather than harking back to the events of 1922.

Notes

1   C. Leitz., *Nazi Germany and Neutral Europe* (Manchester, 2000); N. Wylie (ed.), *European Neutrals and Non-Belligerents During the Second World War* (Cambridge, 2001). In addition, see D.L. Wheeler, 'Allied relations and negotiations with Portugal' at www.usembassyisreal.com

2   See Wylie, *European Neutrals*, p.247 for reference to Spain's 'desperate need' for fuel, and p.340 for the premium placed on securing access to German coal and raw materials.

3   P. Canning, *British Policy Towards Ireland, 1921–1941* (London, 1985), pp.296–303.

4   Canning, *British Policy*, pp.296–9.

5   GSRGM 43436, 'Chief Officers' Conference' , minute of meeting, 28 January 1940.

6   NA Department of Foreign Affairs (hereafter DFA) P23.1, Reihill to Williams, 2 September 1940.

7   NA DFA P23.1, Leydon to Smith, 8 December 1940.

8   TNA POWE 26/398, memo on export policy to Spain, 1939.

9   J. Colville, *The Fringes of Power: Downing Street Diaries 1939–October 1941* (London, 1985), p.363.

10 TNA T161/1402, Churchill to Wood, 5 December 1940.

11 TNA T161/1402, Churchill to Wood, 27 December 1940.

12 TNA T161/1402, undated memo, Wood to Churchill, December 1940. Treasury minute, 16 December 1940.

13 A. Bullock, *Bevin* (London, 1967), pp.52–3.

14 S. Broadberry and M. Harrison, *The Economics of World War 1* (Cambridge, 2005), p.142.

15 M. Abbenhuis, *The Art of Staying Neutral: The Netherlands in the First World War* (Amsterdam, 2006), p.130.

16 T. Kristiansen, 'The Norwegian merchant fleet during the First World War, the Second World War and the Cold War', paper delivered to 30th ICMH conference, Rabat, August 2004.

17 P.G. Murphy, 'Reconstruction of the Pigeon House electricity station', *Transactions of the Institute of Civil Engineers* (TICE), 62 (1939–40), p.143.

18 TNA POWE 26/408, minutes of meeting of lord president's coal committee, May 1941.

19 TNA MAF 83/215, 'Coal exports from GB as affected by cereals switch', minute of meeting, 24 January 1941.

20 NA DFA P23, note of phone call, Leydon to Smith, 23 January 1941.

21 NA DFA P23, report by Leydon, 28 January 1941.

22 TNA CAB 72/25, minutes of meeting, 5 March 1942.

23 TNA T161/1402, Smith to Dunnet, 30 July 1941, Treasury to Food, 8 August 1941.
24 TNA T161/1402, report of meeting, 7 February 1941, Treasury memo, 21 March 1941.
25 NA DFA P23, report by Leydon, 25 July 1941.
26 C. Crowe, R. Fanning, M. O Kennedy, D. Keogh and E. O'Halpin (eds), *Documents on Irish Foreign Policy: IV, 1932–1936* (Dublin, 2004), p.xxiv.
27 TNA T161/1402, Kingsley Wood to Lloyd, 29 October 1941.
28 TNA T161/1402, Wood to Churchill, 20 February 1941.
29 TNA T161/1402, Wood to Churchill, 11 March 1941.
30 NA DFA P23, copy letter Rank to Woolton, 22 March 1941.
31 TNA T161/1402, report of meeting, 22 May 1941.
32 TNA T161/1402, undated memo, Wood to Churchill, December 1940. Treasury minute, 16 December 1940.
33 TNA T161/1402, report of meeting, 28 August 1941.
34 TNA T161/1402, Cranborne to Kingsley Wood, 2 September 1940.
35 TNA T161/1402, Churchill to Wood and Dominions Secretary, 7 September 1941.
36 TNA T161/1402, Kingsley Wood to Churchill, 2 September 1941.
37 TNA T161/1402, minute of meeting, 11 September 1941 contains this report.
38 TNA T161/1402, report of meeting, 11 September 1941.
39 TNA T161/1402, Jenkins to Dunnett, 23 August 1941.
40 TNA T161/1402, report, 10 September 1941.
41 Ibid.
42 TNA T161/1402, J. Colville to H Wilson-Smith, Treasury, 14 September 1941.
43 T. Grey, *The Lost Years* (Dublin, 1997), p.143. F. Forde, T*he Long Watch: The History of the Irish Merchant Marine in World War Two* (Dublin, 1981), p.38.
44 *Economist*, 19 January 1942.
45 NA DFA P23.1, note of meeting, 10 October 1941.
46 NA DFA P23.1, note of meeting, 10 October 1941, note of phone call, 22 October 1941.
47 TNA T161/1402, report of meeting, 11 October 1941. See also Forde, *The Long Watch*, p.37.
48 R.J. Hammond, *Food: The Growth of Policy* (London, 1951), pp.175–8 for this issue.
49 T161/1402, report of meeting, 11 October 1941.
50 Canning, *British Policy*, p.310.
51 See Note 12 above.
52 TNA T161/1402, report of meeting with Dockrell.
53 NA DFA P23.1, note of phone conversation, Leydon to Robson, 4 December 1941.
54 NA DFA P23.1 passim.
55 NA DFA P34, Leydon to Boland, 4 May 1943.
56 R. Fisk, *In Time of War: Ireland, Ulster and the Price of Neutrality* (Dublin, 1983), p.455.
57 TNA CAB 72/25, minute of meeting, 5 March 1942.
58 The initial offer was for wheat delivered to Halifax. The final offer was for wheat delivered to Dublin.
59 TNA T161/1402, Kingsley Wood to Arthur Greenwood, 7 May 1942.
60 TNA T161/1402, copy memo, 8 May 1942.
61 TNA MAF 83/355, Hand to Browne, 17 July 1942.
62 TNA MAF 83/355, minutes of meeting, 5 March 1942.
63 TNA CAB 72/25, minutes of meeting, 1 May 1942.
64 TNA MAF 83/355, minutes of meeting, 29 May 1942.
65 TNA CAB 72/25, minute of meeting, 29 May 1942.
66 B. Girvin, *The Emergency* (London, 2006), p.322.

67 NA DFA P33, Forsyth to Leydon, 17 May 1944.
68 TNA MAF 83/1114, Foreign Office to Norman Smith, 27 July 1942.
69 D. Bourgeois, 'Relations Economiques Germano Suisses: Un Bilan Economique de 1944', in *Business Helevetique et Troiseme Reich* (Zurich, 1998), p.104.
70 TNA MAF 83/355, 'Supplies of coal to Éire for maintenance of exports', letter from Drinagh co-op to Ministry of Food, July 1941.
71 NA DFA P23.1, note of phone call, 31 October 1941.
72 TNA MAF 83/355, Norman Smith to Cheyne, 1 July 1941.
73 TNA MAF 83/355, minute sheet, 30 October 1941.
74 TNA CAB 72/25, position paper EPE (Economic Policy Éire) 42/3, 27 April 1942.
75 M.J. Kennedy, *Division and Consensus: The Politics of Cross-Border Relations, 1925–1969* (Dublin, 2000), pp.78–87.
76 GSRGM 50541, Bredin to Johnston, 26 January 1942.
77 This ministry was established in June 1942 with Maj. G. Lloyd George as minister.
78 TNA MAF 83/355, Smith to Browne, 1 April, 1 June 1942.
79 TNA MAF 83/355, minute sheet, 15 July 1942, Townsend to Browne, 17 July 1942.
80 See Chapter 2, Note 37.
81 TNA MAF 83/355, minute sheet, 7 August 1942.
82 Ibid.
83 TNA MAF 83/355, Woolton to Lloyd George, 18 August 1942.
84 GNR working timetable 1943 shows two trains per day from Drogheda to Belfast.
85 NA DT S12921, Seán McEntee to Taoiseach, 22 July 1942, Teastas práinneach form F1, 2 Meán Fóir [September] 1942, R.C. Ferguson to Maurice Moynihan, 10 December 1942.
86 TNA MAF 83/355, Vanderpeer (Agriculture and Fisheries) to French (Food), 24 August 1942.
87 TNA MAF 83/355, Lloyd George to Woolton, 31 August 1942.
88 GSRGM 54811, 'Chairman's letter to Minister for Power and Fuel', Bredin to Johnston 23 July 1942, note of phone call 12 August 1942.
89 GSRGM 54811, Reynolds to N. Smith, 18 August 1942.
90 TNA CAB 72/25, EPE 42/21, 20 November 1942.
91 *Railway Gazette*, 18 December 1942, p.615.
92 TNA MAF 83/355, memorandum to Economic Committee on Éire, 24 November 1942.
93 TNA MAF 83/355, minute of Economic Committee on Éire, 3 December 1942.
94 TNA MAF 83/355, minute sheet, 10 October 1943.
95 TNA MAF 83/355, Selbourne to Cranborne, 12 October 1943.
96 TNA MAF 83/355, Browne to Knight, 17 December 1942, Knight to Browne, 28 December 1942.
97 TNA CAB 72/25, position paper EPE 42/3, 27 April 1942.
98 TNA CAB 72/25, Knight to Browne, 19 March 1943.
99 GSRGM 59480, 'Lubricating oil supplies', Bredin to Leydon, 31 March 1943.
100 TNA MAF 83/355, minute sheet references by Denis Browne, 23 April and 14 June 1943.
101 IRRS Library, GSR Weekly Circular, bound volumes 1941–1945.
102 K.B. Nowlan and T.D. Williams, *Ireland in the War Years and After, 1939–1951* (Dublin, 1959), p.33.
103 W.H.B. Court, *History of the Second World War Coal* (London, 1951), p.374.
104 See Note 98 above.
105 L. Caruana and H. Rockoff, 'An elephant in the garden: The allies, Spain and oil in World War II', National Bureau of Economic Research working paper 12228. I am grateful to Cormac Ó Gráda, UCD for this reference.

Plate 1: Unloading turf from converted passenger coaches at Kingsbridge (Heuston) station (courtesy of Gerry Beesley).

Plate 2: A trainload of turf awaiting departure from Portarlington
(courtesy of ESB Archives).

(9617).U9311.Wt.4958/P4343.3.5000.3/43.W.P.W.Ltd.Special.

SERIAL NO. 3231

Supplementary Soap Ration Card.

EXTRA ALLOWANCE FOR...........................MONTHS.

Date of Issue...*1st. Octr. 1943.*...

Name of Holder...*Patrick Scully*...............................

Address...*49 Annamore Park, Cabra, Dublin*...

Occupation of Holder...*Coalman on Briquetting Plant*...

Name and Address of Employer...*G.S.R. Broadstone.*...

INSTRUCTIONS.

1. Each of the Coupons on this Card may be exchanged for the same quantity of soap as is obtainable in exchange for an ordinary soap coupon.
2. To obtain the soap you must hand up this ration card to the shop-keeper, who will remove the correct number of coupons. On no account remove coupons yourself as this will render them invalid.
3. When the coupons have been used the Card must be returned with an application for a new Supplementary Soap Ration Card.
4. This Card may be used only by or on behalf of the person named above.

John Leydon
Secretary

Dept. of Supplies.

GALLUANACH SOAP	GALLUANACH SOAP	GALLUANACH SOAP

Plate 3: Workers on the briquette plants were allowed extra soap rations (courtesy of IRRS).

Plate 4: A locomotive crew at work. This photo post-dates the emergency
when such large lumps of coal would have been unknown
(courtesy of IRRS).

Plate 5: From left ash rake, dart and picker for breaking clinker, shovel
(courtesy of David Carse).

GREAT SOUTHERN RAILWAYS

AIR RAID PRECAUTIONS

NOTICE TO PASSENGERS

On receipt of an Air Raid warning do not try to leave the train while it is in motion.

If the train stops away from a platform do not attempt to leave the train unless advised by the Company's staff to do so. If advised to remain in the train pull down all Blinds and Curtains as a protection against flying glass, and lie on floor if space permits.

If train is at a platform get out at once and go to the nearest Air Raid Shelter. If there is no such Shelter passengers should scatter away from buildings, and take cover.

THE GENERAL MANAGER,
KINGSBRIDGE, DUBLIN.

(5,000 F 4/1 5/43)

Plate 6: Air raid precautions notice (courtesy of IRRS).

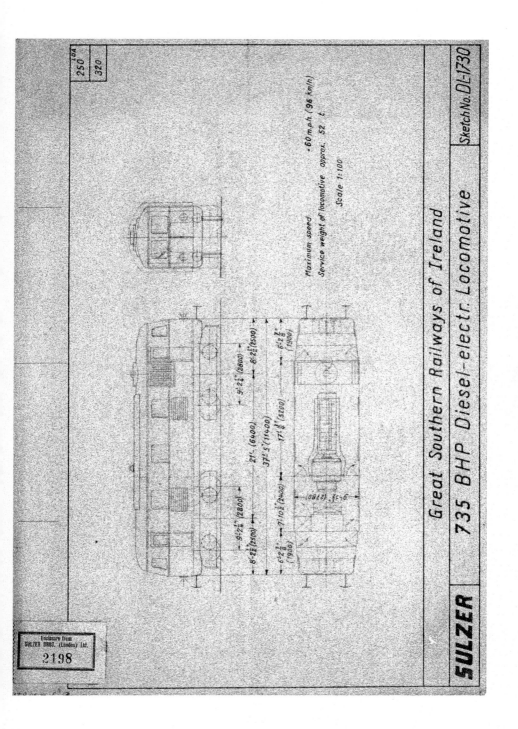

Plate 7: Sulzer sketch of a Diesel locomotive (courtesy of IRRS).

Plate 8: Kingsbridge goods yard. During the emergency period the railway became a predominantly freight operation (courtesy of Sean Kennedy).

5

Turf

Domestic fuel played a central role in maintaining civilian morale. Norman Smith remarked following a visit to Dublin in August 1941: 'The pinch has not really been acutely felt yet but it needs little imagination to realise what the situation will be when cold weather sets in and houses with no alternative means of heating or cooking (as in those of the poorer classes) are unable to obtain coal.'[1] When coal imports ceased in 1941, turf became crucial to survival, and was substituted for coal on a scale inconceivable in peacetime. While most turf burned today is in briquette format, sod turf was the mainstay of the Emergency fuel supply. During the Emergency, turf changed from being a smallholder crop largely harvested in the western countries to one produced on an industrial basis in the midlands by an imported labour force. The size of turf harvest and the long distances to be covered meant that the railway system was vital. However, problems quickly arose as turf had to compete with other harvests such as grain and sugar beet for railway resources. The government set priorities through an Emergency Powers Order setting out which traffic would have first claim on railway wagons.

The war caused shortages of domestic fuel throughout Europe. Even Switzerland with its abundant hydro-electricity restricted the use of domestic hot water to one day per week.[2] Railway companies throughout Europe were under pressure to transport large amounts of fuel to urban consumers. In Sweden, 'From a technical point of view it was possible to replace imported fuel by domestic fuel [timber]... In practice however, this was impossible because of the fact that such a transition would create impossible demands for increased transport, more labour and greater storage space.'[3] These constraints applied equally to the use of turf in Ireland during the Emergency years. Turf traffic stretched the capacity of the Irish railway system as did the transport of coal in Britain and the transport of wood in Sweden.

Ireland had some advantages in finding substitutes for imported coal. The country was almost self-sufficient in electricity, with Ardnacrusha's output able to meet demand for most of the year. The fledgling Turf Development Board, established in 1935, had laid the basis for a modern peat extraction industry. The weakness of the Irish position lay with the dependence of utilities such as railways and gas companies on high-quality British coal. The ESB was dependent on imported coal to maintain supplies when Shannon water levels were low. Delays in the completion of the Poulaphouca hydro-electric scheme and in the delivery of harvesting equipment for Clonsast bog hampered Ireland's moves towards self-sufficiency in fuel. While neutral countries such as Switzerland, Sweden or Argentina made extensive use of timber, Ireland, as the first two lines of the poem *Cill Cais* remind us, had been a relatively under-forested country since the early eighteenth century.[4]

'Cad a dhéanfaimid feasta gan adhmad,
tá deireadh na gcoillte ar lár?'

Under the 1928 Forestry Act planting was encouraged and the felling of trees restricted. Planting increased from 1934 onwards, but the stock of mature timber in the country[5] was insufficient for timber fuel to play the role that it did in Sweden when Germany restricted coal exports.[6] The London *Times* of 7 October 1939 wrote of Ireland that 'The only commodity of which a real shortage is possible is timber. Native supplies are scanty.'[7] By 1942 it was considered that 'For military reasons it is essential to prohibit indiscriminate felling of trees [where] cover would be of value in the event of hostilities,' and a prohibition was imposed on felling within 30 feet of a road.[8]

Traditionally, turf was burned as domestic fuel in the vicinity of bogland. The more widespread use had been discussed in the transactions of learned societies for almost a century and had figured in official publications of the Dáil and Castle administrations.[9] However, by 1921 'All the experiments had failed and... the bogs were being used then as a fuel source only when coal was unavailable.'[10] The TDB was the first serious state-backed effort to develop turf as an industrial fuel, and its early days are described by C.S. Andrews in *Man of No Property*. Andrews wrote: 'Broadly there are two types of bog in Ireland – blanket bog and high bog. The blanket bogs are confined to the west [and] are relatively shallow... The high bog which is deeper and more variable in quality... is to be found in the Bog of Allen and the central Plain.'[11] The problems of exploiting the midland bogs were 'a problem of shortage – first, a shortage of labour; secondly, a shortage of existing face banks, and thirdly, there are large virgin bogs of deep turf which are undrained.'[12] The logistical contradiction was that the best available turf was farthest from the east coast, where potential demand was greatest, often in bogs of smaller area, while the turf nearest the east coast was difficult to harvest.

Andrews had worked towards the establishment of a national distribution network for turf, securing a preferential rate from the railway companies. In the year ending October 1935 the GSR carried 10,686 tons of turf.[13] The GNR kept any reservations on this initiative to itself and its traffic manager recommended that a request for a low rate be granted 'as a gesture of good intentions in connection with a project not expected to materialise'.[14]

The TDB put increased emphasis on high-quality turf, and by September 1939 had acquired the experimental bog at Turraun, County Offaly and was developing bogs in Lyracrompane, County Kerry and Clonsast, near Portarlington. In 1939 the TDB re-opened a turf briquette factory in Lullymore, County Kildare. This factory used a patented process to manufacture briquettes from machine-harvested turf dust and had operated briefly during the late 1930s, before the venture ran out of cash.[15] Sir John Purser Griffith, long time advocate of turf and developer of Turraun bog, told C.S. Andrews: 'The future of the bogs rested in the production of macerated turf to be burned in power stations sited on the bogs.'[16] It was decided to build a turf-fired power station in Portarlington, but the project was suspended due to wartime materials shortages, being revived in 1945 and expanded to a network of turf stations in the midlands.[17]

This was the state of the turf industry in June 1940 when Britain reduced the export of coal, causing the Irish government to introduce coal rationing at half a ton per household per month.[18] The increased use of turf became an issue of survival. For turf enthusiasts such as Frank Aiken, minister for defence, this was an opportunity to substitute turf for coal on a scale inconceivable in peacetime conditions. C.S. Andrews and Hugo Flinn, the parliamentary secretary to the minister for finance, were the driving force behind these efforts. Flinn was an electrical engineer with a business background and was, according to Andrews, 'an improbable Fianna Fáil supporter [and] the man in the gap', despite his 'irascibility, rudeness and indifference to the feelings of his subordinates'.[19] The government expected public utilities to co-operate with efforts to substitute turf for coal, and the seeming reluctance of railway and gas undertakings to successfully adopt turf led to accusations of technological conservatism. In October 1942 the Emergency Scientific Research Bureau suggested that 'the possibility of damage to retorts should not deter the [Dublin Gas] company from using turf for the manufacture of gas.'[20] This view continued in a post-war context where 'The government, and especially Seán Lemass, overrated the potential and especially the short-term potential of turf, and dismissed the often valid objections of the ESB as bureaucratic obstructionism.'[21]

In April 1941 the 'Turf Development Board scheme for increasing turf production' was launched under the direction of Hugo Flinn, and a multi-agency turf executive was appointed. Its function was to oversee a scheme utilising the county councils to produce what was termed 'national' turf, which was carried to urban centres on the east coast and to Cork and Limerick. Fuel Importers Limited, originally established to procure coal imports, broadened its remit and distributed turf in the cities. No major role was assumed for the railways as it was assumed that:

> The turf-producing counties would work for the winter on turf and coal coming into the country...would be reserved for the use of the non-turf counties...the problem resolved itself down to the distribution of turf within the turf counties and as the hauls involved would seldom exceed 20 to 25 miles the job was largely one to be done by road transport...In July 1941 the Turf executive was informed that the prospect of coal arriving in quantities sufficient to meet the requirements of the non-turf areas were not likely to be realised...As the largest surplus was produced on the extreme western seaboard and as long distance transport would be required, the railway companies were at once called in to deal with this new aspect of the problem.[22]

This was a parallel of the situation on the Swedish railway system where 'the task of supplying Stockholm with fuel hitherto met by shipping imported coal has now fallen heavily on the railways.'[23] Transport costs were a large element of the final cost of turf in the cities. In summer 1941, turf delivered to the bog roadside in Mayo at a cost of 12 shillings per ton retailed at 44 shillings per ton in Dublin if delivered by rail and up to 66 shillings per ton if delivered by road using scarce petrol.[24] The nearest turf to the eastern seaboard was in the midland bogs which were largely undeveloped in 1942.[25] Therefore, in 1941 and 1942 Mayo, Kerry and Donegal were particularly important sources of supply.

The Turf Executive told the transport companies that the amount to be moved by rail would be at least 500,000 tons.[26] A short season was envisaged, beginning in June with as much as possible to be moved before the grain harvest in September. The extensive programme of rail, road and canal transport was planned before the severe cuts in coal quality began to hit the GSR. On 10 April 1941 the government used the Emergency Powers Act to suspend part of the Road Transport Act 1933 and allow unrestricted haulage of turf. Although this went against a policy of restricting private road transport, the railway companies did not protest. The GSR road freight manager wrote to Bredin: 'If matters develop on the lines ... anticipated the demand for transport would be very much greater than the company could possibly meet ... relaxation would, to my mind, be imperative sooner or later.'[27]

The TDB promoted and co-ordinated harvesting through a network of parish councils, guaranteed a price to producers, and used the county councils as the turf-harvesting apparatus. The Mayo county surveyor, T.P. Flanagan, described how after Hugo Flinn addressed a conference of parish council delegates in Castlebar he 'immediately followed up this meeting with a circular to all clergy and to all Parish councils ... I next arranged a series of meetings in the principal turf-producing parishes.'[28] A setback threatened when 'Dublin merchants and local speculators got busy ... they confined their activity to the better bog areas within a reasonable distance from a railway station ... They ascertained the county council prices and contracts and in all cases offered higher prices.'[29] Such speculative acquisition of turf drove prices up and could not be tolerated.[30] Transport and transport costs were an integral part of the equation of getting turf to the urban consumer. The country was divided into turf and non-turf areas. It became an offence to move turf by rail, canal or lorry out of a turf county without a licence. Three successive orders under the Emergency Powers Act delineated increased areas until the turf areas comprised all of Connaught, together with Clare, Kerry, the midland counties and parts of Limerick, Waterford and Cork. This meant, for example, that it was illegal to consign turf without a licence to either of the Cork city stations or to any station in Waterford east of Dungarvan. According to Flanagan, this order 'was the master stroke which saved the situation for the outlying districts and gave some hope of turf at reasonable price to the poor'.[31]

The GSR was accustomed to handling seasonal traffic. Livestock peaked in the autumn and coal peaked during the summer stocking season. Grain was carried from late August, while the four sugar factories were served by the beet campaign which ran from October to January. The movement of such traffic is best visualised as a single logistical system, involving a balanced flow of loaded and empty vehicles. This meant that empty lorries had to be on the bog on time to lift the turf and these, in turn, had to meet empty wagons in the stations, before they could make their return trips to the bog. The supply of empty wagons was in turn determined by the speed of unloading on the east coast.[32] The GSR owned approximately 4,000 open trucks,[33] but wagon shortages were beginning to emerge in 1938 and it was inevitable that these would worsen when the turf season overlapped with the beet season, which absorbed 50 per cent of the GSR's open trucks.[34] In late 1939 an unsuccessful attempt was made to procure steel to build new wagons. The only way of resolving the capacity problem was to increase the load of existing vehicles or to adapt non-freight carrying vehicles. A programme to fit creels to existing open wagons, almost doubling their capacity, began in May 1941 and continued until 850 wagons were converted. During the foot-and-mouth outbreak of 1941 it was proposed to convert 700 cattle wagons for turf use and 378 vehicles were converted before the programme was stopped at the insistence of the Department of Agriculture.[35] In October 1941 a similar programme was started involving removing the roofs of old passenger coaches, enabling them to carry turf, with sixty-six coaches being converted. The coaches had a passenger train brake and were formed into six block trains of eleven coaches each, thus allowing a higher speed and a quicker turnaround. A coach train took six hours forty-five minutes from Galway, compared to nine hours by traditional goods train.

Special turf trains commenced running in summer 1941 with three trains per day from Mayo.[36] These trains were operated from Donegal, Mayo, Roscommon, Longford, Kerry and Offaly to Dundalk, Drogheda, Dublin, Wexford, Waterford and Cork, and were supplemented by wagons of turf hauled on the scheduled goods services. From August 1941 Donegal turf was arriving daily in Dundalk by the GNR. By the end of August five turf specials were arriving in Dublin daily from the west and four special trains were operating daily to Cork, Waterford, Limerick and Wexford.[37] Cork was served from Glenbeigh, County Kerry and Limerick from Athlone, while Drogheda was served from Mayo through Claremorris and Enniskillen.[38] From Flinn's point of view turf was the most important traffic on the railway. In September he reported to de Valera: 'From Laois, Offaly and Westmeath are now coming in about 300 tons per day. It is hoped to double this amount within the week. We will drive this to the limit both of transport and of available supplies, and in the process we will learn the limits.'[39] At this point it seemed that the transport campaign was going well as on 20 September Flinn informed the GSR of his 'appreciation at what you have done and the promptitude with which you have attended to the matters raised'.[40] However, by 16 October Flinn reported to de Valera that a serious deterioration had taken place:

> The present position is definitely unsatisfactory. Improvement was being made up to the third week in September when deterioration set in largely due to inferior fuel on the railways. This became both short in quantity and thoroughly bad in quality, culminating in practical suspension of traffic about 10 October...At the same time we received intimation from the railway company that due to the imminence of the beet traffic they were withdrawing the lorries which had been used by us for transport to railhead...Yesterday we received an intimation from the Great Southern Railways that owing to the fact that they had received 14,000 tons of coal from England they had withdrawn the whole of the wagons previously used for turf transport for the purpose of distributing this coal.[41]

Lemass defended this reallocation of wagons on the grounds that the coal concerned came from windfall cargoes carried in ships bound for Spain and Portugal which had missed convoys and which needed to be turned around quickly.[42] The shortage of railway wagons caused inter-departmental tensions. Flinn wrote to the taoiseach that '[The] lack of direction on this matter was prejudicing transport of turf...On 19 September this matter was again raised and a meeting was held...The general tenor of this meeting was unsatisfactory from the point of view of priority for turf.'[43] Turf deliveries by rail slowed due to declining coal quality, and in October Flinn secured 1,000 tons of coal from army reserves for the GSR for turf transport.[44] This did not, however, solve the long-term problem, which was an insufficiency of wagons to meet peak seasonal demands. On 27 October T.P. Flynn, assistant secretary in the Department of Industry and Commerce, wrote to J.P. Candy that 'There are many objections to a directive, but I think we shall have to face something of this kind...Livestock is first because trains must have priority in running. The scheduled programme of beet can scarcely be interfered with. Grain and flour, being food for the people, must, I think, precede fuel. Coal comes before turf because the rapid turnaround of the few steamers available is dependent on the immediate removal of the coal by railway wagons.'[45]

On 29 October Flinn told the Dáil that there were 2,000 lorries engaged in turf transport in the turf areas, but that they were only usable in the inner belt which was rapidly being exhausted. He continued: 'The only place where there is a large quantity of turf to be tapped is in the distant areas and over rail, and if the position is to be made secure in the non-turf areas over the winter it depends upon adequate rail traffic . . . the point has now been reached where priorities will have to be set.' Noting that it took a gallon of petrol to move a ton of turf twenty miles, Flinn stressed to the Dáil how important it was 'that the largest possible use should be made of the railway system and that the largest amount of its stock as possible shall be rendered available for this purpose'.[46] Flinn's performance in the Dáil was impressive and he seemed in control of his brief. However, two weeks later he was privately much less sanguine in a memo to de Valera: 'The collapse which we envisaged is now complete . . . the only turf which we found it possible to arrange . . . on this day consisted of a train which by special permission of the Archbishop of Tuam was to be loaded at Cloonaskeragh, County Galway. Owing to very bad weather conditions it was impossible to unload this train.'[47]

Flinn's demand for prioritisation of turf received a setback on 3 November when an inter-departmental meeting concluded that 'the majority of departments were opposed to a definite number of wagons being allocated.'[48] This defeat was compounded on 5 November when the GSR advised Candy that they were again suspending turf haulage in order to facilitate the distribution of coal from boats that had arrived in Dublin. Flinn wrote to Lemass immediately asking for details of recent coal shipments in order to allow him to make a judgement on the chaotic state of turf deliveries.[49] He followed this on 6 November with a memo to the taoiseach seeking a definite wagon allocation and concluding that 'the justification or otherwise of the help given in the past and proposed to be given in the future must be judged by the actual effective service which [the GSR] shall in fact show itself capable of giving to the State during this emergency.'[50] Flinn went on to suggest the appointment of a controller of railways. This is the first suggestion of governmental control of the GSR. The covering note is annotated 'feicithe ag an dTaoiseach' ('seen by the Taoiseach').

The problems being faced by the TDB and the GSR were not unique. In Britain a major constraint on railway coal-carrying capacity was the supply of empty wagons.[51] In winter 1941 'a general priority to coal such as had been given the previous winter was not again granted.'[52] There was a need to strike a balance between the demand for fuel transport and the demand for transport for other commodities. In fact the carriage of seasonal traffic posed capacity difficulties in peace and in wartime. In the case of Welsh coal, 'Every September throughout the nineteenth and well into the twentieth century shipments to Italy and parts of France were well nigh stopped as all the wagons normally used for carrying coal were required for fruit-harvesting operations.'[53]

The debate on priorities was resolved on 10 November when an Emergency Powers Order was approved by cabinet setting out the commodities that would have first claim on the company's freight services and their stock of wagons. Priority was accorded to livestock, beet, grain, coal and turf in that order.[54] However, livestock and grain did not compete with turf for open wagons. This meant that in the allocation of open wagons, turf had a priority behind coal and beet as long as the four beet factories were in operation. Flinn lost the battle for a quota of wagons to be exclusively allocated to turf. A similar situation occurred on Britain's railways in 1943 when 'the threat to the movement of coal through a shortage of wagons was so serious that the Railway Executive Committee suggested a ban on the use of mineral wagons for general traffic ... [this was] rejected on the grounds that it would give overriding priority to coal traffic.'[55] Flinn grudgingly informed the taoiseach on 14 November that he had decided to accept the priority order, advising that the Department of Industry and Commerce was now responsible for a sufficiency of empty wagons at loading stations.[56]

In Britain the Ministry of Transport had learned a good deal about coal movement in the first winter of the war.[57] Similarly in Ireland, in November 1941 a conference of county surveyors was convened to analyse the 1941 season.[58] The most significant lesson learned was the need to match production to available transport capacity. The meeting noted that in Donegal 'transport facilities were incapable of moving the present surplus before July 1943', while in Kerry 'transport facilities limit the quantity which can be delivered to Cork city to 10,000 tons per month.' In Clare it was anticipated that 'serious transport difficulties would be in the north-west and the county surveyor should concentrate on the remainder of the county.' It was decided to abandon harvesting in Donegal and suspend county council cutting in west Galway in the hope that the labour released would go to the new bogs being developed in Kildare and Offaly.[59] Donegal had the largest backlog of untransported turf and was serviced by the GNR, which was relatively untroubled by coal problems. In September 1941 the GNR chemist, Bratt, reported on the difficulties being encountered in Donegal: 'I have been unofficially told that next year's programme for Donegal is in the melting pot ... suggestions are being made that instead of cutting turf next year the turf-cutting population should be transplanted en masse to the midlands.' In November the chief mechanical engineer stated that '*all* [my emphasis] our special turf trains can always be coaled at Derry without interfering in any way with the coal stocks in Éire.'[60] The logistical problems with Donegal turf occurred between the bog and the railhead, and the GNR experience in Donegal shows what the GSR might have achieved with reasonable coal.

By November 1941 so much turf had been transported that an unexpected lack of demand for the fuel in urban areas led to a review of turf transport.[61] In mid-January it was decided to suspend all road transport except from Clonsast, to re-allocate turf wagons to carry firewood, and to suspend all rail haulage of turf for six weeks.[62] These moves were a belated recognition of the constraints which the Irish climate imposed on turf harvesting. The transport of the 1941 turf harvest can be compared with the transport of timber in Sweden. Ollson observes: 'Heavy use was made of the Swedish transport network ... more wood ... [was] cut mainly in Northern Sweden ... but in that event far more wagons and engines would have been required than were available to transport the wood to the consumers in southern Sweden.'[63]

One million tons of turf had been harvested in 1941 but according to Andrews 'much was lost due to the misguided policy of late cutting and the inadequacy of the transport system.'[64] By March 1942 Flinn's new thinking was indicated in this memo to the taoiseach:[65]

> One of the principal lessons learned from the turf campaign of 1941 is that of transport conditions and limitations; and the main conclusions are:
>
> 1. Under existing conditions of transport there is a period – say from November to February ... in which long distance transport of turf by rail or road is undesirable.
> 2. That transport should be continuous throughout the year except for that intermission.
> 3. That really large provision for any winter must be the transport in the spring, summer and autumn of the previous year's harvest.
> 4. That any large dependence on a current harvest must include heavy rail transport during the wheat and beet seasons.
> 5. That the maximum capacity of the transport system is relatively small.

Turf competed with other commodities for locomotives, wagons and track space. The most important of these were grain, beet, livestock and coal traffic from Irish mines. In February 1942 Candy informed the transport companies of the plan for the coming season which involved moving a million tons of turf between March and September. The GSR estimated that this would take 800 wagons per day. Some revision was necessary as the unloading capacity at the five main unloading points was 350 wagons per day, and the maximum loading capacity of the twenty-eight designated stations was 400 wagons per day. On 4 March a lower target of 800,000 tons was set, divided between the GSR, the GNR and the Grand Canal Company, which received thirty new horse-drawn barges to serve the expanding midland bogs.[66] The programme commenced in March and intensified in May with a programme of 230 wagons a day plus a twelve-coach train. The GSR circular to staff stressed that:

> The operation of the programme will entail the use of approximately half of the stock of coal trucks, and the success of the scheme depends on each station loading only its own quota daily. If the quota for any point is exceeded it will result in overloads at some points and shortages at others. There is little margin available for turf for consignees other than Fuel Importers.[67]

This circular illustrates the high proportion of the wagon fleet dedicated to turf, and the balance between public and private turf.

Such an intensive programme required a high availability of wagons. The availability rate for covered wagons stood at 94 per cent for the last six months of 1944.[68] The rate for open wagons, crucial for the turf harvest, would have been higher, given their simpler structure. Given this level of use, and the shortage of materials for repairs, the availability rate compares well with that of 93.3 per cent in November 1938,[69] or 96 per cent in Britain during 1944.[70] The British wagon fleet was subject to bombing and requisition by the military. However, British railways had access to materials for repair, maintenance and new construction which were unavailable to the GSR. The record of the GSR in the area of wartime wagon availability stands up well, especially given the shortages of materials and lubricants and the need to use native timber.[71] The Milne report of 1948 noted that 7 per cent of the wagon stock was under or awaiting repair and described this as satisfactory having regard to the materials shortages.[72] The British railway system, under direct government control since September 1939, faced similar problems in moving coal out of the coalfields. Prior to the war a significant amount of Britain's coal was transported in small coasters,[73] but after the outbreak of war most of this traffic was transferred to rail. The railway system did not cope easily with this transfer, and according to the official history 1940–1 was 'the critical year', observing that 'the transport crisis was primarily a railway crisis.'[74]

Contemporary reports show the severity of the difficulties faced by the GSR: '8.00 p.m. special Limerick to Waterford of 14/5/42 left at 1.25 a.m. 15/5/42, arrived Clonmel [50 miles] 11.00 a.m. where engine failed and crew took rest.' On the same day a serious disruption of traffic was reported 'due to the inability of engines to function. Five Kerry and nine midland specials did not run, no engines being available.' In June 1942 harvesting was suspended for three days in Kerry due to the widespread failure of locomotives.[75] In a typical report on these events driver Hayes reported: 'When working a turf special Farranfore to Mallow, I had a load equal to 32 wagons. I informed Inspector Crowe that I would take 25 wagons to Mallow. He informed me that I should take 32. The engine failed at 31.5 milepost.' These problems were not unique to Ireland. In February 1941 a British administrator wrote: 'Droitwich gas were in a most serious problem and Mines Department arranged for 14 wagons to leave on 13 February and 12 to leave on 18. It is now 25 February and no-one in the kingdom can tell me where those wagons are.'[76]

On 11 June 1942, Industry and Commerce conveyed its dissatisfaction with the working of the turf programme and with breach of the directives issued to the company on wagon allocation. Bredin replied:

> I learn with amazement that the discharge of wagons ceases on Friday evening and does not commence until the following Monday morning ... on arrival of turf wagons at North Wall, varying numbers of wagons are marked off for shunting into the different merchants' yards. Furthermore that these merchants are permitted to select their wagons and if the contents of a particular wagon are not suitable [it is handed] back to Fuel Importers for discharge at the dump ... it is impossible to ensure a regular flow of empties ... unless the wagons are discharged promptly at North Wall.

Bredin was alluding to the use of a scarce public resource for the private business needs of fuel merchants. Candy replied to Bredin:

> North Wall has always been a troublesome spot for us. The labour there is difficult and strikes are of frequent occurrence. A half day on

Saturdays must be paid as a full day and a full day as double time and we find Saturday afternoon working is most unsatisfactory ... These difficulties will be solved when we open Liffey Junction discharge sidings ... meanwhile we are putting up with an admittedly unsatisfactory organisation at North Wall.[77]

This exchange illustrates the disruptive effect of peaks or surges on any logistical system. Thus between 21 July 1941 and 27 October 1941 deliveries to Dublin peaked on seventeen occasions. These were concentrated towards the beginning of the week, being Monday on four occasions, Tuesday and Wednesday on three occasions each. This pattern of imbalance was self-sustaining as empty wagons arrived back in the turf counties late in the week. Systemic inefficiencies were built into the system as long as harvesting worked on a five- or six-day basis while the rail transport part worked on a six- or seven-day basis.[78]

Empty wagons were scarce, and were mainly allocated to turf destined for Fuel Importers Limited. The allocation of empty wagons was a sensitive and crucial issue to smallholders trying to sell turf to the non-turf counties. In September 1942 two Kerry TDs, Fionán Lynch and Fred Crowley, made representations on behalf of constituents. In his reply, Bredin observed that in the twenty-one weeks ending 26 September, 235,635 tons of turf had been moved, of which 176,000 was for Fuel Importers Limited. He went on:

Suppliers are made up of producers and middlemen. The volume of traffic railed by the former is small. The great bulk of it is purchased by speculators ... and it is this group which is most clamant in its demand for wagons. These demands are invariably accompanied by complaints of preferential treatment ... Misrepresentation not infrequently plays a part in the endeavour to secure as large a proportion as possible of the wagon supply ... It can be appreciated ... with demand so much in excess of supply that it is not possible to satisfy all parties.[79]

Allegations of irregularity in the supply of wagons caused the demotion and transfer of a GSR employee on the West Clare section in 1942. When a similar complaint was made in 1943 a head office team was sent to investigate. They reported:

Most of the 400 producers in the area marketed their turf through agents ... the turf is ... purchased and consigned in the name of the agent, all of whom are local people and some of whom produce small quantities of turf. The present system is that wagons are allocated only to producers of turf, who record their name with the stationmaster, and are then given wagons strictly in accordance with their order on the list. The advantage of this ... is that it precludes agents from gaining control of the wagon supply and using such advantage to depress the purchase price to the producer. We recommend the continuance of this system, and are strongly of the opinion that no allocation of wagons should be made to agents, except insofar as they are also producers.[80]

These reports illustrate a number of issues. They give us a glimpse of social tensions in rural society during the period, while demonstrating the necessity for, and the effectiveness of, the restrictions on the movement of turf. They also show that by late 1942 the railway system was transporting turf effectively. There would have been no point in making such representations in the chaos of late 1941 and early 1942.

Following the sudden death of Hugo Flinn in January 1943,[81] responsibility for all turf matters passed to the Department of Supplies. C.S Andrews was appointed turf director and the turf executive was stood down. A Finance memo observed that 'it seemed to be the accepted view of those members of the executive ... that the body did not progress very satisfactorily.'[82] With the reallocation of responsibility the volume of correspondence on the transport of turf specials dwindles almost to nothing in the GSR files. This may indicate Andrews' different management style and the fact that the national turf campaign had reached equilibrium.[83] Bredin wrote a valedictory note to Candy which may be taken as a tactful coded reference to Flinn: 'I would like to say the efforts made by you personally and by your staff to simplify our many difficulties have been a great satisfaction to me.'[84]

In April 1943 John O'Brien described the coming season as 'much the same as in 1942, and having regard to the improvement in operation since last year, and the experience which has been gained it is assumed that the facilities ... provided for other traffics will at least equal those provided last year.'[85] It was anticipated that the GSR would move 398,600 tons of turf by rail in addition to 12,000 tons by road from Laois and Offaly to Dublin and a similar amount from Cork, Kerry and Clare to Cork city. The season commenced in April with eight trains per day, rising to sixteen per day between June and September, when the beet season commenced. The

GSR was able to give an estimate of the wagons needed for other traffic, which would be jeopardised by the full implementation of the turf programmes (see Appendix II).[86] From 1942 the centre of gravity shifted eastwards as the midland bogs were opened up. In 1942, Portarlington, Moate and Inny Junction were the only stations east of the Shannon loading turf. By 1944 almost twenty-two of the fifty stations supplying Dublin were east of the Shannon.[87]

Most complaints that survive in the GSR files relate to deliveries to Dublin, which was supplied from the midlands and the Mayo line. Kerry, the largest turf-producing county, supplied Cork and Wexford without generating significant complaints. There was one ignominious exception at Whit 1942.[88] Harvesting was suspended for three days due to widespread failure of locomotives. At one point there was a failed train in every station between Mallow and Killarney. However, in general the Kerry operation had a creditable record, given that the run from Cahirciveen to Enniscorthy was 202 miles, or thirty-five miles longer than the mileage from Ballina to North Wall. The higher level of complaints from some areas may be explained by the fact that certain turf was unloaded in Dublin under the noses of Candy and Andrews. In addition, the Mayo programme was a source of constant contention between the GSR and the county surveyor, who had released 400 tons of coal to the GSR in the darkest days of 1941. The failure of the GSR to deliver sufficient empty wagons to Mayo was a source of constant rancorous correspondence between Flanagan, Candy and Bredin. However, there is no trace of these tensions in the paper Flanagan delivered to the Institute of Engineers of Ireland in December 1942.

Just as coal transport caused a crisis for British railways in the winter of 1940 – the first winter of real war – the first turf season of 1941 tested the GSR system to the limit. The confusion and chaos of the hastily organised 1941 campaign was to be expected. Turf transport regularised in 1942, and had normalised by the beginning of the 1943 season. During this period the main emphasis of harvesting shifted from the western counties to the newly developed midland bogs with their imported labour force. The difficulties with wagon supply were broadly similar to the problems that affected Swedish timber transport or British coal transport, although those in charge of the programme in Ireland were obviously not to know this. In fact, the weaknesses in the rail transport campaign concealed the inefficiencies in the 1941 turf campaign. This is illustrated by the case of Donegal, which had the greatest amount of turf left on the bog at the end of 1941 despite an efficient transport campaign by the GNR using its British coal allowance. The turf transport system became more efficient during 1942, as seen in the correspondence about the working of North Wall depot, where the GSR shifted blame back to the merchants. It was not until 1944 that Bórd na Móna adopted a policy of completing the harvest in the early summer. Their quarterly report of September 1944 makes the telling point: 'The factor which has mainly contributed to the improved supply position... is that stock building commenced at a much earlier date, which allowed railway facilities, then more freely available, to be used to capacity.'[89] By September 1945 Bórd na Móna explained the necessity of 'starting the stock building much earlier to allow the full programme to be completed by the end of September when transport services were absorbed ... in beet and other priority traffic.'[90] It took four seasons to assimilate the lesson that the turf could not be effectively transported at the same time as the beet and cereals harvests. While the management of the GSR had been making this point since 1942, they were the most politically naive players in the turf logistics chain. Turf harvesting was managed either by county surveyors or by the Turf Development Board, both closely attached to political institutions at local or national level. Distribution in the urban centres was controlled by Fuel Importers Limited, whose chairman John Reihill made 'generous subscriptions to Fianna Fáil party funds [which] had brought him to the attention of Seán Lemass'.[91] The GSR was not the only weak point in the 1941 turf season, but at the time it seemed to attract a disproportionate amount of blame. Perhaps the weaknesses in turf transport combined in the official mind with the perceived failure of the GSR to use turf as a locomotive fuel.

Strategic Emergency traffic competed for scarce railway resources in a manner unknown in peacetime. Even the narrow gauge West Clare section was under pressure and turf had to be carried in cattle wagons as 'practically the entire stock of open wagons is engaged on the transport of phosphate rock between Ennistymon and Ennis.'[92] To the extent that particular commodities had identical seasonality they increased the problems associated with handling them. The successful movement of a harvest cannot be taken for granted. The German potato harvest of 1916 was partially lost due to a shortage of transport;[93] similarly, the 1941 beet harvest in Germany was partially lost due to demands made on the railway system by Operation Barbarossa;[94] in France in 1945, 'sugar beets were rotting in French fields because there was no coal to transport the beets to refineries.'[95] A national distribution network for turf was established during the Emergency and the railway system was the backbone of this system. The return of peace saw turf from the newly developed midland bogs established as an urban fuel and delivered by road. Rail transport of turf was an Emergency measure and declined after 1945 until the last rail loading point for domestic turf at Cahirciveen ceased to function in 1949.[96]

Prior to 1939, turf enthusiasts foresaw a wide range of non-fuel uses, with 'turf as fertiliser, turf as animal litter, turf as brown paper, turf as hardboard'.[97] The Emergency years saw the launching of a range of experiments with varying degrees of success. Perhaps the most costly failure was the attempt to manufacture charcoal from high-quality Turraun turf. By August 1943 the exchequer was faced with a loss of between £150 and £350 per week on the operation.[98] A proposal to transfer the operation to the TDB was opposed by the Department of Supplies on the grounds that such a transfer would put the department . . .

> . . . in a position of trying to transfer embarrassments which are ours as well as the Bureaus to other people who are in no way responsible for the lamentable position in which we find ourselves . . . The analogy with the Department of Defence and Phosphorous is quite false. Defence wants phosphorous . . . At present nobody has any use for turf charcoal.[99]

The desperate conditions during the Emergency created a climate of forgiveness for failure and the misallocation of resources, provided the supply objectives were met. Similar failures occurring in peacetime would have caused the Department of Finance to call a halt and to hold up the failed trials as an example of the danger of enthusiastic experimentation. The sum of these Emergency experiences allowed Bórd na Móna to eliminate the arcane and the uneconomic from its post-war plans and concentrate on machine-harvested turf, converted to either briquettes or electricity on the bog. By the late 1950s this was refined into a new production system harvesting the top few millimetres, which were then transported by rail to nearby power stations or briquette factories. The network of narrow gauge lines operated by Bórd na Móna serving bogs, factories and power stations is the second largest rail network on the island of Ireland. This is the long-term legacy of the Emergency on turf exploitation and transportation.

The short-term success of the Emergency turf campaign was that the non-turf counties and in particular the cities were kept supplied with fuel, much of it rail transported. The 'what might have been' can be seen in the Dutch 'hungry winter' of 1944–5, where the shortage of food was exacerbated by the cutting off of occupied Holland from the Limburg coalfields. 'It is impossible,' wrote the Swiss Red Cross, 'to describe the radical and dire consequences the lack of coal is having for the Netherlands and how incredibly primitive life has become.'[100] Despite the disappearance of British coal from Ireland, households throughout the country received an adequate fuel ration throughout the Emergency. The turf concerned was mainly remote from the consumers, and the railway functioned as the national grid on this occasion. When compared with the experience of Holland in 1944, this was no mean achievement and justifies C.S. Andrews' claim that 'no-one died of cold during the Emergency or had to eat uncooked food.'[101]

Notes

1 BNA T161/1402, minute of meeting, 11 September 1941 contains this report by Norman Smith.
2 NA INDCOM ES 225, 'Emergency measures in Switzerland', DFA to Supplies, 10 January 1941.
3 S.O. Ollson, *German Coal and Swedish Fuel, 1939–1945* (Goteborg, 1975), pp.301–7.
4 N. O'Carroll, *Forestry in Ireland: A Concise History* (Dublin, 2004), p.13.
5 Ibid., p.7. The stock was 25,000 acres, mainly planted in the late eighteenth century.
6 Ibid., p.30.
7 *The Times*, 7 October 1939, 'Éire and the War'.
8 NA DT S12792, Department of Defence memo for government, 13 April 1942.
9 C.S. Andrews, 'Some precursors of Bórd na Móna', *JSSISI*, 24, 2 (1952), pp.132–55. C. Ó Gráda, *Ireland: A New Economic History* (Oxford, 1995), pp.321–4 and fn 30, p.511 for a list of publications.
10 Ó Gráda, *Economic History*, p.323.
11 C.S. Andrews, *Man of No Property* (Dublin, 1982), p.159.
12 *Dáil Debates*, vol. 85 col. 2097, 4 March 1942.
13 *Irish Times*, 15 January 1936.
14 GNRGM 33/940, 'Peat traffic', Lockhart to Stephens, 19 August 1937.
15 Andrews, *Man of No Property*, pp.166–7.
16 Ibid., p.134.
17 Ibid., p.202.
18 *Irish Press*, 4 June 1940, 'Coal rationing starts today'.
19 Andrews, *Man of No Property*, p.180.
20 C.J. Gallagher, *The Gasmakers* (Dublin, 1985), p.169.
21 M. Manning and M. McDowell, *Electricity Supply in Ireland: The History of the ESB* (Dublin, 1984), p.101.
22 NA DT S12417B, report on transport of turf to non-turf areas, 28 November 1941.
23 *Railway Gazette*, 6 March 1941, p.345.
24 Institute of Civil Engineers of Ireland (ICEI), *Emergency Fuel* (Dublin, 1942), p.115.
25 See M.M. Field, 'The politics of turf, 1939–45', unpublished MA thesis, University College Dublin, 1990.
26 GSRGM 49103, 'Restrictions on movement of turf', minute of meeting, 16 April 1941.
27 GSRGM 49103, Stewart to Bredin, 15 April 1941.

28 ICEI, *Emergency Fuel*, p.115.
29 Ibid., p.117.
30 Andrews, *Man of No Property*, p.175.
31 ICEI, *Emergency Fuel*, p.118.
32 R.H. Walters, *The Economic and Business History of the South Wales Steam Coal Industry* (New York, 1977), p.338.
33 GSR Sec. 15413/1, 'Transport Supplies Limited', memorandum of agreement with Bank of Ireland, 16 March 1938.
34 GSRGM 50802, 'Fitting of creels to 50 railway wagons for turf', Bredin to Candy, 9 January 1942.
35 GSRGM 50802, Morton to Bredin, 22 May 1941, Secretary of the Department of Agriculture to Bredin, 30 April 1942.
36 GSRGM 50938, 'Daily return of working of turf specials', circulars, 17 and 29 October 1941.
37 NA DT S12417B, report by Flinn to An Taoiseach, 28 November, 1941.
38 GSRGM 50938, Floyd to Bredin, 29 October 1941.
39 NA DT S12417B, Flinn to Taoiseach, 15 September 1941.
40 GSRGM 50802, Hourican to Bredin, 20 September 1941.
41 NA DT S12417B, Flinn to Taoiseach, 16 October 1941.
42 NA DFA P23.1, note of meeting, 6 November 1941.
43 NA DT S12641, Flinn to Taoiseach, 30 October 1941.
44 NA D FIN S008/007/42, Defence to Finance, 19 January 1943.
45 NA DT S12641, T.P. Flynn to J.V. Candy, 17 October 1941.
46 *Dáil Debates*, vol. 85, cols 97–8, 29 October 1941.
47 NA DT S12641, Flinn to Taoiseach, 14 November 1941.
48 NA DT S12641, Departments of Agriculture, Defence, Industry and Commerce, Supplies, Lands and the OPW attended.
49 NA DT S12641, Flinn to Lemass, 6 November 1941.
50 S12641, Flinn to Taoiseach, 7 November 1941.
51 C.I. Savage, *Inland Transport* (London, 1957), p.626.
52 Ibid., p.231.
53 Walters, *South Wales Steam Coal*, p.338.
54 GSR unnumbered file, 'Priority Order 1941', containing SI 504, 1941.
55 W.H.B. Court, *History of the Second World War Coal* (London, 1951), p.365.
56 NA DT S12641, Flinn to Taoiseach, 14 November 1941.
57 Savage, *Inland Transport*, p.231.
58 NA DT S12641, decisions of conference of county surveyors' 1942 production proposals.
59 Ibid.
60 GNRGM 124/2 contains this correspondence.
61 NA DT S12417B.
62 NA DT S12417B, Flinn to Taoiseach, 25 November 1941, Williams to Flinn, 17 January 1942, Flinn to Lemass, 22 January 1942.
63 Ollson, *German Coal*, p.288.
64 Andrews, *Man of No Property*, p.174.
65 NA DT S12417B, memo from Flinn to Taoiseach, 2 March 1942.
66 GSRGM 55802, 'Calibration of barges for the Grand Canal Company'.
67 GSRGM 53300/1, 'Wagons for turf haulage', traffic manager's circular, 1 May 1942.
68 GSRGM 62759, 'Wagons under or awaiting repair', memo to Bredin, 5 December 1944.
69 GSRGM 33685 'Wagon supply', minutes of Chief Officers' Conference, 12 November 1938.

70 Savage, *Inland Transport*, p.626.
71 IRRS Archives, mechanical foreman's record book, Waterford. See notice June 1944 extending oiling frequency of wagons.
72 *Report on Transport in Ireland* (P9201), 1948, p.65.
73 H.C. Brookfield, 'A study in the economic geography of the pre-war coastwise coal trade', *Transactions and Papers of the British Institute of Geographers*, 19 (1953), pp.81–94.
74 Savage, *Inland Transport*, pp.191, 215.
75 GSRGM 53300/12, 'Emergency turf transport, Kerry area', report of J. Byrne, 10 June 1942.
76 BNA POWE 26/410, report week ending 26 February 1941.
77 GSRGM 53300/1 for this correspondence.
78 Graph of deliveries contained in S12417B, 28 November 1941.
79 GM53300/1, Fionán Lynch, TD and Fred Crowley, TD to GSR, 18 and 29 October 1942.
80 GSRGM 53300/19, 'Allocation of wagons: W. Clare section', Bredin to O'Brien, 8 April 1943, Kirwan to Bredin, 19 August 1943.
81 *Irish Times*, 29 January 1943.
82 NA DT S12417 A, minutes of interdepartmental meeting, 19 February 1943.
83 See GSRGM 53300/9, 'Turf transport, miscellaneous correspondence' for reduced volume of correspondence.
84 GSRGM 53300/9, Bredin to Candy, 22 March 1942.
85 GSRGM 53300/18, 'Turf transport arrangements for 1943 season', O'Brien to Bredin, 7 April 1943.
86 GSRGM 53300/18, minute of meeting, 12 May 1943.
87 GSRGM, Traffic manager's circular 1 May 1942; 53300/21, 'Proposed turf containers' (1944).
88 See GSRGM 53300/12 for details of this episode.
89 NA DF S/99/11/44, 'Turf Development Board reports of operations and activities', report for quarter ending September 1944. (These quarterly reports run from 1944 to 1947.)
90 NA DF S/99/11/44, report for quarter ending September 1945.
91 Andrews, *Man of No Property*, p.171.
92 GSRGM 53300/19, Kirwan to Bredin, 7 April 1943.
93 A. Offer, *The First World War: An Agrarian Interpretation* (Oxford, 1989), p.29.
94 A.C. Mierzejewski, *Hitler's Trains: The German National Railway and the Reich* (Stroud, 2005), p.114.
95 C.J. Potter, 'Europe's coal problem', *Proceedings of the Academy of Political Science*, vol. 21 (January 1946), pp.28–40, at p.32.
96 GSRGM 50802, Secretary, Bórd na Móna to F. Lemass, 4 June 1949.
97 Ó Gráda, *Economic History*, p.323.
98 S12912, 'ESRB turf charcoal', Department of Supplies minute, 7 August 1943.
99 Ibid.
100 H. van der Zee, *The Hunger Winter* (London, 1982), p.189.
101 Andrews, *Man of No Property*, p.180.

6

Road Transport

The operation of various transport modes is over-simplified in many accounts of Emergency Ireland, showing how the popular memory of the Emergency has been uncritically incorporated into the historical narrative.[1] Petrol almost disappeared, horse-drawn transport made a comeback, and, in general, transport was a severely rationed commodity. The restrictions in road transport in Ireland were more severe than those in Britain, being similar to the restrictions applied in Continental Europe. This chapter will examine how the GSR coped with these restrictions. The number of licensed motor vehicles on Irish roads fell from 73,813 to 26,188 between 1939 and 1943, and by early 1941 most of the vehicles remaining on the road were buses and lorries.[2] The GSR was the largest single lorry operator in the state, owning 450 vehicles, all of which assumed a critical role in ensuring the nationwide distribution of goods and in collecting the key harvests of grain, turf and sugar beet.[3] The company also operated the majority of bus services south and west of a line from Dublin to Sligo. Therefore, the road sections of the business are central to understanding the company's response to the Emergency.

Petrol rationing schemes had been prepared in many countries before the war.[4] The British rationing scheme was announced in January 1939[5] and implemented from 23 September.[6] Fuel rationing was introduced in Ireland a week later.[7] No petrol was on sale in Germany except for military purposes from 27 August 1939.[8] Petrol engines were then commonly used in heavy vehicles in preference to the newer and more economic diesel engines. The GNR bus fleet was 65 per cent diesel powered compared to the less prosperous GSR whose fleet was 10 per cent diesel powered.[9] In February 1941 the Department of Industry and Commerce indicated that while it had not been necessary to place any restriction on deliveries of diesel there was no guarantee that this would remain the case.[10] Table 5 shows the decline in imports, with a critical shortage of petrol and a less severe shortage one of diesel fuel.

Table 5 Oil fuel imports 1939–1944

Year	Petrol m galls.	Index 1939	Diesel m galls.	Index 1940
1939	43	100	n/a	n/a
1940	32	74	11.5	100
1941	18	41	8.75	76
1942	13	30	7	59
1943	9	21	5.5	47
1944	n/a	n/a	6.5	55

Source: NA EHR 2/3, which contains the figures on which this table is based.

After the virtual suppression of private motoring in early 1942, further cuts were directed at commercial vehicles. Efforts were made to stretch a diminished supply by experimenting with alternative fuels and later, when these experiments did not live up to expectation, by introducing traffic management measures. These three measures of petrol rationing, experimentation with alternative fuels and traffic management were adopted both in Britain and in Ireland. On 5 September 1939 the Department of Industry and Commerce met the two railway companies and the DUTC to consider 'an agreed proposal for the restriction of petrol supplies to omnibuses'.[11] The GSR expressed a concern that 'the smaller operators throughout the country with their small horsepower vehicles and irregular service would probably obtain excessive supplies.'[12] Railway company representatives 'endeavoured to discuss the advantageous position of the Railway system proper for carrying a large proportion of traffic... without very much more expense, but Mr Ferguson on two occasions waived [sic] this matter aside, saying the matter of coal supplies was another day's work.'[13] How much this view was driven by concern for the public good as opposed to a desire to disadvantage competitors is open to conjecture. Two of Ferguson's subordinates remained after the meeting proper to hear the GSR representatives say that 'coal supplies could be obtained more easily than petrol supplies, the latter coming across the ocean... while the Welsh coal is less than 150 miles from our ports' – an ironic statement in view of subsequent developments.[14]

Petrol substitutes became common in most European countries from 1939. A Dutch observer described 'German cars and trucks... propelled by enormous gas balloons on their roofs or by odd looking stoves on wheels.'[15] These 'stoves' were producer gas units. The producer gas process involved fitting a retort and drawing air through a bed of incandescent carbon, either anthracite or wood charcoal. The ensuing reaction produced a gas that could be used as fuel together with carbon monoxide which posed obvious dangers.[16] The development of gas producers for vehicles began in France and was later taken up in Germany, Sweden, Russia, Australia and South Africa.[17] In 1937 the British government established a committee to consider alternative road fuel, while the Mines Department established another committee at the outbreak of the war.[18] On 10 November 1939 Geoffrey Lloyd, MP, minister for mines, inspected a London bus fitted with a gas producer unit, described by the London *Times* as 'a curious contraption...a cross between a field kitchen and a mobile tar burner'.[19]

On 25 August 1939 an enterprising manufacturer sent a brochure on producer gas to the Irish authorities, who forwarded it to GNR general manager George Howden who replied that he considered the claims in the catalogue to be quite unreliable.[20] On 17 October 1939 Bredin reported to the GSR board that some work had been undertaken on the design of a producer gas unit that would shortly be manufactured and tested.[21] The GNR commenced experiments in October 1939 on an obsolete bus but suspended them in December pending the results of the GSR experiments. In July 1940 Howden instructed that the trials be resumed: 'I am very anxious to reach a convincing result on this controversial subject without delay.' A number of well-publicised test runs were made with the bus in early August.[22] These early co-ordinated experiments by the railway companies gained some experience in the design, manufacture and operations of gas producer units but were otherwise inconclusive.

On 28 December 1940 a notice appeared in the daily newspapers announcing fresh restrictions due to 'unforeseen circumstances'.[23] This was due to the severe restrictions in petrol supplies by the British. In January the petrol ration was reduced from eighteen to three gallons per month.[24] As a result, all forms of private motoring came to a standstill.[25] On 7 January 1941 the Department of Supplies asked the railway companies to prepare proposals for 25 per cent and 50 per cent cuts in road service levels, advising them that 'very drastic reductions are being made for lorry owners operated by concerns other than railway companies...greater than that made in the case of the railway companies.'[26] On 1 February the GSR announced the end of all services undertaken directly by road and not feeding into the rail network while on 6 February it curtailed bus services.[27] The *Irish Press* of 3 February 1941 announced that going by train to the races was 'just like old times'. In *The Irish Times* of 4 February the motoring columnist wrote that the uptake of gas producer plants had been less than anticipated due to the drawbacks of a loss of power of 30 to 40 per cent, and increased engine wear. Faced with severe shortages of fuel, some lorry owners exported their lorries to Northern Ireland, where lorries were scarce and petrol was available. This practice was taken so seriously that at one stage the confiscation of the vehicles and the prosecution of the owners before a military tribunal was contemplated.[28] In the event it was decided to control the sale of lorries under the Emergency Powers Act. McElligot of Finance considered that 'if non-political offenders are to be brought before that body I would suggest those who infringe foot and mouth regulations as far more worthy of attention.'[29]

In February 1941 C.S. Andrews approached the GSR stating that the TDB had been 'trying to manufacture a suitable grade of turf charcoal but quite frankly we haven't any experience and we are only learning as we go'. The GSR sent its report to Andrews and warned that inferior charcoal would lead to disastrous results, 'whereas if the turf is properly selected and thoroughly carbonised...the results obtained equal or exceed those obtained from the best anthracite.'[30] Thus at the same time that Bratt of the GNR was expressing the need for high-quality turf to fuel locomotives, a competing demand was being made for high-quality turf to make charcoal for road vehicle gas producers.

The government established the Emergency Scientific Research Bureau (ESRB) in order to apply scientific knowledge to bear on Emergency-related shortages. It comprised scientists and engineers, mainly from the universities,[31] and met for the first time on 23 February 1941 when it was informed that the taoiseach had instructed them to prioritise the development of substitutes for imported fuel.[32] The ESRB played a minor role in the development of substitute fuels compared to that played by the railway companies who employed chemists (Burnell of the GSR and Bratt of the GNR) and possessed scientific resources on a scale generally unknown in Irish industry. They were therefore donors to, rather than recipients of, bureau expertise. The ESRB concentrated on an expensive and ultimately unsuccessful attempt to produce turf charcoal on Turraun bog, County Offaly.[33] It was estimated that 8,000 tons of turf charcoal could be produced, which was reckoned as equivalent to 1.12m gallons of petrol. This project was plagued by major cost overruns and technical difficulties. The railway companies had offered to design, construct and operate carbonising plants at Turraun and Lyracrompane bogs in exchange for financial assistance with construction costs and a rebate on road tax for the vehicles concerned.[34] While yet another request for support from the railway companies would not have been welcomed by government, the railway company proposal probably had a greater potential for success as the staff involved would have had experience of the commercial application of science, unlike the ESRB directorate whose background was mainly academic.

In January 1941 Bredin reported that an experimental gas producer plant had been constructed in Inchicore. He went on to urge the purchase of two test units as 'if numbers of this unit are now available for export to this country . . . we as a public transport undertaking should procure them rather than they get into the hands of our competitors.'[35] Two lorries were fitted with units from different manufacturers and were displayed to the press in February 1941.[36] In March Bredin reported to the board that the lorries were satisfactory and that the company was now capable of designing and constructing its own gas producer plants.[37] Bredin described the 'almost feverish activity . . . on the part of sheetmetal shops' in fitting producer units and urged that speedy contact be made with the ESRB to secure the maximum amount of raw material for the GSR as 'the more material obtained the less will be available for our competitors.'[38] This shows how commercial rather than strategic concerns were uppermost in the mind of the GSR. The company saw the petrol shortage and the producer gas experiments as another phase in its struggle against road haulage competition. Government policy, on the other hand, was to encourage the maximum use of gas producer units as quickly as possible in order to guard against a sudden worsening of petrol supplies.

In March 1941 the ESRB established a working group consisting of chief chemists of the railway companies and Warner of the TDB. The task of the group was to develop the large-scale production of turf charcoal. The urgency in the project arose from the calculation that, while material existed to construct 3,000 gas producer units, there was only sufficient fuel for 400 units, as anthracite could not be made available for gas producer fuel in sufficient quantities. An illustration of this problem can be seen in the advice from the Castlecomer colliery company that it could meet less than a quarter of its requirements. On the following day Bredin advised the ESRB that in the absence of anthracite it would be useless to proceed with the expansion of the conversion programme.[39] The lack of anthracite caused the virtual cessation of gas producer development. The construction of two gas producers for buses slowed considerably. One of the bus units was substantially completed by July 1941 but it did not enter revenue-earning service until October 1942.[40] The other unit was never fitted to a bus, but was used by the laboratory at Inchicore as an alternative gas source when restrictions on town gas were threatening to interfere with the vital work of locomotive fuel testing.[41]

By early 1942 it was clear that gas producer units were not fulfilling the hopes of 1939. A manufacturers' list of Irish customers showed that the main users of gas producer units were small concerns. Of the 117 concerns listed, 79 per cent operated two units or fewer. Guinness, Jameson, Gilbeys and Odlums had each only one lorry with a gas producer fitted unit. The ESB and the Dairy Disposal Board with twenty-six and thirty-two respectively were untypical of large companies in their use of such units.[42] In contrast the *Railway Gazette* reported in January 1942 that there were 160,000 gas producer vehicles in Germany and German-occupied Europe.[43] Following on the Japanese advances in the Far East, Britain introduced a voluntary conversion programme in April 1942 under the new directorate of alternative motor fuels. Fleet owners were asked to convert 10 per cent of their vehicles. Despite prominent examples such as the conversion of twenty London buses, the programme did not succeed[44] and an order for 6,500 units was cut back to 2,250 in September 1943[45] as 'both passenger and goods operators showed considerable reluctance to take part in the experiment.'[46] Only 725 of the original target of 6,000 vehicles had been converted by June 1944[47] and the following September the programme was abandoned.[48] Southdown Motors reported to its shareholders that 'we have met with a fair amount of technical success, but even on the flat routes we have selected... it is difficult to maintain the schedule.'[49] This reflects the experience of the GSR, whose sole gas producer bus ran in the flat land between Dublin and Garristown where it was reported that 'the plant has given no trouble, but the crew are experiencing difficulties keeping the schedule.'[50]

The limitations of gas producer units meant that in Ireland only 611 non-state-owned vehicles had been converted by 30 May 1942.[51] This was raised with the GSR by the Department of Industry and Commerce in July 1942, when Ferguson enquired as to progress, optimistically alluding to the 'success' enjoyed by the ESB and of the greatly expanded use of gas producer units in Britain.[52] On enquiry the GSR found that 'the ESB are in no way enthusiastic about the matter. They purchased forty plants and only fitted fourteen, twelve of which have been very unsatisfactory.'[53] A report on small operators in Mayo prepared by the local GSR district superintendent concluded that 'almost all the twenty or so users were... most dissatisfied with their performance... cylinders and pistons can be extensively damaged, sometimes with a mileage as low as 7,000 miles.'[54]

The Broadstone and Inchicore workshops of the GSR gave it a unique advantage in that motor spares could be manufactured. In 1943 Bredin ordered that 'nothing should be allowed to interfere with the fullest possible production of motor parts at Inchicore works.'[55] In 1946 it was recorded that the company was making clutch hubs from old tram axles and was manufacturing radiator base plates after a redesign which allowed old bootlaces to replace rubber washers. Piston rings and piston sleeves had been made from rainwater downpipes.[56]

Voluntary effort was insufficient to promote conversion to gas producers at a satisfactory level. In March 1943 civil servants considered how departmental lorry fleets should be fitted in order to maintain public services in the event of total cessation of petrol supplies. The meeting concluded that all departments should convert one third of their fleet to gas producer operation.[57] On 14 April 1943 Seán Lemass told the Dáil that the government had been notified to expect a considerable reduction in fuel deliveries for 1943. On 4 May the *Irish Independent* reported the introduction of a scheme to compulsorily extend the use of gas producer units on privately owned lorries. Fleet owners would be compelled to convert one vehicle in every three.[58] The order was enforced by withdrawing petrol allocations from unconverted vehicles. On 12 October John Leydon (assistant secretary of the supplies branch of the Department of Industry and Commerce and later secretary of the Department of Supplies) warned the Post Office that 'the minister cannot continue to exempt P&T from the penalty imposed on private owners...unless a definite assurance of the completion of the programme is received.'[59]

This mandatory conversion arrangement had implications for the GSR as the largest fleet operator. In early May 1943 it was reported that the manufacture of 100 units was in hand, but in November Bredin expressed his disappointment at the slow rate of conversion – four per week.[60] The project was hastened by allocating some of the conversion to provincial garages – a move that provided us with rare photographic evidence of the conversion process.[61] By this stage the fuel used for gas producer units was anthracite instead of the turf charcoal envisaged in 1941. The GSR secured an additional allocation of anthracite from the British Fuel controller, supplementing supplies from Castlecomer.[62] This shows the change in British attitude compared to that of 1941 when all attempts to secure alternatives to petrol (such as by distilling creosote) were blocked by the refusal of import licences.[63] The Irish compulsory conversion scheme required the conversion of one third of lorry fleets. Despite this, there was a public perception that some conversions were cosmetic and that the vehicles fitted with a producer in fact ran on petrol.[64] The British scheme was less demanding, aiming at the conversion of 10 and later 5 per cent of vehicles. This is an indication of the greater severity of fuel shortages in Ireland. Similarly, while the Irish scheme remained in place until the end of hostilities, the British scheme ended in September 1944.

The shortcomings of peat charcoal had become apparent by 1944 when a report on the Turraun experiment from Industry and Commerce stated that county surveyors were finding it difficult to dispose of the stocks as several lorry owners have reported that they did not find the peat charcoal satisfactory. Professor Hogan reported that 'it could not be claimed that peat charcoal was an ideal fuel . . . two other difficulties . . . were mentioned . . . viz that it cannot be stored in the open and that it does not stand up well to long transport.'[65] Despite this, as late as January 1945 the virtues of turf charcoal as a fuel were being promoted by the motor trade in advertisements for gas producer units with the slogan 'Believe it or not, Dublin to Kildare and back on a bag of raw turf'.[66]

Despite the early optimism, gas producers did not deliver the promised results. While petrol was available gas producers remained a poor second, and petrol remained available in small quantities in Ireland as in Britain. All attempts by government to cajole or persuade the largest fleet operators in the state to convert more of its vehicles failed. In October 1943 the *Irish Independent* reported that only about half of the total number of working vehicles had been fitted, and that this slow progress had 'caused dissatisfaction in official quarters'.[67] Gas producer users had to rely on anthracite or wood charcoal, which was almost as scarce as petrol. A typical case was that of Gallagher's of Killybegs, who in 1944 sought a petrol allowance to facilitate fish exports to Britain as their vehicles 'would not be able to work a service between Killybegs and Teelin with producer gas due to the hilly road'.[68]

By summer 1944 gas producer vehicles were losing their attraction even in mainland Europe. Autotransit was a Swiss company based in Spain which operated seven vehicles between Bilbao and the Franco-Spanish frontier. While *'le penurie du carburant et le rationnment des pneumatiques compliquaient singulierment les operations'* ('the scarcity of oil and rationing of tyres greatly hindered their operations'),[69] in July 1944 the *Railway Gazette* reported that the producer gas vehicles had been gradually eliminated due to the numerous breakdowns associated with them.[70] In March 1945 the Irish post office chief inspector noted that 'the programme would not long survive the return of peacetime conditions.'[71]

The Japanese victories from December 1941 made the fuel situation more acute and led to a shortage of rubber for tyres. On 28 February the *Connacht Tribune* described how:

On top of the transport difficulties caused by the shortage of coal and petrol we now have the shortage of rubber caused by the extension of the war in the Pacific... it is little use evacuating people from the cities into rural areas where essential food supplies are almost non-existent for lack of transport... Business delivery vans could be reduced by compulsory pooling arrangements and a restriction on the number of deliveries.[72]

Private motoring had been eliminated and gas producer units had not lived up to the promises of manufacturers. A more radical approach was necessary, involving the curtailment of the rights of lorry owners to carry goods in their own vehicles. This was a politically sensitive step inviting the opposition of traders and merchants who had invested in lorries, and it laid the government open to charges of caving in to the demands made by the railway companies at the transport tribunal that private road transport should be restricted. Despite assurances from the government that these measures were for the duration of the Emergency, lorry owners and some opposition politicians professed to disbelieve such assurances. Quite simply, the GSR would not have been entrusted with a peacetime monopoly on road freight transport. In a similar vein, the British war cabinet considered that the railway companies should be kept away from the air industry, concluding that 'introduction of rlys [railways] into operating co. [company] is a disaster. They will treat it as they did the canals.'[73] Both governments understood the capacity of the railway companies to strangle competing newer technologies.

In spring 1942 the paramount need to conserve oil supplies meant eliminating most empty lorry mileage, which was only achievable through some form of centralised control. This policy was stated in a British context by Lord Leathers on 6 September 1942 when he said that 'road transport must under present conditions be regarded as a supplement to the other forms of transport.'[74] In an Irish context, from 1 August 1942 the Department of Supplies curtailed petrol supplies to approximately 3,000 trader-operated commercial vehicles.[75] A memorandum from the Department of the Taoiseach described how:

All private lorry owners must cease operating with the exception of GSR lorries, licensed hauliers and exempt area hauliers. The GSR will be obliged to initiate scheduled road goods services and set up depots for the collection and distribution of goods. It is believed that most if not all of the lorries put off the roads will be [hired] by the GSR and the drivers retained to drive.[76]

The scheme was piloted in north Mayo – an area remote from the railway system where turf harvesting created a strong demand for lorries. Road transport in this county was already highly regulated. The Mayo county surveyor had hired most of the available private lorries in the county for turf transport, and had supplied petrol vouchers for the work.[77] The proposal became public in late August 1942, and in early September the Department of Supplies informed the GSR that it would withdraw petrol from heavier vehicles from 1 October 1942 and expected the GSR to 'undertake at once the building up of a substitute transport organisation ... the extension of the ... scheme over the whole country was the ultimate aim of the minister.'[78]

A Fine Gael request for a Dáil debate on the introduction of the order was acceded to, despite the opposition of Seán Lemass,[79] and a Fine Gael motion to have the order revoked was debated by the Dáil on 15 October.[80] Richard Mulcahy argued that the government had erred in not discussing this measure with the House and in not consulting with the National Lorry Owners' Association. Mulcahy was followed by Mayo Fine Gael deputy Patrick Brown, who was also a prominent member of the North Mayo Carriers' Association.[81] Lemass outlined the dilemma faced by the government: if it waited for a problem to emerge it would be accused of lack of preparedness, while if it took action in anticipation of problems it would be accused of unnecessary interference in private enterprise.[82] As to the choice of the road services of the GSR, Lemass said: 'It might be that in times past the organisation might have proved itself not as efficient as they [the government] would have liked to see, but there was no other organisation we could use.'[83] In an attempt to deal with the concerns of private lorry owners, he said that 'the scheduled area scheme has been devised to cope with circumstances created by the Emergency and does not represent any decision in the matter of post-war transport policy.'[84] The motion was put and defeated. An *Irish Times* editorial commented: 'There is no apparent reason why the new system should be a failure. It will mean hardship to private lorry owners and it may be less convenient than the competitive services of today: but it certainly will save petrol and if efficiently handled ought to create little discomfort.'[85] This attitude was mirrored in the provincial press when on 24 October the *Connacht Tribune* editorial stated:

> For more than a year we have been drawing attention to the serious-ness of the transport problem in the west ... we suggested a compulsory pooling arrangement among business firms ... It should have been obvious from the first that the scheme was a necessity

throughout the west and not just in one particular county... Objection may be taken to entrusting this task to a firm which has a virtual monopoly of rail and road transport in the twenty-six counties, but it must be admitted that it is much more likely to make a success of it than any government could do.[86]

On 19 November it was announced that the order covering north Mayo would come into effect on 7 December.[87] *The Irish Times* reported that the government had asked the traders to work out their own co-ordinated scheme, but that they had a strong objection to their customers being serviced by competitors. The editorial summarised the situation as one where: 'Before the war there were more services than were necessary... the people who had goods for transport... enjoyed the benefit of frequent services and of "competitive" rates... If the country's imports of petrol decreases by one half, the number of services weekly will be reduced by one half.'[88] The controlled areas scheme allowed the Department of Supplies to plan for a basic distribution service for goods regardless of variations in the supply of petrol. In January *The Irish Times* reported that monthly consumption of petrol in Mayo had been reduced by 10 per cent from 3,100 to 2,664 gallons. The number of vehicles operating in the county had decreased by 55 per cent from 117 to 65, of which seventeen were GSR vehicles.[89] The scheme attracted the attention of the *Railway Gazette,* whose editorial observed that 'there seems to be no doubt that the general public is better served by the new arrangements.'[90]

On 8 February 1943, the Department of Supplies told the GSR that:

It was the desire of the government that further restrictions in the operation of trader-operated vehicles be carried out without publicity ... It was finally agreed that the new areas to be so dealt with would be the balance of County Mayo and that part of County Galway to the east of a line from Galway city to the east shore of Lough Corrib.[91]

In February 1943 Patrick Flynn, principal officer in the Department of Supplies, stated that 'the GSR should control all road transport required for the turf traffic as the majority of vehicles employed thereon were those owned by the traders which had or would cease to operate through the fuel restrictions; and unless such control was exercised the traders would recommence carting their own goods thus defeating the... scheme.' A concession was made to lorry owners in the areas affected by allowing the unrestricted use of gas producer fitted lorries.[92] The controlled areas scheme involved organising lorry transport along the lines of bus services where all services run to a timetable. The level of service could be quickly adjusted in the light of the fuel available. This was demonstrated in early May when bus services were cut in half[93] but restored a fortnight later when fuel supplies improved.[94]

On 18 May 1943 the GSR and the Department of Supplies discussed the eastward extension of the scheme.[95] It was extended to south Mayo and west Galway in April 1943; in September 1943 to east Galway, Roscommon, portions of Longford, Westmeath, Offaly, Laois and Tipperary; in October 1943 to Sligo and Leitrim; in February 1944 to Clare, Limerick and Kerry and in July 1944 to the remainder of Longford and Westmeath.[96] Each expansion of the scheme was preceded by a Department of Supplies investigation. The designation of a scheduled area generally provoked strong local opposition, led by the National Association of Private Lorry Owners, whose secretary, Michael J. O' Connor, BA, was an assiduous lobbyist. Opposition generally took the form of public meetings, and lobbying of public bodies and TDs with the support of chambers of commerce. On 12 December 1942 the *Connacht Tribune* advertised a public meeting and urged lorry owners, van owners and garage employees to 'come in your thousands'.[97] A strike of lorry owners was suggested in Tipperary, while Westmeath County Council protested against the 'monopoly of transport given to the railway company'.[98]

These protests seldom outlived the introduction of the scheme. Many of the lorry owners affected were hired by the GSR to carry commodities such as turf and sugar beet. In July 1943 Bredin advised that private vehicles would be hired to a much greater extent to haul turf, and ordered that sixty-eight lorries from the fleet of 568 should be withdrawn as a source of spare parts. On 27 July the road freight manager reported: 'There are 27 vehicles of the company working in Mayo, it is envisaged that the majority (if not all) of these will be replaced in the future by private lorries.' The GSR withdrew its lorries from turf haulage in counties where the controlled road areas were introduced. In doing so it withdrew its vehicles from rough, untarred roads, leaving turf haulage with its high maintenance costs to private hauliers. The GSR also withdrew the proportion of its fleet which was most expensive to maintain, and created a reserve of spare parts.[99] The GSR also gained financially as it retained 6 per cent of the payments to hauliers as an administrative charge. The hauliers secured constant work and an assured petrol supply. This process also allowed the national lorry fleet to be managed as a unit, despite the multiplicity of owners.

The balance between hired and GSR vehicles in the three highest mileage counties can be seen in Table 6, which shows the GSR fleet being used mainly for general merchandise haulage, leaving the hired sector to do turf and beet haulage. The GSR reported that it had 'organised in each area a panel of auxiliary hired vehicles... Special attention has in accordance with your instructions, been paid to the selection of vehicles and the extent to which the owners are depending on same for a livelihood.'[100] By 1944 the GSR had hired in 500 privately owned lorries.[101]

Table 6 Hired versus direct lorry fleet, January 1944

	Vehicles	**Gen goods tons**	**Beet tons**	**Turf tons**
Limerick	35	1884	1445	270
Limerick hire	8	0	0	204
Mayo G.S.R.	36	4285	501	36
Mayo hire	20	0	1056	356
Galway G.S.R.	71	7681	2086	328
Galway hire	102	29	14016	566

Source: GSRGM 554183, Dooley to Dept. Supplies, 14 Feb. 1944.

In October 1943 the Department of Industry and Commerce asked the GSR to prepare contingency plans based on 10 per cent and 25 per cent cuts in the petrol ration. A plan was submitted within three weeks, involving a 10 per cent cut by confining all services to one lorry per day, or a 25 per cent cut by lessening the frequency of selected services. The speed with which a plan could be submitted demonstrates the success of the controlled areas scheme in matching lorry miles to available petrol. This was possible only if empty mileage was minimised and all road movements in the affected areas were under central control.

The GSR weekly circular of 22 August 1944 describes the effects of the scheme on the economy of rural Ireland. While the description is for internal consumption and uncritical, it is a useful summary of the effects of the controlled areas experiment. The scheme was described as impartial, steady, relatively cheap and...

... widely appreciated, especially in the western hinterland where large areas formerly served by the travelling shop, with its double profits basis of barter, are no longer dependent on the factors which

> make private distribution largely a matter of chance . . . the travelling
> shop, as such, has virtually entirely disappeared, and is replaced by
> an organised system of supplies depots.[102]

The report concluded that the 'barter system which imposed unnecessary
costs on rural communities has largely been destroyed by the flexibility
and cheapness of the new services'.[103] The process described here is both a
political and a transport process entailing a reorganisation in commercial
and social relations by curtailing of barter and the elimination of travelling
shops. These objectives would have been popular with consumers,
especially those in more remote areas concerned with keeping down
prices, and were in tune with the needs of the Fianna Fáil support base in
these areas. The publication of this article would have put arguments in
favour of the scheme in the mouths of thousands of GSR employees.

Ireland adopted a dual strategy to manage oil shortages. An engineering
solution sought to convert lorries to gas producers and this approach was
championed by the Department of Industry and Commerce, the TDB and
the ESRB. An administrative approach involved designating counties as
controlled areas, a strategy championed by the Department of Supplies.
While these measures had parallels in Britain, the Irish measures were
more stringent, reflecting the more severe oil shortages in Ireland. The
scheduled areas programme dealt with the shortage that existed, while the
gas producer conversion programme dealt with the shortages that were
feared. The controlled areas scheme was more useful for managing a
severe petrol shortage than the gas producer conversion programme.

At the beginning of the war great faith was placed in producer gas as an
alternative to petrol. The raw material for these units was wood charcoal
in Germany or anthracite in Britain. In Ireland the TDB hoped that turf
charcoal would provide a suitable fuel for gas producer units. Gas
producers were, however, highly unpopular with lorry operators, and
widespread adoption could only be secured by compulsion. However, the
blame for the failure to adopt turf fuel was diffused across lorry owners in
general as opposed to being focussed on GSR management as it was in the
case of the use of turf as locomotive fuel. The GSR pioneered the
development of gas producers units, but its motive was to anticipate
demand for materials on the part of its competitors. The company's
capacity for technical innovation demonstrates the strength of its
engineering knowledge and contrasts with the ESRB, whose attempts to
produce quality turf charcoal at Turraun was a costly failure. This failure
did not deter the government from driving forward a programme that

secured the conversion of approximately one third of the country's commercial freight vehicles. In May 1944 a memorandum to the taoiseach noted that 'owing to the fitting of producer gas plants, the time is approaching when the critical factor in road transport will be supplies of lubricating oil rather than petrol.'[104]

The unpopularity of gas producer lorries is shown by the records of the GSR fleet in the controlled areas developed from late 1942. Of the 423 owned and hired vehicles used by the GSR in the controlled areas in January 1944 only seven were gas producer vehicles, compared to eighteen horse-drawn units. Of all the units used by the GSR in the controlled areas, 17 per cent of the directly owned and 22 per cent of the hired units were horse powered.[105] In practice horsepower was the most widely used substitute for lorries. The GNR had eliminated horses by 1939 but owned ten horses in 1940.[106] When horses and drays were reintroduced for local deliveries in March 1942 'there was a very brisk demand for horses... with a result that prices rose and we were faced with considerable difficulty in securing the necessary equipment.'[107] The renewed popularity of the horse and dray is perhaps the most telling testimony to the shortcomings of the gas producer system.

From north Mayo the Controlled Areas scheme spread eastwards and southwards, reaching to within thirty miles of Dublin and gave the GSR quasi-monopoly powers in the designated counties. The scheme was described in the 'Emergency Historical Record' as having 'achieved its main purpose and secured (with the minimum use of petrol tyres and vehicles) an equitable distribution of merchandise even in remote areas'.[108] This programme allowed the Department of Supplies to plan for any eventuality, as outlined by Seán Lemass when he stated: 'That organisation which operates throughout the country is capable of being expanded to meet the minimum transport requirements in every district.'[109] The scheduled areas scheme was primarily conceived as a means of dealing with the challenges of moving the turf harvest which overlapped with the grain and beet harvests. The scheme was piloted in Mayo and spread throughout the turf-producing areas with the exception of Donegal, whose transport situation was unique. It was anticipated that the scheme would be extended eastwards and the *Connacht Tribune* wrote in August 1943 that 'with the continuance of abnormal conditions, the principle of control is likely to be extended gradually to other parts of the country until eventually it will cover the twenty-six counties as a purely emergency plan.'[110] The reorganisation measures adopted in Britain were less exacting, involving the creation of sectoral lorry pools and the Ministry of

War Transport taking control of a number of well-established road haulage firms to provide the operational experience and maintenance facilities for directly running a large road transport operation.[111]

The contrasting experiences of the lorry and bus sections of the GSR during the Emergency is noteworthy. The maladroit handling of the increase in bus fares in 1941 worsened relationships between the company and the government and led partially to the government takeover in March 1942. In contrast the road freight services were used as an agent of government policy and received the grudging support of Lemass in the Dáil when he described them, despite past inefficiencies, as the only organisation which the government could use.[112] The contrast between the rail and the road sections of the business is also noteworthy and underlines the extent to which the failures on the rail side were failures of quality rather than quantity of coal. Unlike coal, the petrol delivered in 1943 could do the same work as the petrol delivered in 1939, allowing fuel shortages to be managed by cuts in miles run. The challenge to road transport operators intensified after the Japanese successes of 1942. Severely restricted, GSR buses continued to provide basic public passenger transport outside Dublin, whose remaining tram routes received a reprieve until 1948. There were no examples of buses drawn by horses, as in Denmark and Holland, or buses running on tram lines due to lack of tyres, as in Budapest.[113] GSR lorry services formed the backbone of a nationwide goods distribution system created from scratch in 1942. The coping strategy was based on the development of a nationwide logistical system rather than on the success of any 'miracle cures' in the form of native alternatives to petrol fuel.

Notes

1   B. Grob Fitzgibbon, *The Irish Experience During the Second World War* (Dublin, 2004), pp.53–4; T. Grey, *The Lost Years: Emergency Ireland, 1939–45* (London, 1997), p.188.

2   M.E. Daly, *The Buffer State: The Historical Roots of the Department of the Environment* (Dublin, 1997), p.393.

3   NA, EHR, vol. 2, p.270 gives a figure of 450 while the ESRB estimated a figure of 700 in a memo on gas producers for road transport and farm tractors, 11 February 1943, contained in NA DT S13126.

4   *The Times*, 25 October 1939, 'The fighting forces must have first call on supplies of petrol'.

5   Ibid., 18 January 1939.

6   Ibid., 23 September 1939.

7   Ibid., 7 October 1939.

8   Ibid., 28 August 1939.

9   GSR F509 report of meeting, GSR, GNR and Department of Industry and Commerce, 5 September 1939.

10 GNRGM 267/7, 'Curtailment of lorry services due to shortage of petrol supplies', memo, 7 January 1941.

11 GSR F509, report of meeting, 5 September 1939.

12 Ibid.

13 Ibid.

14 Ibid.

15 H. van der Zee, *The Hunger Winter* (London, 1982), p.17.

16 *Railway Gazette*, 16 January 1940. The formula is $C + \frac{1}{2}O_2 + 2N_2 = CO + 2N_2 + 52950$ BTU.

17 M.A. Hogan, *Producer Gas for Internal Combustion Engines* (Dublin, 1943), p.2.

18 C.I. Savage, *Inland Transport* (London, 1957), p.435.

19 Ibid., 10 November 1939.

20 GSRGM 48414/4, 'Bellay gas producers', Howden to Morton, 27 September 1939, Flynn (Industry and Commerce) to Morton, 2 September 1939.

21 GSRGM 48414/4, Bredin to Morton, 17 October 1939.

22 GNRGM 39/1507, McIntosh to Howden, 14 December 1939, Howden to McIntosh, 27 July 1940, McIntosh to Howden, 7 August 1940.

23 *Irish Times*, 28 December 1940.

24 *Irish Times*, 10 January 1941.

25 *The Times*, 14 January 1941.

26 GNRGM 267/7, Williams to Howden, 4 February 1941.

27 *Irish Times*, 31 January 1940; *Cork Examiner*, 6 February 1941.

28 NADT S11903, 'Cabinet committee on emergency problems', note, 11 August 1941.

29 NADT S12338, McElligot to Ó Cinnéide, 24 April 1941.

30 GSRGM 48414/2, 'Turf charcoal', Andrews to Morton, 15 February 1941, Morton to Andrews, 4 March 1941.

31 GSRGM 48414/3, 'Correspondence with ESRB', lists the bureau membership as: J.J. Dowling, professor of technical physics, UCD; J.J. Drumm of Drumm battery fame; M.A. Hogan, professor of mechanical engineering, UCD; J.H. Pole, professor of physics, TCD; T.S. Wheeler, state chemist. J.J. Lennon, secretary of the industrial research council, was secretary.

32 R.J. Bradley 'The Emergency Scientific Research Bureau: An analysis and evaluation of the scientific and technical impact of the ESRB', unpublished PhD thesis, Trinity College Dublin, 1992, p.128.

33 NA DT S12912 details these experiments.

34 GSRGM 48414/2, Morton to Lennon, 29 March 1941.

35 GSRGM 48414/6, 'Gas producers used in lorries', Bredin to Morton, 10 January 1941.

36 *Irish Press*, *Irish Times*, 15 February 1941 for description and photographs.

37 GSRGM 48414/6, report by Bredin to board meeting, March 1941.

38 GSRGM 48414/3, Bredin to Morton, 11 March 1941.

39 GSRGM 48414/3, Agent, Castlecomer to Bredin, 10 March 1941, Bredin to Lennon, 11 March 1941.

40 GSRGM 48414/1, 'Gas producer plants trailer units', Morton to Coyle Insurance, 15 May 1941.

41 GSRGM 48414/1, Ginnety to Bredin, 19 November 1942.

42 GSRGM 48414/4, Bellay technical manual, 7 November 1942.

43 *Railway Gazette*, 16 January 1942.

44 *The Times*, 3 June 1942.

45 BNA MT 84 55, 'Producer gas'; graph of production mk. vi and mk. vii units.

46 Savage, *Internal Transport*, p.436.

47 BNA MT 84 55, Graph of production of units by Briggs Ltd.
48 *The Times*, 14 September 1944.
49 *The Times*, 26 June 1943.
50 GSRGM 48414/1, Ginnety to Bredin, 10 November 1942.
51 *Dáil Debates*, vol. 87, col. 867, 3 June 1942.
52 GSRGM 48414/6, Ferguson to Bredin, 15 July 1942.
53 GSRGM 48414/6, McNally to Bredin, 8 July 1942.
54 GSRGM 54842/3, Costello (District Superintendent) to Bredin, 26 March, 7 April 1943.
55 GSRGM 48414/12, 'Fuel for gas producer units', minute of meeting, 1 November 1943.
56 IRRS archives, Luke diary, section P.
57 NA FIN/ S/041/0006/43, Posts and Telegraphs to Finance, 6 July 1943.
58 *Irish Independent*, 4 May 1943.
59 NA FIN/S/041/0006/43, Leydon to Posts and Telegraphs, 10 October 1943.
60 GSRGM 48414/12, Bredin to Ginnety, 4 May 1943, minutes of meeting, 1 November 1943.
61 GSRGM 61304, 'Publication of photographs of staff fitting gas producers: Galway'.
62 GSRGM 48414/12, Johnston to Bredin, 25 May 1943.
63 GSRGM 50713, 'Proposed distillation of hydrocarbon oil from creosote', Burnell to Bredin, 24 September1941, Irish Tar distillers to Meadows, 8 May 1942.
64 K. O'Nolan (ed.), *The Best of Myles: A Selection from Cruiskeen Lawn* (Dublin, 1968), p.300.
65 NA DT S13474, Industry and Commerce to Taoiseach, 1 May 1944.
66 *The Leader*, 25 January 1945.
67 *Irish Independent*, 26 October 1943.
68 GNRGM 200/217, 'Fish from Ballyshannon', CDR to Department of Supplies, 1 March 1944.
69 G. Kreis, *La Suisse Pendant la Deuxieme Guerre Mondiale* (Zurich, 2000), p.52.
70 *Railway Gazette*, 11 July 1942.
71 NA FIN S/41/0006/43, report by chief inspector, 11 March 1945.
72 *Connacht Tribune*, 26 February 1942.
73 BNA CAB 195/3, War cabinet secretary's notebook, 8 March 1945.
74 GNRGM 61/6a, 'Northern Ireland petrol and rubber supplies', traffic officers' report, 22 February 1943.
75 GSRGM 55183, Minute of meeting, 7 September 1942.
76 NA DT S12958, memo for government, 1 September 1942.
77 ICEI, *Emergency Fuel* (Dublin, 1942), p.138.
78 GSRGM 55183, Minute of meeting, 7 September 1942.
79 NA DT S12958, Smith to Mulcahy, 22 September 1942.
80 *Irish Press*, 2 October 1942.
81 *Dáil Debates*, vol. 88, cols 1298–1303, 15 October1942.
82 *Dáil Debates*, vol. 88, col. 1307, 15 October 1942.
83 *Dáil Debates*, vol. 88, col. 1319, 15 October 1942.
84 *Dáil Debates*, vol. 88, col. 1319, 15 October 1942.
85 *Irish Times*, 15 September 1942.
86 *Connacht Tribune*, 24 October 1942.
87 *Irish Independent*, 19 November 1942.
88 *Irish Times*, 8 December 1942.
89 *Irish Times*, 26 January 1943.
90 *Railway Gazette*, 22 January 1943.
91 GSRGM 54842/3, 'Reorganisation of road transport, Galway', minute of meeting, 8 February 1943.

92 GSRGM 54842/3, Minute of meeting, 8 February 1943.

93 *Irish Press*, 3 May 1943.

94 *Irish Independent*, 13 May 1943.

95 GSRGM 55183, Bredin to O'Brien, 30 June 1943.

96 NA EHR 2, memo 'Internal transport' from Industry and Commerce to Department of An Taoiseach, October 1945.

97 *Connacht Tribune*, 12 December 1942.

98 *Irish Times*, 15 September 1943.

99 GSRGM 55183/1 describes this process.

100 GSRGM 55183, Dooley to Department of Supplies, 14 February 1944.

101 NA EHR 3, vol. 2, p.270.

102 GSR weekly circular 2928, 22 August 1944.

103 Ibid.

104 NA DT S13474, Unsigned memo to assistant secretary, 5 May 1944.

105 GSRGM 55183, 'Provision of extended road transport', Dooley to Department of Supplies, 14 February 1944.

106 GNRGM 267/7, memo, 7 January 1941.

107 GNRGM 244/2, 'Horse lorry services, Dundalk', Foley to Lockhart, 11 March 1942.

108 NA EHR 2, memo 'Internal transport', Industry and Commerce to Department of An Taoiseach, October 1945, p.7.

109 *Irish Times*, 16 October 1942.

110 *Connacht Tribune*, 14 August 1943.

111 Savage, *Internal Transport*, p.541.

112 See Note 97.

113 *Irish Independent*, 23 January 1941 (Denmark); *Railway Gazette*, 7 April 1944, p.369 (Amsterdam), 12 June 1942, p.658 (Budapest).

7

Mobilisation

A French historian has described the railway system in the Second World War as 'a weapon in time of war...a means of military transport of evacuation or of supplying the civilian population the railway system through its rediscovered monopoly experienced exceptional traffic, mobilising...all material and human resources available to it.'[1] While railway timetables shaped the 1914 mobilisation,[2] the 1920s and '30s witnessed such a rapid development of reliable motor transport that in 1940 'most of the logistical support for the Wehrmacht was handled by road'.[3] This chapter describes the role of the GSR in Emergency defence. The company provided military transport and planned for the evacuation of civilians from Dublin. Its workshops provided engineering services for military and civilian customers while its labour force formed a pool of recruits to various military and civil defence groupings. However, in contrast to their counterparts in belligerent countries, the Irish railway companies did not face the prospect of their workforces being denuded by conscription and mass recruitment.

In mid-1937 the Department of Defence was considering measures to cope with the threat of air raids, and in August two representatives visited the London Midland and Scottish Railway (LMSR) in London, where the Irish representatives told their hosts that 'they had not...reached the stage where they were ready to communicate with public bodies on the matter.'[4] The LMSR reported this immediately to the GSR, who gained advance notice of the 1938 Air Raid Precautions Bill. The legislation applied to the cities and to the boroughs of Dun Laoghaire, Drogheda, Dundalk and Wexford and placed special obligations on essential undertakers (gas, water, electricity and transport companies) to prepare a plan to maintain services in the event of air attack. The act also obliged transport undertakings to co-operate with measures to evacuate the civilian population. In July 1939 W.H. Morton, GSR general manager, reported that five members of staff had attended the civilian anti-gas school in Griffith Barracks. On 19 August 1939 an Air Raid Protection (ARP) scheme was submitted by the company, consisting of an overall master plan for all GSR activities together with a sub-plan for each location. The overall plan was co-ordinated by an active ARP committee, established in August 1939 and which had met six times by the time war had broken out. A network of ARP squads was quickly established and the secretary of Dr Steevens' Hospital asked the Kingsbridge ARP organisation to provide cover for the hospital as 'the male staff of the hospital is totally inadequate to provide fire fighting and decontamination duties.'[5]

Following the fall of France in June 1940, the Irish army hastily put together 'General Defence Plan number one' subsequently described as 'a hasty reaction to a rapidly developing situation and does not reflect the more professional plans drafted... in October 1940'.[6] On 28 June 1940 T.J. Flynn, assistant secretary of the Department of Industry and Commerce, wrote to the GSR requesting that it urgently prepare instructions for staff 'in the event of hostilities breaking out in this country'. Flynn attached instructions that had been prepared by the GNR for its staff in Éire and asked the two companies to ensure the two sets of instructions were as uniform as possible.[7] Instructions were issued to staff on 4 July, outlining the arrangements in the event of enemy action by land, sea or air and applied to drivers, guards, stationmasters and in particular to signalmen, who, in addition to regulating traffic, constituted a widely scattered chain of observers in communication with each other by phone or telegraph.[8] Signalmen were given a special telegraph code to carry the air raid warning within a twenty-five mile radius. Trains were to be stopped coming into danger areas, and hurried in leaving if they could get clear within a reasonable time. In the event of an air raid, passengers were to be evacuated from stationary trains and conducted to a shelter, and if no shelter was available they were to be advised to scatter. Trains containing passengers were to be shunted into tunnels at Phoenix Park, Dalkey, Dun Laoghaire and Cork.[9]

At this point Germany was seen as the most likely invader, with a landing feared in the south-east. On 2 July the signal inspector in Waterford was approached by the military for advice and assistance in disabling the bridges over the Barrow (linking Waterford to Rosslare) and the Suir (linking Waterford to Mallow) should the need arise. On the same day the military authorities visited the Waterford locomotive superintendent seeking information on 'engine power, staff and facilities available... and discussed ways of destroying engines, rolling stock and cranes which could not be removed'.[10] The preparations were put to the test a week later when an Irish air corps plane was struck by lightning and three occupants baled out with two landing near Geashill, County Offaly. Unaware of the origin of the plane, the Tullamore stationmaster kept signalmen on duty (to relay information) until the Gardaí gave the all clear and held a bus in readiness 'to convey armed forces if necessary to the area confirmed'.[11]

During July 1940 plans were drawn up for the destruction of rail bridges in the event of invasion.[12] These preparations involved the preparation of bridges for fitting of demolition charges. On 23 July 1940 GNR traffic at Ballybay was held up for some hours when a Lieutenant Kelly informed the stationmaster that a bridge was mined and traffic would have to be stopped. When the company's general manger George Howden raised the matter with Department of Defence headquarters the following day he was told that 'the whole matter arose out of the over zeal of a junior officer who has been put right in the meantime.'[13] He was assured that the bridges to be mined would be discussed with GNR engineering staff and that the same programme applied to the GSR. Egan of Defence wrote to Morton on 29 July 1940 advising him that 'in certain contingencies the destruction of bridges ... may become necessary as a military measure ... It is regretted that your company was not approached ... at an earlier stage but that the minister understands that ... your local officials have been approached by the military officers in the district.' This letter also outlined the arrangements proposed for making the Barrow and Suir viaducts unusable and for 'the removal of rolling stock from Waterford ... Rosslare and Wexford to points further north'.[14]

This focus on the south-east reflected the anticipated location of a German landing. On 3 August the Waterford locomotive superintendent reported that two officers had recently called and indicated that 'a serious view is being taken of the possibility of such an invasion and to ask that all engine power, 15 ton travelling crane and breakdown vans be moved to Kilkenny and Bagenalstown at very short notice ... they request that one engine be always in steam on each road leading out of the shed so as to be available to haul other engines ... in the direction mentioned above.'[15] This shows the imminence with which a German invasion was expected and the hurried nature of the evacuation envisaged. These hurried preparations had a tragic result on 22 August when Private William Larkin was killed by the morning passenger train from Wexford near Glenealy, County Wicklow when preparing a bridge for demolition. The driver told the inquest that the train was travelling at 55 mph at the time.[16] Arrangements were then made for GSR lookout men to accompany soldiers on bridge duties. The programme for preparation of bridges for destruction continued in less vulnerable areas during 1940 with bridges in Westmeath and Galway being tackled in November.[17]

On 30 December 1940 the Cork district superintendent reported that arrangements had been completed for evacuation of rolling stock, activated by code words that would be changed monthly. Code one meant: 'there is a possibility that scheme for evacuation of rolling stock including travelling cranes be put into effect at an early date.' Code two signified: 'it appears necessary that execution of evacuation scheme will become necessary', while code three signified: 'the evacuation scheme will be put into effect at once.' The receipt of code one was to trigger the movement of all surplus rolling stock northwards from Cork. Code two would trigger the evacuation of remaining goods wagons and the mobilisation of parties of men to disable fixed cranes and the lifting bridges over the Lee. Code three would trigger the commencement of the evacuation of all remaining vehicles. The Goold's Cross to Cashel branch was earmarked for storage of rolling stock from the Cork area. A similar scheme was prepared for the Kerry area which was to be activated in the event of a landing between Bantry Bay and the River Shannon. Engines and rolling stock in north Kerry would move through Limerick to Roscrea, while those in south Kerry would go to Mallow and wait there until they could go north to the Cashel branch without conflicting with movements from Cork.[18] The authorities suggested that the GSR should develop its own sections of the Local Defence Force (LDF) to evacuate locomotives and stock and render Limerick works unusable. One of these sections was to be armed in order to cover the operations of men arranging evacuation and demolition.[19] The main role of the GSR in Irish defence planning was therefore to deny its equipment to an invading force. A priority was given to evacuating locomotives. Without locomotives, the rest of the railway system was useless, as the Irish track gauge of 5 feet 3 inches was wider than in the rest of Europe, meaning that replacement locomotives would need significant alteration.

Planning for the destruction of railway facilities began in summer 1940 in Waterford, and later spread to less vulnerable areas. The vaguer plans of the two more northerly command areas reflected military and political uncertainties over who an invader might be. This contradiction was sharpest in the Eastern command, where Commdt. Grey reported that 'certain arrangements for LDF action at Dundalk have been made.'[20] When asked to expand on this laconic observation Grey explained: 'The places from which we require rolling stock to be removed will differ according to the situation. In the case of an advance across the border we should be anxious that Dundalk and Clones traffic should be cleared to Dublin...If we were confronted with landing of airborne troops near Dublin it would not be desirable that railway traffic should converge on the city. In that case movement should be outwards to Dundalk, Clones, Mullingar and Arklow.'[21] The decision to work through the LDF in Dundalk rather than the GNR itself was an indication of the delicate circumstances facing a company that straddled the border.[22] On 21 June 1940 the GNR was approached by Maj. Lillis about the use of its facilities in the deployment of troops. The company responded, setting out a number of options.

> Assuming the troops and equipment to which you referred arrived by train in Dundalk it would be possible without detraining to continue their journey westwards by rail as far as Cavan...As an alternative the rail journey could be continued to Enniskillen and thence...to Collooney where a direct connection is made with the GSR leading northwards to Sligo or southwards to the west of Ireland. If [it] is decided that the troops are to be detrained at Dundalk, it would be possible within two and a half hours, or three at the most, to concentrate 98 buses and 80 lorries belonging to the company and these could convey 4,540 troops...It will be appreciated that under certain circumstances there might be some refusals to drive troops not belonging to Éire...but such numbers would...be small.[23]

Both options involved an agreed southwards deployment of troops. The rail route described involved multiple border crossings, while the road option involved troops detraining in Dundalk for onward deployment. This could only be in a southerly direction. It is clear that Lillis' discussions with the GNR concerned a southward deployment of British troops with the co-operation of the Irish government. The Irish authorities took certain risks in making this approach to the GNR as news of such a request would have quickly made its way to the political or military authorities in Northern Ireland. Perhaps this was one of the reasons why de Valera stressed to army Commanders Dan McKenna and Hugo McNeill and Garda Deputy Commissioner W.R.E. Murphy that 'any request to an outside power for aid in resisting an invasion could (and should)[24] be made by the government only and in no circumstances should any such request be made by our forces.'[25]

While no longer enjoying the commercial predominance it had in 1914, by 1939 the railway companies were still among Ireland's major employers. There had been little recruitment in the 1920s and '30s, so the railway labour force contained much fewer men of military age in 1938 than in 1914. Nevertheless, enlistment arose as an issue immediately on the outbreak of war. On 4 September 1939 in the civil engineer's department 'a labourer named Radcliffe... asked for a privilege ticket to London to enable him to join the British Army.'[26] The ticket was issued 'without any comment'. The call up of reservists provoked questions from staff and their unions about conditions attaching to enlistment in the Irish and British forces.

On 5 September 1939 Cecil Watters, the Irish officer of the National Union of Railwaymen (NUR), raised the position of reservists, presuming that 'similar arrangements to those made on previous occasions would operate'.[27] Men enlisting in 1914 could expect their jobs to be held open, their seniority retained, their pension contributions maintained and, in the case of men with dependants, their military pay topped up with an allowance.[28] A board sub-committee considered the NUR request and recommended the application of the 1914 arrangements, with the exception of an allowance which was deferred until cases arose. The main board rejected this recommendation and referred the issue to the government, enclosing a draft reply to the union which stated: 'The international relations of this country render present circumstances much different from those obtaining in 1914–1918 and I regret, therefore, that the GSR cannot give any guarantee [but that] men called up by our own government might be regarded as on a different footing.' Leydon replied: 'You may take it definitely that our position in respect to neutrality would not be prejudiced if you decide to reinstate employees who, being reservists of the British Forces, rejoin their units during the war. If therefore you are not prepared to grant the concession... it is clearly most desirable that your refusal should be based on some other ground than that indicated in the draft reply which you sent to me.'[29] By assuming that restrictions on foreign enlistments would be put in place, the GSR board was applying a stricter and more technically correct interpretation of neutrality than that applied by the government. Following Leydon's letter the board approved a proposal keeping jobs open for all volunteers in the Irish forces and for British reservists.[30] In practice the arrangements applied to voluntary enlisters as well as to reservists in the British forces. Notwithstanding these arrangements, there was no mass rush to enlist. In comparison with the estimated 800 who enlisted from the GS&WR alone in the previous war,[31] approximately 300 GSR employees enlisted in both armies between 1939 and 1945.[32]

The topping up of army pay had been left in abeyance, but when employers such as the civil service and Dublin Corporation decided to top up the military pay to their staff[33] the Railway Clerks' Association sought a similar arrangement for a member who had been mobilised in the Irish forces. The request was declined.[34] The approach of the GSR to staff members joining the Irish forces anticipated by some months the general duty placed on employers in the 1940 Defence Forces (Temporary Provisions) (No. 2) Bill.

Those who enlisted had different motivations at different times. An early motivation was compulsion, with reservists being called up in September 1939. Patriotism also played a part for those volunteering for the Irish army, although low pay soon put the patriotism of breadwinners to the test. The search for adventure must have motivated some who joined the British forces, but a sense of duty was also important. In September 1939 Porter Bird from Kingsbridge obtained special leave to visit a sick relative in England and wrote directly to Morton from the Young Men's Christian Association (YMCA) in Swansea that he had enlisted 'owing to the fact that me being an ex-British serviceman from the Great War it was only my duty to do so'. The British authorities wrote to ex-servicemen who were not reservists asking them to re-enlist. Two permanent way workers in the Claremorris area wrote:

> Having received recently a letter from the War Office London as regards our position as ex-servicemen . . . we would gladly accept this invitation provided we get permission and would be assured of our jobs from the company when the war is over. We also wish to ask would the company permit our two sons to work temporary in our places till we return.

In June 1940 Porter Stack from Tralee wrote to a director seeking information on release terms. 'I am a British ex-serviceman and my reason for writing to you personally is to keep my business private.' In December 1942 Major Tynan of the British Legion wrote to an ex-army colleague in the GSR seeking information on release terms on behalf of a company employee who had been a prisoner of war during the previous war and had learned to speak German. While these letters illustrate the pull of duty, they also show how limited was knowledge on arrangements on release for the services among the staff. The arrangements agreed by the board were not published in the weekly circular. Any matter that railway management wanted to communicate to their staff was published in this booklet, which staff had to sign for.[35]

Many Irish reservists were released at the end of 1939, only to be called up again after the fall of France in mid-1940. Irish army pay was low, especially for those with families. A porter described how even after moving to cheaper accommodation, 'by being called up in the defence of the state I am losing about £1–6 per week which is rather a big sacrifice for a working man.' A fitter's helper wrote that his wages had dropped from 58/4 to 19/10 per week. Similar letters pointed out that other employers supplemented the pay of those serving. A fireman wrote that he lost about 65/0 per week as a result of enlisting. He enclosed a letter from his wife which read: 'I cried last Saturday night when I had to give the kids dry bread going to bed. It is all right for you. You get your grub and a few bob. But to hear them crying for grub and you haven't it or no way of getting it.' He applied 'for immediate discharge from the army . . . so that I may safeguard my family from further ill treatment'.[36]

Table 7 shows that 85 per cent of those enlisting in the Irish army did so in 1939 and 1940, after which enlistment practically ceased. There was a lower but more consistent pattern of enlistment in the British forces in the early years of the war and a sharp increase in 1943. The diverging pattern between different departments is shown in Table 8. The predominance of the locomotive department reflects the employment of large numbers of apprentices and boy labourers on contracts of finite duration with a high likelihood of dismissal on the expiry of their apprenticeship contract or when they reached twenty-one.[37] Some 36 per cent of all those enlisting came from Inchicore works, of whom 54 per cent enlisted in the British forces.

Table 7 GSR employees enlisting in Irish and British forces.

Year	Irish	British
1939	87	18
1940	71	12
1941	9	18
1942	6	7
1943	6	65
1944	5	7
1945	1	1

Source: GM 41819.

Table 8 Total enlisting and percentage joining British forces.

Department	Number enlisting	Percentage British forces
Locomotive	159	54%
Traffic	46	28.2%
Bus	40 (two served in both)	34%
Permanent way	39	25.6%

Source: GM 41819.

The pattern of enlistment among clerical staff is more balanced between the Irish and British armies. Eighteen staff joined the Irish army up to December 1943, while fourteen (including one woman) joined the British forces in the same period. Clerks had a greater tendency to secure commissions but the officer experience did not necessarily fit them for mundane clerical tasks on their return.[38] In the case of one ex-commandant, the traffic manager wrote: 'The real problem is that [this individual] appears to have enjoyed a substantial salary in the army and resents having to accept the moderate salary appropriate to the position he now holds.'[39]

The treatment of servicemen seeking to leave differed between the two armies. From late 1940 the Irish army received many requests for discharge from soldiers unable to support a family on army pay. Returns from the British forces were much rarer and were generally cases of desertion or in rare instances on medical or fitness grounds. A mechanical inspector who served for a few months as a pilot officer (technical) in the RAF received a medical discharge on the basis of being 'run down'. A boilermaker failed the hearing test for flying and was rejected by the RAF but was denied discharge papers as the British authorities wanted him to go to the merchant navy where his skills were particularly scarce. He returned to Ireland in 1944 and was re-employed as a new hand, losing several years seniority.

The issue of desertion arose especially among boy labourers and apprentices. A spate of desertions occurred from late 1943, with one boy writing: 'I am home on leave from the RAF and have no desire of going back.' Military pay books were not accepted as evidence of service, and cases involving the reinstatement of men without discharge papers were referred to Bredin. On 17 February 1944 Ginnety wrote to Bredin: '[This] apprentice is unable to produce his discharge papers... the man's father is employed as a fitter's helper... and has made representations that his boy be allowed to resume. The circumstances under which this application is made is that the boy's mother insists on his remaining at home.' In another case Ginnety wrote: 'The works manager received a deputation yesterday asking for this boy to be allowed to complete his apprenticeship... I attach a copy of application received from the lad's mother.' In yet another case the Inchicore branch of the St Vincent de Paul Society made representations on behalf of an RAF deserter 'whose father, an employee of the company, had served as an artillery man during the Great War'. Of the nine cases of desertion, eight arose among apprentices or boy labourers; reinstatement was granted in six cases and refused in two. An apprentice painter who had enlisted without permission was refused reinstatement despite having a medical discharge from the RAF. Those reinstated all had the support of parents, union delegations or the St Vincent de Paul. Adults were treated differently, and a labourer who enquired about overstaying leave was told that discharge papers were necessary to secure re-employment, as was a bus driver who sought to remain at home as his sick wife 'prevailed upon him not to return as he is due to go to Burma'.[40] Of the thirty-four staff recorded as joining the RAF, over a quarter deserted.

Desertion remained a live issue until January 1945 when Bredin sought the advice of the Department of External Affairs. He wrote: 'It was clear that the men in question had simply deserted... the mere absence of a proper discharge was not a difficulty. The characters of the men were already known to the company. The real problem was that if they refused to take the men back CIÉ would appear to be trying to coerce the men to re-join their units whereas if they accepted them they would appear to be conniving with if not encouraging desertion.' F.H. Boland of External Affairs replied that 'anything that looked like penalising the men for deserting from the armed forces of another country which they had originally joined as volunteers would be hard to justify in principle.'[41]

In January 1944 the board decided that each application for leave to enlist would be subject to board approval.[42] As reinstatement after service in the Irish forces was a legal entitlement, the decision was aimed at stopping the flow of recruits to the British forces. Only sixteen requests to enlist in either army were subsequently made. Most of those seeking to join the Irish forces were facilitated, but only one request to join the British forces was approved. Some of those refused joined the British forces without permission and were regarded as having dismissed themselves. Those joining the Irish army without permission were told that their case would be considered when the time arose. The flow of GSR staff to the RAF in 1943 might have been a political embarrassment but it also had the potential to increase staff numbers if returning servicemen, who in the interim had been replaced, reclaimed their jobs. In March 1945 an apprentice fitter applied for permission to enlist in the Royal Navy as an engine room artificer. Bredin wrote: 'As consent to release might impose a liability to re-employ him, consent should not be given in this case.'[43]

Only a single fatality can be traced among GSR staff who served in the war, that of Patrick Coombes, a boiler washer from Inchicore and a naval reservist who was lost on HMS *Hood*. While it is impossible to establish with certainty how many men served among all the constituent companies of the GSR, 150 names are recorded on the memorial plaques of the GS&WR in Heuston and its Midland Great Western Railway (MGWR) counterpart in Broadstone depot.

The numerically most significant enlistment of GSR staff was in the Local Security Force (LSF), established in June 1940. The force was organised and controlled by the Gardaí and was divided into an armed and uniformed Group A and an unarmed group B. On 6 July, as men began to enlist in local groups, G.J. Murphy the chief engineer wrote to Morton: 'I think it would be in the best interests of the country if members of this department (and possibly the members of other departments also) were not accepted for service in the Local Defence Force, Group A. If hostilities should break out the railway would very probably suffer and the members of this department should be available for railway service ... According to a recent number of the *Railway Gazette* it would appear that the English railway companies have been forming their own local defence volunteer units and I think it would be of benefit to the country and the company if the same idea was adopted.'[44] On 31 July 1940 the Garda authorities approached the railway companies and asked them to form a Railway branch of the Local Security Force drawn exclusively from railwaymen. This request was nearly a month after Murphy's letter and a week after unions had written to the company regarding time off for parades and lectures.[45] A precedent for this body was the Railway Protection and Maintenance Corps, which recruited railwaymen to protect railway installations during the civil war.

Enlistment in the LSF had the potential to be mass based and was managed by the GSR and the GNR in a manner similar to the British companies in 1914 where they secured an agreement that railwaymen could only enlist with permission of their superiors. A circular was issued by Morton on 12 August asking railway workers to enlist in the LSF and explaining that men deemed essential to the working of the railway (locomotive crew, bus and lorry drivers, signalmen, guards and stationmasters) would not be allowed to join Group A.[46] Approximately 4,000 GSR staff responded enthusiastically to the appeal. A typical reaction came from the staff at Mallow who met and submitted a list of fifty-three volunteers. Of these, thirty-five volunteered for Group A, of whom eight had served with the IRA or the Free State army and one with the British army.[47] The company considered the applications of 910 volunteers for Group A and refused permission to enlist to about 600, due to their status as essential workers or as ARP volunteers. The majority were reallocated to Group B.

There was a general waning of enthusiasm for LSF service, with only 84,000 of the 148,000 who had enlisted still active by Christmas 1940.[48] This applied equally to the GSR units, where the fact that LSF members were engaged in general rather than railway patrolling acted as a deterrent to continued activity.[49] The result was a patchy response, especially in the Dublin area where considerable difficulty was encountered in getting the hundred or so volunteers needed to form an Inchicore/Kingsbridge LSF section, despite the fact that Broadstone had an active and effective section.

Group A was taken over by the military authorities on 1 January 1941 to become the LDF.[50] In September 1942 the O/C of the Kingsbridge company of the 44th rifle battalion LDF wrote to Bredin that 'all our men are in the company's employment and are officered by responsible members of the clerical staff.'[51] This mirrored the practice in the regular army where clerks secured commissions. The rank and file were mainly workshop staff. Of the forty-nine men whose grade can be identified requesting leave for LDF summer camps between 1942 and 1944, thirty-nine were either workshop or clerical staff. The railway operating grades are represented by a solitary train guard. Some railwaymen in the southern command area joined LDF bridge demolition squads attached to viaducts over the Blackwater, Lee and Bandon rivers, but attempts to form LDF units in Limerick to protect and assist with withdrawal of stock and demolition in time of invasion shows how the grand scheme of August 1940 failed to materialise.

The pool of staff available for LSF service was reduced by a number of factors. ARP squads accounted for 10 per cent of staff in the areas affected. In the Dublin area nearly 1,700 men were issued with passes in connection with the evacuation scheme. This pool was narrowed further by the establishment of the track warden service in February 1941. This service reflected the desire of Murphy, the chief engineer, for an LSF group under railway control. It was established following a suggestion from the ARP committee that there should be a rapid response group who would respond to air raids. It was proposed that when an air raid warning was given each track warden would go to a predetermined vantage point and warn approaching trains in the event of bombing before making themselves available for repairs. Morton approved the proposal on 6 February, subject to sufficient emphasis being placed on the voluntary nature of the commitment. The following day Murphy wrote to his divisional engineers outlining the scheme, and while he stressed the voluntary nature of the commitment, he left his divisional engineers in no doubt that 'it will be necessary for you … to get as many of the permanent way staff as possible to volunteer.' The persuasive powers of the divisional engineers were effective, as by September 1941 it was stated that 'all permanent way inspectors and most gangers and milesmen have volunteered to act as track wardens.'[52]

The overlapping demands of the ARP, LSF and LDF made rationalisation necessary,[53] and in January 1943 an effort was made to combine LSF and ARP functions in one organisation. The GSR studied the efforts of the GNR, which had built up an effective combined LSF/ARP organisation in Dublin with over 200 members,[54] and used the GNR organisation as a model to relaunch its ARP and LSF units. An assurance was given that railwaymen members of the LSF would be confined to railway service. The relaunched Inchicore LSF unit[55] carried out night patrolling of railway installations until the end of the war.[56] Despite the early hesitancy, there was a high level of participation in LSF, LDF, ARP and St John Ambulance units. The weekly circular of 8 July 1944 congratulated the Broadstone division of the St John Ambulance for its success in retaining trophies at an industrial first aid competition held in Belfast. The following week's circular described an active LDF platoon based in Cork's Capwell garage which provided part of the transport element of the 48th battalion. In Tralee an active uniformed LSF section numbered over 100 men, but the circular noted that 'the group was self contained and operates in conjunction with the local town company as and when required.'

The attitude of railway management to the various voluntary defence forces was one of conditional co-operation. The action of Murphy in converting the LSF in his department to a track warden service under his control was a typical example showing the primacy of railway operation. This was the approach adopted by the GNR in Northern Ireland where drivers, firemen or guards were not allowed to volunteer for the Local Defence Volunteers established under RUC auspices in June 1941.[57]

Indeed, the northern railway companies fought a running battle with the Ministry of Labour and National Service to have railways declared a reserved occupation. George Howden of the GNR was advised to back off by his colleague Maj. Pope of the NCC who wrote that 'we have not a very strong case to put to the minister of Labour.'[58] As in the previous world war, railway management prioritised the running of trains and any initiative which threatened to strip manpower from that activity was resisted, both in the neutral and the belligerent parts of Ireland.

The railway companies owned the most extensive engineering workshops in Éire and had carried out defence work during the First World War. In October 1938 Leydon summoned Morton to a meeting and informed him that 'the Irish Government had told the British Government that they would raise no objection to contracts for airplane parts or munitions being placed in this country, and particularly with the railway companies.'[59] Shortly afterwards, Morton met Ernest Lemon, the director general of aircraft production. Lemon was vice-president and formerly chief mechanical engineer of the LMSR.[60] The two men would probably have known each other through shared membership of engineering institutions. Lemon suggested that the ministry 'should put down an aircraft assembly plant in Foynes and that Éire should be made into a regional sub-contracting area'.[61] Lemon was making similar suggestions to British railway companies and allocated the construction of Hurricane wings to the LMSR workshops.[62] A proposal was developed involving the manufacture of wings at Inchicore and Dundalk on sub-contract to Short's in Belfast. The matter did not proceed further, presumably as such a venture would have threatened neutrality as much as British possession of the Treaty ports.[63] The External Affairs file on the matter was destroyed in May 1940.[64]

During the Emergency the GSR carried out engineering work for military and civilian bodies in Northern Ireland and in Éire. On 4 June 1940 Maj. General Hugo McNeill approached Bredin requesting assistance in the manufacture of mines and armoured cars. Work commenced immediately and on 11 June Morton wrote to the Department of Defence advising them of arrangements.[65] A number of military orders were undertaken, of which the best remembered is the manufacture of armoured cars on Ford chassis. Stressing the urgency of this work, Morton urged Bredin to proceed 'with the utmost speed... Overtime to the fullest extent may be incurred.'[66] The work reflects an urgent move to adapt the army to modern warfare. Apart from the armoured car order, the bulk of the expenditure was on the adaptation of field kitchens for motor haulage, the manufacture of anti-aircraft mountings for Vickers and Hotchkiss machine guns, the sale and conversion of sixteen buses to field ambulances and the manufacture of 5,000 hand grenades. In the uncertainty after the fall of France, McNeill moved quickly to mechanise the army and to give it some anti-aircraft protection, placing orders with Bredin on 4 June that were not confirmed by Defence until nearly a month later. The work was charged at the rate of time and materials plus two thirds, the rate charged to the War Office during the First World War. In 1942 a request to tender for the manufacture of eight more armoured cars was declined, perhaps a reflection of the demands the fuel shortage was placing on engineering facilities.[67]

During the Belfast blitz of May 1941 York Road station and workshops of the LMSR Northern Counties Committee were severely damaged, with twenty-four coaches and 260 wagons being destroyed. While the LMSR sent over forty replacement coaches from Britain, it could not supply replacement wagons and the NCC turned to the GNR and GSR for help. The unburned parts of 150 wagons were salvaged and sent to Dundalk and Inchicore for remanufacture.[68] The work was under way in early June, when the GSR ARP committee visited York Road, and Pope thanked Morton for the help with the wagons.[69] The NCC owned the port of Larne and served the port of Belfast, both of which had a crucial strategic role, especially after the arrival of US troops. By rebuilding the wagons destroyed in the Belfast blitz, the GSR and GNR helped in keeping Allied forces in Northern Ireland supplied, while lessening the demands on engineering capacity in Britain.

In another initiative related to the Belfast blitz, on 22 April 1941 the Department of Industry and Commerce met the two railway companies and the DUTC to discuss the hire of buses to the Northern Ireland Road Transport Board (NIRTB). The DUTC stated that they had no buses available, so the matter fell upon the railway companies. T.J. Flynn of the Department of Industry and Commerce stated that, while the buses were sought for the evacuation of children, they might be used on regular services as he understood that trams had been destroyed in the recent blitz on Belfast. The GSR agreed to provide forty buses with the GNR providing the balance.[70] The vehicles concerned had their GSR and GNR markings obliterated until their return in 1943, when the NIRTB took delivery of new buses.

While it might be argued that aid to civilian transport undertakings did not constitute a breach of neutrality, it was undoubtedly the case that the lending of buses assisted the war effort, given the large number of munitions workers in need of transport to work. A more extreme stretching of the bounds of neutrality was the manufacture by the GNR at its Dundalk works of armoured railcars for patrolling the railway lines of Northern Ireland. After a prototype was tested in Belfast and returned to Dundalk for alterations, a further seven vehicles were ordered and although the fitting of the armour was undertaken in Belfast, the lead role in the manufacturing was undertaken by Dundalk works. The GNR sought and received an export licence for delivery of these vehicles to Northern Ireland.[71] This was a very elastic definition of neutrality.

Not all cross-border co-operation was approved. In 1942 Defence approved the hire of a locomotive to the BCDR but vetoed the hiring of fifteen coaches to the GNR, insisting that the coaches could not travel within Northern Ireland. The military authorities were unaware that permission sought was retrospective as some of the coaches were in use on a workman's train between Strabane and Enniskillen. The GSR coaches were returned south and used on Dublin suburban services where they released coaches for work in Northern Ireland.[72] However, they continued to work into Northern Ireland until 1942 when complaints from the northern blackout authorities resulted in the coaches being confined to Éire.[73] Both Switzerland and Sweden had lent wagons and locomotives to the Reichsbahn but this was to deliver coal to their respective countries.[74] The GSR coaches (described by the GNR traffic manager as absolutely essential in October 1943) on Malahide or Drogheda services would have stood out not least by their dilapidated condition, leading any knowledgeable observer to wonder whether the coaches they released were carrying troops from Omagh to Belfast docks or workers to the aircraft factories along the shores of Lough Neagh.[75]

In 1936 during the Spanish civil war, 40,000 Spanish children in Madrid and other cities vulnerable to bombing were evacuated to Valencia, Murcia and Cartagena, with further evacuations to Mexico and the USSR later in the war.[76] All the combatants planned for the evacuation of civilians from cities vulnerable to air attack, and planning for this eventuality had commenced in the UK in 1938.[77] In Northern Ireland a joint committee of the three railway companies and the NIRTB met in July 1939 and planned the evacuation of approximately 60,000 civilians from Belfast, submitting an interim scheme on 7 September 1939.[78] Frank Aiken convened a meeting of the transport companies and other interested parties in December 1938 'to consider measures for evacuating children, old people and the sick and infirm and the equipment of hospital trains'.[79] No further progress was made until November 1939 when the government decided to conduct a survey of those likely to be evacuated from Dublin and Dun Laoghaire.[80]

The organisation of an evacuation scheme was the subject of inter-departmental discussions in May 1940. On 31 May 1940 (shortly after the bombing of Rotterdam) Finance urged that a scheme should not be adopted citing, *inter alia*, the social and educational difficulties which would be caused by evacuation.[81] Frank Aiken, minister for co ordination of defensive measures, and Seán Moylan, his parliamentary secretary, decided to progress the matter through the cabinet committee on emergency preparation before proceeding to full cabinet.[82] On 3 June the committee considered a memo prepared by Defence and decided that evacuation schemes should be considered as a matter of urgency.[83] On 13 July the development of a plan was approved, with the priority task being the compilation of a list of potential evacuees and hosts. The slow rate of progress was probably a reaction to the failure of the British evacuation arrangements of 1939, described as 'military, male and middle class... [with] considerably less than half the evacuable population... [taking] advantage of the scheme... and over half of those who actually went [returning] home by the end of the year'.[84]

Irish evacuation planning remained lethargic, despite the shift of the Luftwaffe to night attacks on British cities in September 1940. The preparation of a final plan had to await the registration of potential evacuees. On 16 November an ARP report noted that 'arrangements will be discussed with the transport companies as soon as information is available on requirements.'[85] This process was completed in February 1941. Potential evacuees comprised unaccompanied school-age children, children under school age, to be accompanied by their mothers or a female guardian, and expectant mothers. The reception areas consisted of Roscommon, Longford, Wicklow (excluding Bray, Wicklow town and Arklow), Leitrim, Meath, Kildare and parts of Westmeath and Laois.[86] A memorandum for government dated 9 January 1941 lists provision of transport facilities as one of the outstanding actions, while referring to the situation in Britain where 'many British evacuation schemes were failures ... The idea that people will readily rush their families out of the cities is not borne out by what happened in... Manchester where only 10,000 of 80,000 children were evacuated following the recent heavy attack on that city... The acceptance by the Government of making the scheme attractive is therefore essential to its success.'[87] On 22 January the *Irish Press* announced that evacuation plans were ready.

It was not until 19 February 1941 that the Departments of Industry and Commerce and Defence first met the railway companies and outlined their needs. The railway representatives agreed to the appointment of liaison officers and promised every co-operation to Maj. Lillis, officer commanding civilian and military transport, who stated: 'The military did not intend to assume control of the railways, but that their use of them would be limited in extreme emergency to some troop movements . . . the question of evacuating civilians was also discussed when it was noted that when particulars of the reception areas were available . . . the Dept of Industry and Commerce . . . would get in touch with the railway companies.'[88] Preliminary evacuation plans were submitted within days, with the bus department submitting a proposal providing 32,000 seats within the first twenty-four hours of the evacuation. The rail scheme was less detailed as the destination points were not known but it involved the despatch of twenty-one trains from Kingsbridge, Westland Row and Broadstone.[89] In March the detailed work of preparing the road evacuation scheme commenced jointly with the DUTC, and by May 1941 arrangements had been made for the transport of 51,300 people in the first two days. In early June the plan was extended, with 10,000 to be evacuated on the third and subsequent days until 155,000 people had been evacuated by day twelve.[90] This extension may have been related to the bombing of Dublin's North Strand on 30/31 May 1941 when over forty people were killed.[91]

Billeting of evacuees had been made compulsory under an Emergency Powers Order and those with substantial houses could expect a visit. On 8 May 1941 the accountant prepared a memo recommending that a request by Alexandra College to lease the company-owned hotel at Malranny should be accepted 'rather than risk commandeering by government for evacuees'.[92] The stationmaster in Drumshanbo was informed that as he lived in a five-roomed house he would have to take three children and a woman in the event of evacuation. He protested, as did his colleague in Ballinlough. Although these were the only two examples, they might reflect the situation in Britain where a willingness to welcome evacuees was in inverse proportion to house size and social status.[93]

In late August the scenario changed again, and a so-called panic evacuation was proposed, involving the evacuation of 221,000 over three days with 123,000 being evacuated on the first day. The ARP authorities agreed to give twenty-four hours' notice of evacuation and required that all other services would be suspended.[94] The planning process was reviewed at a conference chaired by Aiken on 22 November 1941, and the arrangements were regarded as inadequate. On 15 December 1941 J. Linnane of Defence phoned:

> He feared that [the GSR] did not understand the very grave position at the moment and the inadequacy of [its] evacuation arrangements ...the military wanted to evacuate 160,000 people within some eleven hours, but the scheme the company had put forward would involve three days, and if the company's schedule were kept, there would be a repetition of the appalling conditions that prevailed in Belfast...If the company's proposals were to be followed it would impose on the military the task of feeding etc. of these thousands of evacuees at the evacuation centres. He wants to ask the company to make more adequate arrangements and he stated that the government is very gravely concerned about the position at the moment.[95]

At a meeting held later that day, the Department of Defence indicated the government's requirements. In June 1941 ARP headquarters had requested and received a table of all GSR locomotives, carriages and wagons, categorised by region and with an estimate of the number of vehicles necessary to run a basic service.[96] With this information the military drew up a framework evacuation plan and presented it as a *fait accompli* to the GSR, which was left to work out the details. This was for an evacuation of 145,434 people, 54,013 by train to counties Meath, Westmeath, Longford, Leitrim and Roscommon, 50,437 by bus to destinations in the same counties and 40,984 by train to destinations in counties Wicklow and Wexford. The departmental representatives outlined their requirement for a scheme of evacuation to commence at two hours' notice. Neither Kingsbridge nor Amiens Street stations could be used and the scheduled train service would be suspended. A total of ninety-six trains would be necessary, of which fifty-five would leave for the west from Liffey Junction with the balance of forty-one departing southwards from Westland Row or Harcourt Street. Some 360 coaches would be used to make up thirty-six separate trains each carrying 1,000 passengers. There would be nineteen trains to Galway line stations between Mullingar and Ballinasloe, ten to the Navan and Kingscourt branch, twenty-four to the Mullingar to Sligo branch and twelve to the Athlone to Claremorris branch. The return to Dublin of the ten trains to the Navan and Kingscourt branch was prohibited. Nine of the Galway line trains, together with three from the Sligo and Claremorris branches would return empty to Dublin via Clara and Portarlington to form further trains. There was no question of the GSR being asked for its opinion

– it was being told, in detail, what to do by the military authorities. In order to make this programme work the GSR drew up an action programme, which was approved by Bredin on 23 December.[97]

This panic evacuation was on a much larger scale than any operation undertaken by the GSR and involved moving on the first day five times more people than travelled for the 1939 All Ireland hurling final where 21,000 seats were provided.[98] The evacuation arrangements bore the hallmarks of the tactical use of railways by the military to mobilise and concentrate troop formations. 'Concentration comprised [trains] that could be timed meticulously... Train movements would be fewer and slower than in peacetime and would follow a quite different pattern [requiring] uniform speeds and [train] lengths... standard times were set for feeding men and animals and for fuelling and watering engines.'[99] This pattern of traffic would require the suspension of normal railway traffic management (block working) as required by the 1889 Regulation of Railways Act. The speeds planned for the western evacuation special trains were on average between 16 and 23 mph, compared to between 28 and 32 mph in the 1942 working timetable.[100] The requirement of the military authorities was for a plan developed in accordance with a military template specifying resources, duties and contingency arrangements. This was new to railway management and may have been the source of some tensions. P.J. Floyd, the traffic manager, was an experienced railway operator but was over sixty-five, and was immediately affected by the board's decision of January to apply compulsory retirement at sixty-five. His successor, J. O'Dowd, wrote to Bredin on 7 February 1942 that 'no provision has been made for the allocation of engines, carriages or trucks... No provision has been made for supplying trains for purely military purposes.'[101] Whether this letter reflects a lack of preparedness on Floyd's part or the actions of a newly appointed manager seeking to impress his superiors, Bredin annotated the letter to the effect that no action need be taken.

Work continued on the preparation of a plan and on 24 February a department of Defence memo reported that 'the transport companies have prepared schedules for an evacuation of 145,000 in eighteen to twenty-four hours ... The western sector from which 68,000 have to be removed presents greatest difficulties ...a complete clearance of the 54,000 allocated to Liffey Junction is the best possible in view of military restrictions on return of trains.'[102] Completed plans for the rail and bus evacuations were submitted on 6 May 1942 at a cost of £2,300 for the road scheme and £20,000 for the rail scheme.[103] The bus-based evacuation was simpler, as the bus companies had already arranged to call in their drivers and move buses to a place of safety in the event of an aerial attack on Dublin.[104] The preparation of an evacuation plan meant filling these empty buses. The GSR and DUTC planned to carry 50,000 evacuees on 200 double-deck and 100 single-deck buses from embarkation points at Ashtown and Griffith Avenue to destinations in Meath, Westmeath, Longford, Cavan and Leitrim. The rail scheme took longer to perfect but operated an average speed of 20 mph compared to the 10 mph planned in the bus scheme. The narrowness of some roads prevented returning buses passing outgoing buses, thus precluding night-time operation.[105]

While the bus plan remained unchanged, the geographical scope of the rail plans was altered on a number of occasions. The western plan was rebalanced with evacuees being diverted to more westerly destinations in early 1943. The westernmost destinations moved from Ballinasloe to Athenry on the Galway line, from Castlerea to Westport on the Mayo line and from Ballaghadereen to Collooney on the Sligo line. The number of trains sent to the Kingscourt line was halved to five. The development of more long-distance destinations was intended to spread the burden of evacuees more evenly and was also facilitated by the availability of better fuel by the early part of 1943. The south-eastern evacuation plan was changed significantly on a number of occasions. While in March 1942 an additional 15,000 evacuees were allocated to destinations in counties Wexford and Carlow using the line between Macmine Junction (south of Enniscorthy) and Bagenalstown, two months later the decision was reversed as the line concerned was the route for evacuating locomotives and rolling stock in the event of an invasion.[106]

In 1943 a supplementary scheme was prepared which saw the 5,000 Bray evacuees being redistributed by road to counties Wexford and Carlow. On 27 April the department advised: 'It has been decided not to use Westland Row ... as an embarking point and to entrain at Lansdowne Road station the 10,000 evacuees hitherto allocated to Westland Row' (in addition to the 5,000 evacuees already allocated to Lansdowne Road). In November 1943 the line from Westland Row to Dun Laoghaire was abandoned for evacuation purposes. The final version of the plan completed in April 1944 envisaged an evacuation of 28,000 people via the south-eastern section from Harcourt Street, Ranelagh and Milltown and 4,000 from Dun Laoghaire and Dalkey. In May 1942 Bray, only seven miles from Dalkey, was planned as an evacuation destination for 11,000 people, while in April 1944 Dalkey was to be evacuated and Bray was only a staging point for onward transfer of evacuees to destinations in

Carlow and Wexford.[107] These changes show the increasingly pessimistic assumptions underlying evacuation planning as the war progressed.

There were no evacuation plans for locations outside Dublin. The matter was pursued in a somewhat desultory manner in June when approval was given for a preliminary survey for the evacuation of Cork, Limerick and Waterford. Nothing seems to have come of these surveys, perhaps because of the conflict between evacuation of civilians and evacuation of railway equipment. In response to a demand for an evacuation plan for Cork, the Department of Defence stated in August 1942 that any evacuation programme would have to rely on such GSR buses as were not needed by the military. The memo added that defence would not consider giving its plans to public companies (such as the GSR) for security reasons.[108]

Providing the 360 coaches for the evacuation plan was not a problem, as even before the service cuts of July 1941, 450 of the 813 GSR coaches were classified as spare and used for seasonal peaks in traffic.[109] The original plan to await the arrival of trains from the provinces to make up evacuation trains made the evacuation plan vulnerable to disruption of the Dublin to Cork line. It was therefore decided to store the evacuation trains in the greater Dublin area. One of the double tracks between Liffey Junction and Clonsilla was converted to a 5.5 mile-long siding, and on 4 November 1942 the cabinet directed that carriages for evacuation trains were to be moved immediately to this siding.[110] When the GSR received this instruction it approached Industry and Commerce with a view to having the instruction deferred until the threat of air attack was imminent. On 27 February Defence agreed to an alternative arrangement in view of the importance of this section of track in ensuring continuity of turf supplies to the capital.[111] The revised arrangement saw the holding of 190 coaches in eight stations in the Dublin area. Parked in such locations as Leixlip and Naas, the coaches provided a dry if musty shelter for courting couples, some of whom were summoned to Naas district court in May 1943 when the district justice said: 'I hate to spoil romance in Naas but if this kind of thing occurs again, the culprits will go to Mountjoy.'[112]

The development of an evacuation plan was more complex than the traditional railway task of carrying passengers from one place to another. Additional tasks ranged from the issue of identity permits to staff to the provision of emergency coal and water arrangements and the feeding of all evacuees. It was proposed to serve a hot drink and some food to evacuees and facilities (including trench latrines) were put in place in the embarkation stations of Liffey Junction, Sydney Parade, Dalkey, Milltown and Ranelagh. Provision was also made to provide each evacuee with a 2 lb loaf of bread, to be loaded in the van of the train before it was filled with passengers.[113] It was also planned to send 'a quantity of flour sufficient for the needs of evacuees for a period of one week. The total amount required is approximately 357 tons... each train to carry 2.25 tons in the guard's van.' Lorries supplied the bus evacuation areas.[114]

Defence planners envisaged widespread destruction in central Dublin, and their assumptions became increasingly pessimistic as the war progressed. In 1941 it was envisaged that neither Kingsbridge nor Amiens Street stations would be usable and that there would be extensive damage to water mains (as shown by the numerous correspondence about mobile water pumps). The arrangements for provisioning the evacuation with flour involved a north side and a south side mill and three alternates in the event of the nominated mill being put out of action.[115]

The late start of evacuation planning allowed the Irish to learn from the failures of the British scheme of 1939. However, the snail's pace of progress in the Department of Defence meant that no evacuation plan existed during the period of highest risk between the fall of France and the invasion of Russia. The planning of the evacuation scheme by the general civil servants in the Department of Defence was laborious and ineffective. Transport preparation did not commence until the registration of evacuees was completed. While the details of transport could not have been finalised until the final numbers and destinations were known, it seems strange that the transport companies were contacted so late in the process. Inordinate amounts of time were devoted to minor matters. For example, in 1941 the Department of Defence agreed to make available 800 tons of good coal for evacuation trains but the matter was not finalised until 1944.[116] In a review of the evacuation scheme undertaken in early 1943 the army described the transport element of the scheme as workable, but in respect of the scheme as a whole concluded: 'The scheme is incomplete, and does not indicate much prospect of reaching finality.'[117]

The Irish railway system was of less importance than the British system in the First World War and was not considered worthy of government control until 1916. By 1939 the tactical role of the Irish railway system had diminished even further, given the developments in motorised transport. While in 1914 the time involved in detraining meant that railways were considered uneconomic at distances of under 100 miles,[118] the development of reliable motor transport meant that by the Second World War the critical distance for rail deployment had moved to 200 miles.[119] When Major Lillis told the GSR in February 1941 that the army would not take over the rail system except in case of extreme emergency he was reflecting the limited role that railways would have in a motorised war. For Irish defence planners the main role of the GSR was to put as much rolling stock as possible out of reach of an invader by evacuation or immobilisation.

A more extensive role was envisaged for the railway companies in the area of civil defence. The GSR was expected to enrol and maintain its own ARP and LSF units. In this area the concern of railway managers in 1940 was the same as in 1914 – they sought to minimise the enlistment of their skilled operation and maintenance staff as much as possible. There was no great difference between the behaviour of the GNR in Northern Ireland and that of the GSR in Éire in securing this objective. However, the most important tactical role of the GSR was to evacuate the civilian population of Dublin in the event of bombing. Under the 1939 plan it was proposed to evacuate 14 per cent of Belfast's population of 438,000 and 21 per cent of London's population of 8.6 million.[120] The initial Dublin plan proposed to evacuate 11 per cent of the population of 473,000, rising to 31 per cent in December 1941 and 34 per cent in March 1942.[121] While these plans were ambitious, the planning process was cumbersome and luckily for the citizens of Dublin these extensive plans were never put to the test.

Notes

1 G. Ribeill, 'Les chantiers de collaboration socials des federations legals des cheminots (1939–1944)', *Le Mouvement Social*, no. 158 (1992), p.87.
2 A.J.P. Taylor, *War by Timetable* (London, 1969).
3 A.C. Mierzejewski, *The Most Valued Asset of the Reich* (Chapel Hill, 2000), p.82.
4 GSRGM 38403/2, 'Air raid precautions ARP', Irwin (LMSR) to Morton, 18 August 1939.
5 GSRGM 38403/8 details this process. Copy of ARP scheme, IRRS archives.
6 C. Mangan, 'Plans and operations', *Irish Sword*, no. 19 (1993–4), p.49.
7 GSRGM 45841, 'Emergency preparation', Flynn to Morton, 29 June 1941.
8 GSRGM 48541, Circular 156.
9 GSRGM 38403, 'ARP scheme key copy', circulars 157, 158, 159, 160.
10 GSRGM 48541, Bredin to Morton, 1 July 1940.
11 GSRGM 48541, B. Cantwell to Floyd, 11 July 1940.
12 GSRGM 45841, Egan to Morton, 29 July 1940.
13 GNRGM 1023/53, 'Mining of bridges by military authorities', Foley to Howden, 23 July 1940, memo by Howden, 24 July 1940.
14 GSRGM 45841, Egan to Morton, 29 July 1940.
15 GSRGM 45841, Tyndall to Bredin, 3 August 1940.
16 *Irish Times*, 24 August 1940.
17 GSRGM 45841, Captain J. Kennedy, Athlone to Morton, 6 November 1940.
18 GSRGM 45841, Walsh to Floyd, 30 December 1940.
19 GSRGM 45841, Report of meeting, 21 March 1941.
20 Military Archives (hereafter MA) Emergency Defence Planning (hereafter EDP) 66,

'Immobilisation of rolling stock', Grey to GHQ, 5 May 1941.

21 MA EDP 66, Grey to GHQ, 13 May 1941.

22 MA EDP 66, Memo: 'Railway rolling stock removal and immobilisation', 5 March 1942.

23 GNRGM 204/1, 'Information supplied to Éire military', Howden to Lillis, 22 June 1940.

24 Text within brackets scored through in original.

25 NA DT S11903, Minute of conference, 15 July 1941.

26 GSRGM 41819/2, 'Staff joining the forces, miscellaneous correspondence', memo, 4 September 1939.

27 GSRGM 41819/1, 'Members of staff joining armed forces', C.D. Watters to Morton, 5 September 1939.

28 P. Rigney, 'Military service and GS&WR staff, 1914–1923', *JIRRS*, no. 161 (2006), p.532.

29 GSRGM 41891/1, Morton to Leydon, 9 September 1939, Leydon to Morton, 13 September 1939.

30 GSR general board minute, 4571, 5 October 1940.

31 Rigney, 'GS&WR staff', p.540 estimates a figure of 755.

32 This is based on a database constructed from file GSRGM 41819 and its fourteen sub-files.

33 GSRGM 41891/1, Note of civil service arrangements, undated, LMSR circular, September 1939; *Irish Independent*, 9 July 1940 re. Dublin Corporation.

34 GSRGM 41891/1, J.T. O'Farrell to Morton, 23 October 1940. Memo referred to is 3 October.

35 GSRGM 41819/2, Bird to Morton, 25 September 1939, Eagleton and Brennan to Ffolliot, 31 October 1939, Stack to Nugent, 10 June 1940, Tynan to Henry, 22 December 1942.

36 GSRGM 41819/13, 'Staff called up for military service' contains these cases.

37 GSRGM 41891/2, 'Staff joining post, 27.6.42'.

38 GSRGM 41891, 'List of salaried enlisting since 1939', 20 December 1943.

39 GSRGM 41819/13, Stewart to Lemass, 6 November 1946.

40 GSRGM 41819/13 contains these cases. Names are omitted for confidentiality reasons.

41 NA DFA 241/83, leathan miontuairisc (minute sheet), 30 January 1945.

42 GSR board minute 5978, 12 January 1944.

43 GSRGM 41819/13, Campbell to Bredin, 4 April 1945, Bredin to Ginnety, 9 March 1945.

44 GSRGM 45819/2, 'Local defence force: Possible dislocation of railway system through employees joining', Murphy to Morton, 6 July 1940.

45 GSRGM 45819/1, 'LSF, FIRRW [Federation of Irish Rail and Road Workers] and NUR re-facilities for employees', FIRRW to Morton, 2 July 1940.

46 GSRGM 45819, 'Local Security Force Railway section', memorandum, 27 November 1940, Circular 159, 12 August 1940, GNR circular 784, 31 July. Circulars are identical.

47 GSRGM 45819/1, 'Local Security Force: Return of enlistment', list of those enlisting Mallow station.

48 K. Kearns, *The Bombing of Dublin's North Strand, 1941* (Dublin, 2009), p.27.

49 GSRGM 45819, Murphy to Morton, 3 January 1941.

50 GSRGM 45819, Memo, 28 December 1940. This move was 'announced in today's press'.

51 GSRGM 45819/14, Goodman to Bredin, 28 September 1942.

52 GSRGM 38403/63, 'Track warden service', circular, 7 February 1941, 12 September 1941.

53 GSRGM 38403, Memo for board, 9 January 1943.

54 GSRGM 56258, 'Proposed co-ordination of all auxiliary defence forces', report by W. Plumer, 19 January 1943.
55 GSRGM 56258, Chief Superintendent Casserly to Bredin, 24 February 1943.
56 GSRGM 45819/22, Ginnety to Bredin, 12 January 1945 re. supply of torches for LSF patrols, Inchicore.
57 GNRGM 1023/31, Memo for board, 24 July 1941.
58 GNRGM 105/1, 'Reservation of railway employees', Pope to Howden, 5 January 1943.
59 GSR board minute, 7 October 1938.
60 H. Hartley, 'William Arthur Stanier, 1876–1965', *Bibliographical Memoirs of Fellows of the Royal Society*, vol. 12 (1966), pp.488–502.
61 GSRGM 38351, 'Manufacture of munitions or aeroplane parts for the British government', memo from E.J.H. Lemon to Sir Donald Banks, permanent under-secretary, Air Ministry, 28 October 1938.
62 Hartley, 'Stanier', p.500.
63 GSRGM 38351, Morton to Leydon, 2 November 1938, Bredin to Morton, 21 November 1938.
64 C. Crowe et al., *Documents on Irish Foreign Policy, vol. V* (Dublin, 2006), p.506.
65 GSRGM 4555/1/1, 'Manufacture of equipment', Bredin to Morton, 6 June 1940, Morton to Bredin, 11 June 1940, Defence to Morton, 26 June 1940.
66 GSRGM 45551/1/1/c, 'Fitting up of field kitchens', Morton to Bredin, 19 July 1940.
67 GSRGM 45551/10, 'Construction of armoured cars', Bredin to Defence, 8 June 1942.
68 Board minute, 4909, 6 June 1941.
69 GSRGM 38403/69, 'Bombing of Belfast York Road station', Pope to Morton, 11 June 1941.
70 GSRGM 49180, 'Hire of omnibuses to NIRTB', minute of meeting, 22 April 1941.
71 Mallon collection, Mechanical Engineer's index 1940, p.134, file 40/728, file 40/758, file 40/757, index 1941, p.455, file 40/757.
72 GNRGM 97/6, 'GSR coaches in NI', Ferguson to Morton, 28 June 1941, Lockhart to Howden, 15 July 1941.
73 Mechanical engineer's index 1942, p.453, file 39/406/4.
74 For Sweden see S.O. Ollson, *German Coal and Swedish Fuel, 1939–1945* (Goteborg, 1975), p.177, for Switzerland see *Railway Gazette*, 15 May 1942, p.577.
75 GNRGM 97/17, 'Demurrage hire of GSR coaches', Lockhart to Shanahan, 22 October 1943.
76 I. Lozano and D. Burgos, *Los Railes del Exilio Ninos de Morelia* (Madrid, 2007), p.46.
77 T.L. Crosby, *The Impact of Civilian Evacuation in the Second World War* (London, 1986), pp.20–1.
78 GNRGM 1023/SB, 'National emergency evacuation of children and certain adults from Belfast'.
79 GSRGM 38403/8, Memo, 31 July 1939.
80 NADT S11986A, Memo for government, Department of Co-ordination of Defensive Measures, 27 May 1940.
81 NADT S11986A, Finance memo, 31 May 1940.
82 NADT S11986A, Moylan to Aiken, 7 June 1940.
83 NADT S11903, Minute of cabinet committee on emergency preparation, 3 June 1940.
84 A.D.H. Owen, Review of 'Evacuation survey: a report to the Fabian society', *Economic Journal*, no. 200 (1940), p.503.
85 NADT S11986A, Report, 16 November 1941.
86 GSRGM 48438, 'Evacuation of civilians', Department of Defence leaflet, February 1941.

87   NADT S11986A, Memo for government, 9 January 1941.

88   GSRGM 48438/1, Memo of meeting, 19 February 1941.

89   GSRGM 48438/1, Stewart to Morton (road), 20 February 1941, Kirwan to Morton (rail), 22 February 1941.

90   NA DT S12405, ARP weekly progress report, 10 June 1941, 24 June 1941.

91   GSRGM 43438/1, Morton to Reynolds, 5 July 1941, minute of meeting, 18 July 1941.

92   GSRGM 48320, 'Hotels: Proposals to lease out buildings', Hartnell Smith to Morton, 8 May 1941.

93   GSRGM 48438/3, 'Exemption of stationmasters' houses in designated areas', memos to traffic manager from stationmaster, Drumshanbo, 10 July 1941, stationmaster, Ballinlough, 22 July 1941.

94   GSRGM 48438/1, Undated memo, ARP branch to GSR.

95   GSRGM 48438/1, Minute of telephone call, 15 December 1941.

96   GSRGM 45841, 'Air raid precautions invasion plans', Morton to Major A. Lawlor, 27 June 1941.

97   GSRGM 48438, Minute of meeting, 15 December 1941, note by Bredin, 23 December 1941.

98   GSR weekly circular 2674, week ending 9 September 1939.

99   D. Stevenson, 'War by timetable? The railway race before 1914', *Past and Present*, no. 162 (1999), p.167.

100 For train speeds see schedules in file and GSR working timetable, 1942.

101 GSRGM 48438, O'Dowd to Bredin, 7 February 1942.

102 NA DT S11986A, Memo for government, 24 February 1942.

103 GSRGM 48438, Bredin to Egan, Stewart (GSR) and Martin (DUTC) to Defence, 6 May 1942.

104 NA DT S11986A, Memo for government, 24 February 1942.

105 NADT S11986A, 24 February 1942.

106 MA EDP/66 railways.

107 GSRGM 48438, Quigley to Bredin, 7 October 1943.

108 NADT 11986A, Memo, 27 August 1942.

109 GSRGM 45841, Morton to Major A. Lawlor, 27 June 1941.

110 NADT S11903, Minute of meeting, 4 November 1942.

111 GSRGM 48438/2, Egan to Bredin, 21 January, Bredin to O'Brien, 1 February, Egan to Bredin, 27 February 1943.

112 *Evening Mail*, 14 May 1943.

113 GSRGM 48437/7, 'Provision of facilities for intending evacuees', Defence to Bredin, 9 September 1942, district engineer to Bredin, 25 September 1942.

114 GSRGM 43438/8, 'Transport of flour to reception areas', Linane to Bredin, 6 May 1942, schedule dated 22 July 1942.

115 GSRGM 43438/8, Memo re. particular of firms nominated to supply flour.

116 GSRGM 48438/4, 'Reserve and storing of coal', passim.

117 MA EDP/40/8, Austin Lawlor to GOC, 19 April 1943.

118 M. van Creveld, *Supplying War: Logistics from Wallenstein to Patton* (Cambridge, 1977), p.114.

119 Ibid., p.143.

120 M. Brown, *Evacuees: Wartime Evacuation in Britain 1939–1945* (Stroud, 2005), p.16.

121 M. Muldowney, 'The impact of the Second World War on women in Belfast and Dublin: An oral history' (unpublished PhD thesis, Trinity College Dublin, 2005), p.41 contains these statistics.

8

Coping Strategies

The period between May 1942 and April 1944 witnessed a stabilisation in the fuel position of the GSR. There was no single cause for this – it was the result of experiments with other fuels, changed operating methods and the locomotive crews becoming accustomed to the fuel available. From a position where it relied exclusively on premium Welsh coal the GSR was forced to get the best results possible from what fuel it could procure. The greatest single factor in the stabilisation of services was briquettes – made from the despised duff coal which had given loco crews such hardship since the summer of 1941. These briquettes were made on second-hand briquette plants imported from Britain which allowed the GSR to use the inferior coal available and gave them a fuel supply system on the continental model. The availability of briquettes caused a virtuous cycle in that it ended the crisis and allowed management to focus on other technical and organisational changes.

Coal briquettes were used widely as locomotive fuel in mainland Europe. In 1938 when the British Foreign Office was considering sanctions against Spain it surmised that 'simultaneous denial of high-quality coal and pitch for briquettes would seriously embarrass the railways.'[1] Briquettes had been used as domestic fuel in Ireland since the development of the Arigna coalfield in the late 1930s.[2] In July 1941 GSR general manager W.H. Morton asked the Department of Supplies about briquette manufacturing plants and was informed that one company was manufacturing and that another was in the process of commissioning a plant.[3] From September 1941 a number of outside firms such as Sisks manufactured briquettes for the GSR with generally successful results. Martin White describes how briquettes began to arrive from a local coal merchant: 'These were made from duff mixed with pitch and turned out very satisfactory.'[4] The GSR concluded that 'a briquetting plant would greatly reduce and almost eliminate the difficulties caused by the general low volatile content of the coal',[5] and decided to establish manufacturing plants under its own control.

In late 1941 and early 1942 three machines were purchased from a Lanarkshire colliery and a London gasworks.⁶ No difficulties were encountered in securing export approval from the British chief censor's office or in securing passports for GSR technical staff travelling to Britain to supervise the dismantling of the machines. The British Mines Department evidently had no objection to allowing the GSR to import briquette plants and they arrived in Dublin in mid-December 1941. The slow process of re-assembly started. The company later told the fitters' unions: 'The new plant was not in good mechanical order – we had no experience of it.'⁷ However, a tentative starting date of late March was given, and by mid-April 'the machine, although broken down and under repair, had produced 3 tons of briquettes which had proven very effective.'⁸

The chaotic train service was in dire need of alternative fuel. A survey of freight trains taken on 11 and 12 April 1942 showed an average delay of nine hours and that 'trains are taking approximately 24 hours en route and instead of reaching their destinations during the early hours of the morning are ... [travelling] during daylight when the wagons should be available for discharge.'⁹ On 15 April the new chairman, A.P. Reynolds, optimistically promised a better service using briquettes to the Irish Cattle Traders' Association.¹⁰ Satisfactory production of briquettes finally commenced in late April, and on the 28th the Cork passenger train successfully used briquettes for the first time. The locomotive inspector reported: 'The engine steamed exceptionally well, maintaining water and boiler pressure ... The fire kept in good condition and there was good lasting in the briquettes used.' Bredin wrote a single word on the report – 'satisfactory'.¹¹ A corner had been turned in the fuel crisis and on 15 May *The Irish Times* reported: 'Cork train only two hours late'.

The successful manufacture of sufficient briquettes to take a train to Cork was significant. However, producing quality briquettes sufficient to run a railway was a different proposition. Manufacturing a briquette to withstand the environment of the locomotive with temperatures of 2,000 degrees and with a draught in excess of 200 mph was a more challenging process than manufacturing a briquette for a domestic grate.¹² A French textbook of 1918 describes how 'briquettes made with low-quality coal will disintegrate into dust before complete combustion has taken place.'¹³ J.H. Dudley, a GSR engineer, described these very difficulties in 1947: 'It is easy now to dismiss these experiments in a few lines but at the time the consequences of each experiment were vital and the success of any one of them would have been extremely important.'¹⁴

The skill and knowledge crucial to briquette manufacture was scarce in Ireland and the engineer in charge of dismantling the plants in Britain was mandated to offer employment to the machine operator but refused the operator's demand for a wage of £9 per week as excessive.[15] The Dublin General Steam Shipping Company supplied technical assistance but with the reservation that as they were 'the pioneers in Éire of the manufacture of briquettes' they wished to safeguard their commercial position after the war.[16] These concerns about intellectual property caused the GSR engineer in charge of dismantling the plants to pass himself off as the employee of a Dublin coal merchant while he was in Britain.[17]

On 6 February 1942 Charles Johnston met a pessimistic Norman Smith of the British Ministry of Mines who told him that 'there could be no increases in quantity or improvement in quality and that present indications were that both would worsen.'[18] The report of this meeting concluded: 'Arrangements have been made for Mr George Lyons when finishing his enquiries...at Silloth to proceed to Newport Mon. to meet Mr Johnston and obtain information which Mr Johnston states he could not convey to the company either by letter or telephone.'[19] This brief note shows the delicacy of the coal supply position at this time. Johnston was by then a conduit for confidential information between the Ministry of Fuel and Power and the GSR. On 16 May 1942 John Leydon recorded that Smith was 'allowing export licences for duff in considerable quantities', and that he had to request more large coal from Smith as 'at present the railway company is not in a position to briquette in large quantities as they have only one plant working, the capacity is limited and it may break down.'[20] The willingness of Britain to supply raw material for briquettes had outstripped the capacity of the GSR to use the raw material.

In May, after briquette manufacture moved from the experimental phase into mass production, a number of changes were made to manage the manufacture and distribution of locomotive fuel.[21] The Department of Industry and Commerce agreed that the company's coal position constituted an emergency and approved the introduction of round-the-clock working in three shifts on the briquette plants.[22] By August, as briquette production increased, the *Irish Press* reported: 'On a few occasions recently the train from Cork arrived at Kingsbridge ahead of schedule.' After the appointment of Reynolds, the *Irish Press* adopted a sympathetic attitude to the GSR and its attempts to use alternatives to coal.[23] (The paper's editorials at this time have been described by Clair Wills as reading like government communiqués.)[24] The new fuel brought improvements in the passenger timetable, and on 29 June an additional daily train to Limerick was introduced, augmenting the 09.00 service to Cork.[25] The *Irish Press* reported: 'Overcrowding disappeared with the new double train service to the south and west which began yesterday.'

As one might expect, briquettes were reserved for passenger trains. However, they were also allocated to 'perishable' trains carrying items such as butter, milk, fish, meat or livestock. These trains were as important as passenger trains as the food they carried was mainly for export, and as such was a central point in any dealings with the British on GSR coal supplies. The seasonal peaks in July and August required special trains of butter from Munster. These trains originated in Tralee and were described in the weekly circular as carrying butter for cold storage – and onward export to Britain. They were scheduled to take nineteen hours when routed through Listowel and Newcastle West or a speedy seventeen and a quarter hours when routed via Millstreet and Mallow.[26] However, most food products were carried in the guard's van of passenger trains or on perishable trains and were high-protein items such as salmon, mussels, eggs and rabbits. In September 1942 the Department of Supplies approached the GSR stressing the need for the speedy collection of rabbits for export during the season, which ran from September to March. The department described how rabbits were brought by hand or cycle to a crossroads or village appointed as a collection station where they were transferred to a depot for subsequent despatch to an export packing station.[27] Clair Wills has surmised that the rabbits provided fur lining for airmen's uniforms, while the meat provided a popular source of non-rationed protein.[28] In May 1943 the Department of Industry and Commerce raised the capacity of perishable trains, following an incident at Mallow where salmon had been refused due to overloading, and Bredin told the traffic manager that extra passenger vehicles should not interfere with legitimate perishable traffic.[29] This vigilance exercised by the department shows the strategic importance of perishable traffic. Only low-quality fuel was available to goods trains so there was little improvement in punctuality or reliability. During May 1942 turf transport in Kerry collapsed, with ten trains abandoned between Mallow and Tralee at one point.[30] In August 1942 the loads of freight trains were cut by 25 per cent. Lighter trains were less likely to stall but more trains had to be run in order to maintain the amount of freight carried.

By September 1942 Inchicore was producing 750 tons of briquettes per week. Two further machines were being overhauled and repaired for Inchicore and Broadstone, with an estimated weekly production of 700 tons.[31] By early 1943 the briquette plants produced up to 2,000 tons a week, or roughly 40 per cent of coal requirements. However, this was not without difficulty. In November 1942 Meadows reported to Bredin that 'the briquette as manufactured in Inchicore is a very poor substitute for those sold commercially. With the quality of the duffs available it would be impossible to make a really satisfactory fuel.'[32] Heavy rain could make the raw material unusable or lead to an excessive level of moisture in the briquettes. This moisture turned to steam in the fire and split the briquettes before the ingredients had combusted. The unpleasant working conditions in the briquette plants, whose workers were among the groups allowed a supplementary soap ration, caused absenteeism, and plants were often shut down due to lack of labour.[33] Nevertheless, 'the briquettes became the backbone of the railway, drivers would try and beg a few extra and hide them on the engine.'[34]

Adapting to emergency conditions involved organisational as well as physical changes. In October 1942 a fuel control system was established.[35] This involved the analysis of each cargo and the grading of the fuel into four categories, with the higher grade A being allocated to perishable and passenger trains, B to livestock, C to turf and general goods trains and D to shunting locomotives.[36] Care was taken to ensure an even geographic distribution of all types of fuel, as 'previously the coal was directed to any depot needing fuel; the result was that one or two depots received large quantities of bad coal ... There is no use in putting first grade coal on the Cork–Dublin train if the Tralee connection is late at Mallow due to inferior fuel, and if the Tralee train again depends on the Cahirciveen connection.'[37]

Late-running trains resulted in higher earnings for locomotive crews, prompting accusations that some crews used the excuse of bad coal to deliberately run late and generate overtime. Martin White describes an incident where 'a man came to me at Dalkey and accused me of deliberately delaying the train to earn overtime ... I think he was very lucky that my fireman did not give him a belt of a shovel.'[38] James Meenan refers to such perceptions in his 1969 Thomas Davis lecture where he said that '[poor running] was at first attributed to the poor quality of the fuel; later it was thought that the fuel was not being handled by the railwaymen as efficiently as it might have been.'[39] A letter to foremen in November 1941 stated that some drivers were going to sheds in the course of their trip and seeking additional coal: 'Such action ... would appear to be deliberate with a view to making overtime.' This letter was displayed on the notice board in Portlaoise and provoked a protest from ASLEF. Bredin later privately described the action of the foreman in displaying the letter as stupid. It was certainly undiplomatic, jeopardising relations between management and locomotive crews, whose life had become much more difficult and physically demanding with the bad coal.[40]

The increased physical demands bore heavily on firemen. Firing a steam locomotive involves throwing in about six shovels of coal at a time in order to achieve a brightly burning fire. Impurities in the fuel fused into a rock hard slag known as clinker, which cut off the air supply to the fire. Removing the clinker entailed frequent fire cleaning or 'baling out' as it became known. This involved stopping, breaking the clinker and shovelling it out using heavy fire irons about 12 feet long, a long shovel, a heavy bar or dart for breaking clinker and a picker for pulling light clinker from the base of the fire. Val Horan writes of this period:

> With bad coal [these locomotives] were just man killers. I remember ...having to clean the fire six times on an overload special [from Athlone] to Athenry and back – 70 miles...With the bad coal the firing method was altogether different...and the fireman never stopped in his effort to keep the fire going. You would...fire all around the box with half shovelfuls. After every third or fourth round you would use the...dart to lever the clinker from the bars to let the air come up...particularly with 'slurry' coal which had the consistency of bog with never a lump in it...When you would pull the picker or the...dart out of the...firebox it would be glowing red for three fourths of its length.[41]

The overtime bill for drivers and firemen, which was about £5,000 in the first half-year periods of 1939 and 1940, had jumped almost six fold to £28,105 in 1942.[42] One reason for this was the late running of long-distance goods trains with a second crew scheduled to take over at a midway point such as Thurles. These crews booked on at their allocated time and awaited their train, which might be running up to eight hours late. When they eventually took over the train they worked it forward on overtime. One response was to instruct crews not to report for work until they were called. In June 1942 the Irish organiser of ASLEF complained that 'at Athlone with the exception of two crews for passenger working all the locomotive staff were rostered to be available as required, [which] interferes very considerably with their domestic and social life.' In September 1942 the company told the unions that 'there were two courses open – to scrap the timetable for goods trains and do away with rosters [or] to agree a period of on call.'[43] Such an agreement was reached in November 1942 with waiting hours between one and five to be paid at half time.[44] This agreement caused overtime costs to stabilise and then decrease.

Table 9 Drivers' and firemen's overtime cost 1942 and 1943.

period	w.e. 8 Feb. 1942	w.e. 28 Dec. 1942	w.e. 8 Feb. 1943
Loco crew o/t	£6597	£6893	£4253
Index	100	104.4	64.4

Source: GSRGM 55202, Table, 19 Feb. 1943.

While company representatives were concerned with overtime costs, locomotive crews were exercised by long hours, transfer to out-depots and securing provisions when away from home. Overtime payments were only a limited compensation in a period of rationing when ration cards and not money was the key determinant in getting scarce commodities. The unions negotiated an arrangement with the Department of Supplies that allowed trainmen staying away from home half an ounce of tea to cover the first three nights, rising to an ounce of tea for those away over three nights.[45] Despite such special concessions, complaints surfaced, such as that from fireman Larkin of Bray, who complained to Reynolds:

> I am one of about two hundred men affected with our families in one town and our lodgings in another. It is almost impossible for any landlady to cater for men in my trade as we have to take sufficient food with us to last us a few days. Under the present system of rationing that cannot be done so we are trying to work heavy trains half hungry.[46]

In the same vein a petition to Reynolds by Broadstone firemen complained: 'At present enginemen are working as much as 48 to 60 hours overtime a week, and often 20 hours on a single trip.'[47] This state of affairs was caused by the large number of special trains. Val Horan writes: 'A look at the timetable of those times gives no idea of the number of trains which were in fact running... Only a few regular goods trains were listed. The method of operation was to send off specials of "overload" [or extra] goods trains as fast as they could be got away.'[48] Issues commonly raised at union management meetings were excessive hours, lack of lodging accommodation and men held away from home for long periods.[49] A typical case in January 1942 involved a Waterford crew taking a Saturday goods train to Kilkenny who returned home on Sunday. They sought payment for the Sunday but were refused on the basis that they should have stayed in Kilkenny and made themselves available for work on the Monday. Following the intervention of the NUR, payment was conceded in December 1942.[50]

In July 1943 the Irish organiser of ASLEF described the difficulties in getting 'full payment for time on duty...after "baling out" [where enginemen] have found themselves stranded in the wilds of the country with no prospects of getting accommodation'.[51] The GSR provided dormitories in fifteen locations, which were used by 34,000 men in the twelve months to January 1942, or 109 men per night based on six-day working.[52] Dormitories ranged in size from twenty-four beds in Athlone or Waterford to six beds in Kingscourt. Mobile sleeping cars with bunk beds were sent to stations on the occasion of big fairs. However, as a train crew consisted of driver, fireman and guard, a twenty-four bed dormitory could cater for no more than eight trains.[53] The traffic manager explained how...

> ...in normal times our men experience difficulties in getting accommodation...but now with the rationing of food, soap etc., as well as the fact that our men have to confine themselves to a certain type of boarding house for obvious reasons their position has become impossible and on certain occasions they could not get any accommodation and were up all night before a fair. The position of enginemen is...very much worse and altogether between lack of accommodation and long hours on duty men working fair specials have a very difficult time.[54]

From a train operating point of view the turning point came in January 1943: 'During December last the poor quality of fuel available resulted in considerable delays...[but] there has been a substantial improvement since January.'[55] In July the traffic manager wrote of the goods service: 'Since February...the position has materially altered for the better, and at present the position is more or less normal.'[56] A daily record of the running of key passenger, mail and perishable trains for 1943 is summarised in Table 10. In January all the trains observed ran late; this was followed by sporadic improvements through the year. The small number of trains makes averages susceptible to wide variations, as in December where the statistics are distorted by two trains arriving ninety and seventy minutes late. The average lateness in 1943 was thirty-two minutes compared to Great Western Railway (GWR) mainline trains to South Wales in the same period which averaged twenty-one minutes late.[57]

Although confined to passenger and perishable trains, these figures are a reliable indicator for train running as a whole, as passenger and perishable trains cannot arrive punctually if they are blocked by goods trains encountering fuel difficulties.

Table 10 Train punctuality on the third of each month 1943.

	Number of trains	Percentage late	Average minutes late
January	8	100	48.5
February	12	58	45.3
March	14	86	27.6
April	8	13	10
May	12	75	45
June	13	62	21
July	15	60	39
August	19	74	37.8
September	19	63	26.6
October	16	81	14.7
November	17	65	27
December	17	35	43.2

Source: CHEM F55, 'Lateness of passenger and perishable trains', 1943.

Improved fuel supplies allowed improved services, and in May the GSR proposed improvements in service to the Department of Industry and Commerce, including direct trains from Dublin to Waterford and Mayo. A second train each way on the Wexford line was proposed due to the 'considerable quantity of milk and other perishable traffic... which curtailed the passenger accommodation'. These measures were approved but government representatives insisted that 'the minimum of publicity should be given and any alterations... should not be advertised as an increased train service.'[58] Other service improvements included a daily return service from Kingscourt to Dublin and the coupling of passenger coaches to goods trains on certain lines.[59] A Sunday service from Westland Row to Bray was also approved, allowing Dubliners to visit the seaside.[60] This generous attitude to passenger services provoked demands for further improvements. The *Connacht Sentinel* commented:

> While we do not grudge the Wexford people this concession we find it difficult to believe that they were ever in such urgent need of an extra train as the people catered for by the Galway line. We would urge the authorities... to put on an extra train each way between Galway and Dublin.[61]

There are few examples of locomotives running during the Emergency period but those that survive give us an insight as to how trains actually ran. One officer in the Royal Engineers gives an account of travelling on a GNR goods train that had just entered Northern Ireland:

> After a while I suggested I might give the Fireman a spell. The locomotive was burning a mixture of coal dust and turf, the latter in chunks about 2 foot long and 9 inches square, carried in a rack at the top of the tender coal space. After going around the firebox with shovelfuls of coal dust I took a chunk of turf and slung it through the firehole. The blast took the turf through the tubes, up the chimney and the remains were deposited on the tender... The trick was to throw the turf downwards through the firehole. The mixture was not at all bad as the turf broke up the layer of coal dust to let combustion air through and clinker was reduced.[62]

In the same period R.N. Clements described a run from Mullingar to Longford:

> Number 662 was fired almost entirely with very bad slack together with a small amount of turf. Leaving Mullingar the safety valves were lifting but in spite of this the effort of running the first 3³/₄ miles proved too much for the Mullingar driver who shut off steam and ran the rest of the way to Clonhugh at 15 mph. A stop was made at this point to raise steam which was just sufficient to bring the train into Multyfarnam. Matt Kelleher of Sligo took over here having brought in the up train from Sligo.[63]

How Bob Clements recorded this run is a bit of a mystery, as he later told Uinseann Mac Eoin that he had been interned in the Curragh between 1940 and 1944 without any parole.[64]

The most comprehensive account is of a run between Dublin and Valentia, consisting of spells on a mainline train between Dublin and Mallow, followed by branch line trains to Valentia. Leaving Dublin, the train consisted of twelve coaches and was hauled by an 800 class locomotive.

> The thirty miles to Kildare took sixty-one minutes, with the sixty-six miles to Ballybrophy taking 124 minutes – six minutes faster than the schedule. By the time Limerick Junction was reached the fire was in

a bad way and a squad of men was out to work to rake out the fire and build it up again, a task which took thirty minutes. Breakfasts and light refreshments were served in the dining car, with a three course lunch of soup, cold meat with potatoes and cabbage and apples and rice costing 3/7 (20 cents).

Between Mallow and Killarney the locomotive was fired with low-quality turf and lost twenty-seven minutes on the run to Killarney, having stopped twice to take on extra supplies of turf. The eventual arrival in Valentia was about two hours late, which was then considered rather good.

On the return journey the writer travelled on the footplate from Ballybrophy to Dublin, which was reached twenty minutes early.

Throughout the engine was driven lightly, this being observable by the low speeds on the up gradients. The engine was fired with ovoids, a small briquette about the size of a horse chestnut. Frequently steam was blown off at 225 lbs pressure and for the most part of the time 220 lbs was registered. Firing was not heavy at any time, and the blast was hardly audible, except when starting at rest from a signal stop at Clondalkin.[65]

These extracts show us how driving techniques were altered to suit Emergency conditions. Timetables were slowed considerably as slow-running trains used less steam and were therefore less likely to fail with bad coal.

A number of ordinary travellers have left accounts of Emergency rail travel. The working diaries of Séamus Ennis record travels between 1942 and 1946 on behalf of the Folklore Commission. In July 1942 he cycled to Galway, breaking the journey in Ballinasloe: '*D'fhág mé Baile Átha Cliath ar a 2.30 pm agus shroich mé Béal Átha na Sluaighe ar a 11.30 pm mar a chodail mé*' ('I left Dublin at 2.30 pm and reached Ballinasloe at 11.30 pm because I slept').[66] He returned from Galway on the bus. A year later he simply recorded: '*Aoine 5 Samhain traen agus bus go Carna*' ('Friday 5 November train and bus to Carna'). There is no mention of any untoward delays. The return journey was similarly uneventful: '*Céadaoin 15 Nollaig bus Ó Charna ar a 8 a.m go Gaillimh agus traen go Baile Átha Cliath abhaile*' ('Wednesday 15 December bus from Carna at 8 a.m. to Galway and train home to Dublin'). Thus a person who travelled regularly in the course of his work cycled from Dublin to Galway in 1942 in preference to the train and returned by bus. In 1943 he used the Galway train with no appreciable delays being recorded. Martin Quigley, an OSS (Office of Strategic Services) operative whose cover was as a representative of US newsreel interests, wrote in his report of 12 July 1943: 'I was pleasantly surprised that I was able to make the trip so pleasantly. The trains are … restricted and quite crowded but nevertheless satisfactory.'[67] On 10 October he wrote in the same vein of a trip to the west: 'The trains in Éire are comfortable enough, if very slow. In most cases there is only one train a day.' This situation does not differ greatly from descriptions of rail travel in Britain during the war years where 'travelling conditions over long distances became progressively more unpleasant as the war progressed … overcrowding to an unbearable degree became commonplace.'[68]

The weekly circular shows us just how little leisure travel was provided for sports fans. The running of trains for sporting events was strictly prohibited under Emergency Powers legislation, but a blanket ban was politically unenforceable. For most of the Emergency special trains were provided for the Curragh or Naas races, and for the All Ireland football and hurling finals. These trains illustrated the different class composition of racegoers and GAA enthusiasts. A typical Curragh race train of 2 October 1943 carried 1,283 passengers, of whom 768 travelled first class. By contrast, of the 479 Cork hurling supporters who travelled to see the 1943 All Ireland final with Antrim, only 68 travelled first class. One commentator noted that, in general, 'many ex-car users forced to use a train travel first class and it is not uncommon to see first and second class full and seats available in third class.'[69]

For the hurling and football championships one special train was provided from each county for the All Ireland fixture. There were no trains for the qualifying matches. This lack of transport did not deter GAA fans from following their county. While only 37,000 turned out to see Dublin play Galway in the football All Ireland of 1942, the arrival of Roscommon as a new force in football meant that its supporters travelled in large numbers to watch the 1943 final against Cavan. Cavan was served by the GNR, which provided eight special trains for the final, which resulted in a draw. The Department of Supplies forbade the running of additional special trains for the replay, so the GSR and GNR were confined to one train. Nevertheless, 47,000 turned out to witness Roscommon's victory in the replay. Roscommon figured again in 1944 when 79,000 supporters attended the final, in which Kerry secured victory. This attendance was the second highest of the decade. Most GAA supporters who travelled to matches in these years did so by bicycle, and Breandán Ó hEithir in *Over the Bar* describes many long cycle trips to matches.

Improved fuel placed a spotlight on the worsened mechanical state of the locomotives. In late 1942 Bredin wrote to the running superintendent: 'It is clear from the nature of these failures that the supervision of the mechanical condition of the locomotives...requires improvement...and I wish to impress on you that the mechanical efficiency of the locomotives is a matter for which you are personally responsible.'[70] This did not produce a significant improvement and the rate of failures of broad gauge steam locomotives almost doubled between January and February 1943.[71] In March 1943 a system of regular mechanical examinations of locomotives was established which aimed to 'reduce failures and to fix responsibility'. The underlying cause of each locomotive failure was recorded, traced and rigorously followed up, with drivers, tradesmen and supervisors being chastised and on occasion disciplined. In addition, monthly records of the coal and oil consumption of each locomotive were forwarded to foremen with instruction that bad performers be specially monitored.[72] The fact that such a system could be established shows that management time was no longer preoccupied with a fuel crisis.

In this period, highly paid work with unlimited overtime was available in Northern Ireland and Britain for skilled craftsmen. This made for turbulent industrial relations. In February 1942 150 fitters in Inchicore went on unofficial strike over the suspension of a colleague. The men struck on a Friday; the thirty men scheduled for Saturday overtime reported for work, but resumed their strike on Monday. The strike was resolved on the following Wednesday when the contested suspension was withdrawn.[73] Despite such glitches, the systematic approach to maintenance introduced in February 1943 led to an improvement in reliability.[74]

Table 11 Broad Gauge steam locomotive failures by quarter 1943 (Q1=100).

Q1 1943	Q2 1943	Q3 1943	Q4 1943
100	75	83	69

Source: GSRGM 55806.

In November 1943 foremen were informed that in each case where enginemen asserted that time was lost due to bad coal a sample of the fuel was to be sent to the laboratory.[75] On 4 December the chief chemist was informed that 'it is essential that your reports should be submitted without undue delay so that disciplinary action may if necessary be taken against drivers.'[76] On 16 December foremen were instructed to examine the locomotives of late-running trains for mechanical defects, to question the driver and to submit a report to the running superintendent.[77] Dealing with a two-hour delay where a high-quality fuel had been issued to the locomotive, the district superintendent advised Burnell, the GSR's chief chemist: 'I propose taking disciplinary action [in this case] in the event of an appeal by the driver or a protest from his trade union that you will verify that the fuel supplied was not such as to account for the bad work performed.' Burnell replied: 'Unless some responsible person has examined and made a note of the physical condition of the fuel...in use, I should not recommend going any further in the matter.'[78] Subsequent reports from the laboratory contained the phrase 'if the sample as received was representative of that which was on the tender',[79] thus avoiding the embroilment of this department in industrial relations issues.

Drivers of late-running trains knew that the fuel would be sent to Inchicore for analysis and could expect an interview with the local superintendent even when it was clear that the crew had done their best. The Waterford area superintendent describes an interview with the driver of a turf special that delayed a passenger train by two hours. 'I have had the man before me and he states the coal he got at Dungarvan was of an exceptionally poor quality...and that the picker was bent double.' In a similar case the Cork superintendent wrote to the chemist that 'the fuel... was of exceptionally poor quality and I am satisfied that the work performed was the best that could be done in all the circumstances.' Some drivers gave a sample of bad fuel to a foreman en route, as on 3 August 1944 when a late-running Waterford driver gave a sample to the foreman at Limerick Junction.[80] There are no records of disciplinary cases involving bad fuel coming through the industrial relations machinery, which adds weight to the view that disciplinary sanction functioned mainly as a deterrent. The Irish organiser of ASLEF wrote:

Fuel difficulties are becoming easier but the shortage of lubricating oil becomes acute. Both the management and the staff are being severely tested and the greatest amount of co-operation between the sides is required in the interests of the state. In general this happy position has been reached and is being maintained. It is apparent that many of the newly appointed younger officers of the company recognise that the co-operation of the staff is something to be desired and one of these officers is to be complimented for his efforts...This gentleman takes a keen interest in the education of engine cleaners and...distributes throughout his district notes dealing with the construction of the locomotive. They are excellently written and are creating considerable interest among the men...Of course there are exceptions to the rule and...a friendly word of warning is sent out to one of these officers who from lack of experience maybe believes that the only way to run a service is by intimidation and terrorism.[81]

By late 1945 the approach seems to have changed, as is seen in the case of a driver of a Dublin to Cork goods train which lost four hours in running north of Thurles where the crew changed. The district superintendent wrote that he was arranging for a locomotive inspector to travel with the driver concerned 'as his work has not been satisfactory'.[82]

The coal shortages forced GSR management to set aside their traditional antipathy and to buy Irish coal. The Irish coal industry grew considerably during the Emergency. The Arigna Mining Company was owned by the Leydon family who, during the late 1930s had invested in an aerial ropeway, a briquetting plant and coal-cutting machinery. Output increased from 25,000 tons per annum in 1939 to 50,000 tons in 1941, by which stage the main constraint on increased production was the availability of labour.[83] In Leinster the long-established Castlecomer Colliery Company was joined by the Slieveardagh Mining Company in Tipperary which was reopened in 1942, and Rossmore Collieries, County Laois, which was opened in 1943. This latter mine was operated by a company owned by Pat Fleming, whose shared experience with Seán Lemass during the civil war engendered a lifelong friendship.[84]

In January 1942 when the GSR was informed by the British that duff for briquette manufacture would be subsumed into its coal allocation, they sought quotes for Irish coal as a way of gaining the maximum amount of fuel for the briquette plants 'due to the difficulties in obtaining coal from Britain'.[85] The coal was tested with various combinations of locomotive smokebox ash, power station ash, silica sand, fireclay and turf mould. These tests took place between 22 August and 9 September 1942 on the Tullow train, which left the main line at Sallins, thus protecting the mainline service from obstruction if the test train failed. The conclusion of these tests was that Irish coal might be used blended with duff as a briquette ingredient up to a level of 15 per cent.[86]

Lower-quality coals such as slack, culm or duff are difficult to dispose of and if unsold must be accumulated in spoil tips which need to be maintained. They are therefore an irritant for mine operators who use whatever means possible to secure a market for them. On 15 September

1942 the stores superintendent was informed by Bredin: 'It has been arranged to procure 3,000 tons of duff coal from Mr Fleming of Athy.' The agreement to purchase was concluded by A.P. Reynolds rather than through the stores manager. However, this departure from normal purchasing procedure seems to have been untypical. The proprietor of a small mine in the Arigna district wrote to Reynolds, in a letter addressed to 'Dear Percy', which continued: 'We are anxious to secure a contract and I trust you will endeavour to secure this for me.' The letter was passed to Bredin, who indicated they were prepared to buy coal but that they would not enter into a long-term contract. When Fleming's contract to supply Athy culm was terminated in January 1943 he raised the matter with Reynolds, who referred the matter to Bredin.[87] Bredin confirmed the decision and in a barbed reference to quality pointed out: 'We have also on hands a quantity of ashes which we have reclaimed from the front end of our locomotives which we are making use of [in the same way as the duff].'

In January 1943 the GSR was anxious to buy as much Arigna coal as possible through its agent, the Dublin firm of Donnelly's. This firm assured the GSR that everything possible would be done 'to obtain as great a weight of coal as possible from the Arigna district'.[88] The phrase 'as great a weight as possible' referred – probably unintentionally – to one of the problems with Arigna coal, which was bought by weight and could be made up of stone, slate and other uncombustible materials. A note from the chief chemist in December 1945 read: 'A box labelled "ex Leydon's pits, Derrynavoggy" was received here . . . on 1/12/1945 containing only slate-like pieces of material, presumably carboniferous limestone, and consequently was not submitted for fuel analysis.'[89] Irish coal could only be economically used when mixed with fine coal from across channel.[90] A similar situation occurred in Argentina, where local coal could only be used successfully when mixed with Brazilian coal.[91] When Arigna coal was reintroduced on the Cavan and Leitrim section of the GSR in mid-1942 average weekly coal consumption increased by 188 per cent.[92] Any hope that it would be more successful in broad gauge fireboxes were dispelled in a report from the Mullingar locomotive inspector, who wrote:

The enginemen in Dromod refuse to take coal from Cull and Gannon as it is useless for any purpose, firebox being full of ashes before 10 miles have been run. If Leydon's coal is sent out, enginemen will take it as a mixture of 3 to 1 with Duff slack and in 75% of cases can run to Mullingar without cleaning out fire, a distance of 37 miles . . . I strongly urge that supplies from Cull and Gannon be dispensed with as same is useless for locomotive purposes.[93]

Quality problems with Arigna coal were exacerbated by adulteration and pilferage. George Burnell visited the coalfield in February 1943 and in his report discussed the problem of 'contamination'.[94] 'Mr Laydon [sic] said that the sieved and picked coal left him and he was of the opinion that it was subsequently mixed with other coal from the neighbourhood before being sent to us...He hinted that one of our employees was suspected of pilfering it.' A later report revealed that the culprits may have used lorries hired and supplied with petrol by the GSR. 'There is the possibility of their being used at night for the illicit extraction of coal from wagons lying at Arigna.' Another shortcoming adverted to by the stores superintendent was that 'seasonal farming operations commencing in March will draw labour from the smaller operators and Leydon is the only one capable of producing a steady output.'[95] Leydon informed the Department of Finance that they expected sales to contract after the war, even to the ESB whom they described as 'a more recent and more fickle customer'.[96] The mine owners had no incentive to maintain quality as they knew that after the war many of their wartime customers would desert them. Similarly, the GSR regarded Irish coal as a wartime affliction, as expressed by Bredin to the store superintendent when he approved a contract 'in order to maintain supplies from this source at least until we can afford to do without them'.[97]

In addition to turf, briquettes and Irish coal, the GSR experimented with a number of alternative fuels. One of the most important resources in allowing the GSR to cope with the decline in coal quality was pitch, a by-product of the British foundry industry which was freely available for export. Between May 1942 and October 1944 27,000 tons, or two-years' supply, was imported for briquette manufacture.[98] It was soon discovered that loose pitch, when added to an ailing fire, could assist locomotive performance. Pitch was described as 'the most disagreeable thing to manipulate in the world'[99] and four Dublin dockers unloading pitch were overcome by fumes and hospitalised in April 1943.[100] Val Horan observes: 'The fumes from the pitch were very hard on the eyes: sore eyes were a common complaint of footplate men.'[101] Despite this, pitch was eagerly sought after by loco crews and dire measures had to be threatened to control unauthorised issue.[102] After pitch was first issued at the beginning of June 1942, coal consumption fell by 12 per cent in the following six weeks.[103] Foreman Ledwith of Mullingar reported: 'There is a supply of pitch at Dromod and since it was put there there has been a noticeable improvement in the running of goods trains.'[104]

In summer 1942 an attempt was made to use liquefied pitch as a locomotive fuel using the well-known technology of oil burning. Burnell wrote: 'Under perfect conditions such as . . . a power house, pitch can be successfully used [but] I have grave doubts as to its exploitation for locomotive purposes.' He recommended that the experiment should not proceed further but that the engineer devoted to it should be retained, 'to embark on an experiment with pulverised native coal'.[105] Pulverisation was a proven way of burning low-quality coal, having been used on locomotives in the years after 1918 when coal was scarce. The engineer in question was not retained, and on Christmas Day 1942 Burnell died. As an experienced industrial chemist who had joined the GSR from the English GWR in 1920s and with his background in railway technology, his loss must have been keenly felt.[106] He was succeeded in his post by his son George.

During the course of 1942 two experiments were undertaken with experimental steam-assisted grates. One was designed by an Irish engineer named MacAllister while the other was supplied by the Diesel Engine Company. Both experiments were unsuccessful as the equipment proved unsuited to the difficult environment of a locomotive. In both experiments Percy Reynolds was involved in procuring equipment, while Bredin assumed direct control over the experiments, transmitting the designers' requirements to his subordinates and demanding telephone reports of progress. This involvement of senior management ensured that the equipment was given more than a fair chance and that any failure could not be ascribed to non-co-operation by the GSR.[107] It would be a mistake, with the benefit of hindsight, to write off these experiments. The success of any one of them had the potential to transform railway operation.

In spring 1944 the pulverised coal proposal was revived. Much work on this process had been undertaken in mainland Europe in the years following the First World War and a review of the issue had been published in the *Transactions* of the Institute of Mechanical Engineers in 1941.[108] The GSR experiment had its roots in the need to acquire high-quality anthracite as fuel for lorry gas producers. In February 1944 P.J. Fleming offered the GSR 250 tons of good-quality Slieveardagh anthracite a week, on condition that they also bought 750 tons per week of culm, or anthracite dust. The GSR needed the anthracite and needed to find a use for its unwelcome by-product. A report concluded that 'unless we can find a satisfactory method of burning culm in much larger quantities than at present, Fleming's offer is of no assistance to us.'[109] The Benbulben

Barytes Company was approached for the materials to adapt a locomotive and in March 1944 express passenger locomotive 402 was modified. This locomotive had a high grate area needed to burn low-grade coal which was fed into the fire by a screw conveyor. Tests commenced in April 1944 and were referred to by Lemass in a Dáil debate on 20 April. Bredin later explained to an equipment supplier: 'We hope to purchase low-grade coal at the pit for...under £1 per ton. If we find we can burn this fuel satisfactorily...we intend fitting sufficient locomotives to consume 1,000 tons per week.'[110] Athy culm cost 16/8 per ton compared to 65/10 per ton for locomotive fuel.[111] The initial results of static trials were encouraging, with the locomotive quickly developing a large amount of steam.[112] When running trials commenced in August problems were encountered, with the ash fusing onto the inside of the firebox, blocking the tubes and forming an insulation blanket. The tests were abandoned after a month as 'in order to obtain sufficient horse power it was necessary to have fuel of a quality not available', and because further alterations to the locomotive were not practicable.[113] However, some of the adaptations undertaken to the firebox were similar to those necessary to convert a locomotive to burn oil, as was done later in the Emergency period. Before the pulverisation experiment, the GSR held 2,310 tons of Athy culm. While about 1,000 tons were used in the trials and in briquette manufacture, in September 1944 this material was reclassified as 'Athy culm and accumulated useless coal',[114] a description that encapsulates much of the Emergency experience with Irish coal.

As the coal supply position in Britain failed to improve during the middle years of the war, an increasingly close relationship developed between the GSR and the Ministry of Fuel and Power. The official war history of the coal industry describes how 'on the Ministry of Fuel and Power fell the direct task of inducing industry to burn more [low-grade] coal. This was no easy task.'[115] It required a laboratory for experimentation and the GSR fulfilled this role. One of the areas of experimentation was with a newly developed brand of domestic smokeless fuel known as phurnacite. This fuel was extremely expensive and special instructions were issued to locomotive crews regarding its use.[116] Deliveries commenced in June 1942 and by October they were running at 3,000 tons per month.[117] Its availability in Éire surprised Donnelly's, the importing agent.[118] The significance of these deliveries cannot be over-estimated as they clearly breached British policy that coal exports to Ireland should be confined to the lowest-quality, unsaleable on the home market. However, as a 'manufactured product' phurnacite was deemed by the Mines Department not to be coal and could therefore be sold to the GSR. This somewhat Jesuitical distinction suited both the Mines Department and the GSR.

In May 1943 Charles Johnston expressed concern to Norman Smith at 'the danger of our being deprived of this fuel now that we have proved its worth and carried out extensive experiments on the use of it as a locomotive fuel'. He continued: 'The loco fuel position was discussed from many angles. He is rather interested in our method for using phurnacite . . . He would like the opportunity of travelling on the footplate of a loco using this fuel. Should you wish to have overalls available, he is 6' tall and of slight build.'[119] This shows that the GSR acted as a laboratory for the Ministry of Fuel and Power. This role continued, and in September 1943 the fuel controller reported that 'numerous tests were being carried out to supply information to the British Authorities on various types of fuel under normal working conditions.'[120] Dudley wrote:

> In 1943 or 1944 certain people in high places in Britain were interested in how it was being done and came here to see it for themselves when Britain was conserving coal for a continental landing . . . it had been represented to them that certain types of fuel could not be used successfully, whilst at the same time our drivers were doing well on them. They had learned how to use them.[121]

In December 1943 a railway enthusiast newsletter noted: 'Not long since, a fuel expert from England turned up to see how the trains were running on ovoids: [a test with] the Cork train from Ballybrophy to Dublin was run at an average 70 mph.'[122] The locomotive used was 800 *Maedhbh*, the premier locomotive in the fleet. Such high speeds were unknown during the Emergency and indicates that a show was being put on for the visitor who was, most probably, Norman Smith.

These events show the relationship that developed between the GSR and the Ministry of Fuel and Power and the way they served both Irish and British needs. By late 1943, those planning the invasion of France knew that the invading armies would need initially to import their own fuel until French mines in the Pas de Calais area came under their control. Those in charge of invasion planning therefore needed to test various types of briquettes and manufactured fuel as these would be the staple fuel of continental railway systems after liberation. It was impractical for such tests to be carried out in Britain due to the unacceptability of delays on the British railway system, which was working near to capacity. The GSR was an ideal testing ground for the

Ministry of Fuel and Power, but the survival of evidence is entirely fortuitous.

The desire by both sides to keep these experiments quiet is understandable, given that both sides were challenging the policies of their governments. The GSR had been refused permission to hire coaches to the GNR for use in Northern Ireland, while on the other hand the Ministry of Fuel and Power was ignoring a decision of the cabinet. There are very few traces of Smith's test run and they survive by chance, such as in Johnston's requisitioning overalls for him, or the chance remark on the scale of the test programme in a report of a meeting dealing with other matters. The evidence is corroborated by contemporary railway enthusiast sources – a privately circulated bulletin in the case of the 1943 visit while Dudley's reference comes from a paper he delivered in 1947 to the Irish Railway Record Society. Taken together, these incidents show the evolving role of the GSR as a testing facility for the Ministry of Fuel and Power.

The success of the GSR in adapting to Emergency conditions should not obscure the widespread detrimental effect of Emergency shortages on public health and welfare. For example, during October 1942 all buses passing through Spiddal, County Galway had to be disinfected due to a typhus outbreak.[123] In September 1943 a Guard giving evidence at an inquest in Dundalk on a boy run over by a train stated that 'trains from Belfast frequently stopped outside the station and children from nearby swarmed on the line begging from passengers.'[124] This decline in public welfare had serious implications for the GSR as an owner and transporter of fuel. The company was vulnerable to theft of anything combustible, be it locomotive coal, turf in transit or timber parts of the infrastructure. The railway line was bordered with wooden fence posts while the rails were laid on wooden sleepers, held in place by oblong wooden keys, which when impregnated with creosote burned particularly well. The trees that grew beside the line (though the sparks from locomotives ensured that they were less numerous than today) presented another source of domestic fuel. For all these reasons the railway system was almost under siege for the duration of fuel shortages.

On 15 August 1941 G.J. Murphy, the civil engineer, wrote to the Garda commissioner reporting fifty-one incidents involving the theft of keys since May. 'These articles are about 6 inches long and 3 inches square and being made of oak and well seasoned are very attractive from the point of view of use of fuel ... the removal of sufficient number of keys ... would leave the rails loose and cause derailment.' The Garda commissioner advised of the difficulties in patrolling the track, but noted that two men had been prosecuted for theft of keys at Killiney and had both been sentenced to a month's imprisonment, suspended in one case.[125] On 1 September 1941 a driver came before the Dublin District Court charged with the theft of a lump of coal weighing 34 lbs which he threw from his locomotive where it struck a member of an LDF patrol. The district justice applied the probation act but described coal as being 'as scarce as gold dust'.[126]

The GSR took a strong line against trespass and pursued court cases against trespassers whose motives ranged from swimming in the Royal Canal to stone throwing, the taking of short cuts and chasing rabbits with ferrets.[127] Of the fifteen cases involving prosecutions taken during 1941 only two were for theft of keys. As the shortage of domestic coal worsened the incidence of theft increased, and of the seventeen prosecutions taken for trespass in 1942 nine concerned the theft of some combustible part of the railway infrastructure.[128] In May a ganger on the Macroom line asked the company to proceed against two local youths, 'as the damage done . . . to fences is appalling. These youths are armed with hatchets and bags and are tearing away the fences everywhere they can.'[129] In June four boys aged between four and nine who lived in Dublin's Beggar's Bush barracks were interviewed in the presence of their parents and admitted to stealing keys. It was decided not to prosecute as the majority of the youths were under seven years of age.[130] In July 1942 alone three cases came before the courts. In Bandon the local Garda superintendent advised a prosecution where two youths had been caught cutting bog alder – a moist and slow-burning tree. Despite the advice of the chief engineer a prosecution was mounted and the probation act applied.[131] Later in the month a brother and sister were prosecuted in Mullingar for theft of turf. The case came to court in November and a fine of 2/6 was applied.[132] On 18 July a labourer leaving Inchicore was stopped and three briquettes were found in his possession. He was brought before the court three days later, but the justice decided not to impose a criminal sentence as the man had admitted to taking briquettes over a period of time and had offered to pay compensation. A request for reinstatement in his job was declined.[133] In August the chief engineer reported: 'About 180 sleepers . . . on the Wexford south branch near the Maudlintown Corporation houses have been chipped with axes by persons gathering firewood . . . 25 of them have been so damaged that their lives have been shortened.'[134] In September the Gardaí raided a house near Cork and found railway keys. The householder was prosecuted.[135] In winter 1942 a milepost was removed from the line between Cappoquin and Lismore,[136] while eight fence posts were removed near Maynooth.[137] More seriously, in August 1942 points were interfered with at Mallow in order to halt turf trains at a signal. Bredin was informed that 'civic guards brought 11 parties male and female to station... These parties were found to be in possession of 16 bags presumably for the purpose of stealing turf.' The case came before the court in mid-October where the defendants were bound over for twelve months on a bond of £10 or, in default, seven-days' imprisonment.[138]

While reports of thefts of combustible railway material decline after winter 1942, the problem continued. The weekly circular of 21 October 1944 records the making of an award to a platelayer who had devised a way of locking keys in place, thus obviating 'a source of worry to the company and of danger to the travelling public'. Fuel theft was probably controlled by the activity of the railway LSF sections, especially after their relaunch in early 1943, referred to in Chapter 7. Theft of fuel reappeared in the bad winter of 1946/7 but it was an irritant rather than a problem. When the running superintendent reported that in Mullingar, where 2,500 tons of coal was held, 'they have had two cases recently of women loading up sacks of coal' and suggested employing watchmen, the memo was annotated: 'The pilferage would need to be substantial to justify this expense.'[139] The best sociological analysis of the problem comes from a report by the investigation branch in Mallow.

> There is undoubtedly a certain amount of fuel pillaged at all large centres... the main offenders in this respect in Mallow would appear to be coalmen, steam risers and... local temporary labourers... the supervisors are decidedly reluctant to interfere with fuel pillaging employees inside and... they give 'the Nelson Eye' to certain trespassers from outside because they do not wish to encourage the displeasure of their own subordinates or town dwellers whom they may know as near neighbours or otherwise... Such an attitude is not confined to Mallow and too often our employees of different ranks are indifferent to trespass and consequent petty pillage of fuel ranging from stray coal to abandoned turf down to whatever can be salvaged from a heap of discharged clinkers.[140]

The GSR was one of the major owners of combustible material in urban Ireland during the Emergency. Fuel Importers possibly held more stocks of fuel but it was held in enclosed defensible areas. The TDB and the county councils owned more turf but much of it was remote from the urban consumer and was often so wet as to be unattractive to the fuel hungry. The pilferage of fuel from the GSR shows the widespread incidence of fuel poverty in Irish society during this period. In addition, the theft of coal and turf is one of the few areas in which women feature in the narrative of the Emergency railway system. Women make a fleeting appearance bearing sacks with which they hoped to get fuel for heat and cooking. These incidents serve as a reminder that Emergency shortages had wide social consequences. Shortage of fuel could mean a shortage of hot water for washing, which when combined with the soap rationing mentioned earlier in the chapter, had its effect on public health. It is of little surprise that infant mortality and the death rate from tuberculosis rose significantly in Éire in the Emergency period.[141]

Between 1942 and 1944 the GSR reorganised its operations to cope with low-quality fuel. The critical action for the GSR was getting the briquette machines into operation. The more radical experiments with turf, liquid pitch, pulverised coal or patent fire grates did not produce a solution but in some cases laid the groundwork for later successful technical developments. Of greater immediate importance were smaller initiatives such as the fitting of drop grates, the issues of pitch or the reorganisation of schedules. These brought an improvement to all trains, not just those that received briquettes. Historians of technology stress the importance of a sequence of small incremental changes in the development of machines or technological systems, and this can be seen in the response of the GSR to the Emergency fuel crisis. The most significant technical innovation was the simplest – the fitting of a dropping section to the grates of locomotives, allowing the fire to be cleaned with greater speed and ease. Jack Woodfull, an Inchicore boilermaker who improved upon the basic design, was recommended for an award of £3, but Bredin sanctioned an increased award of £5 with instructions that the cheque be presented personally.[142] An American historian of technological change writing of steam riverboats in pre-civil war America, highlights the vital role of...

> ... anonymous and unheroic craftsmen, shop foremen and master mechanics in whose hands rested the daily job of making things go and making them go a little better [through] such seemingly small matters as machining a shaft to hundredths rather than sixteenths of an inch or devising a cylinder packing that would increase effective cylinder pressure by a few pounds or altering the design of a boiler so that cleaning... would be necessary only every other rather than every trip.[143]

While the phrase 'Plato's cave' has been used to describe life in

Emergency Ireland,[144] a more appropriate metaphor for the railway industry would be a magpie's nest. The GSR shamelessly begged, borrowed or stole ideas in order to keep the system going. Briquettes came from continental practice; turf burning had been tried on Swedish railways as far back as 1911; while pulverised fuel had been tried in mainland Europe in the years after the First World War. The GSR had access to German scientific knowledge through Burnell, its chemist, and through Bratt, the chemist of the GNR who wrote to Howden: '[The author of this book] is very interested in utilisation of low-grade fuels... He has been very interested in placing before the technical public a translation of Professor Meinke's book on "The Locomotive"... I actually came across [Meinke] in my student days in Darmstadt.'[145] This was not Plato's cave. Far from being 'a ghost of its peacetime self', as Meenan describes it, in late 1943 the GSR was busier than it had been before the war.[146] Passenger services were sparser and slower than in pre-war years but this was the case in most railway systems throughout the globe. By early 1943 the GSR had reached a workable equilibrium with improving passenger and freight services. Complaints about service levels had all but disappeared. However, maintaining this state of affairs depended on a continuing supply of coal and shipping, which would change radically in 1944.

Notes

1   BNA POWE 26/398, FO memo, 'Spanish postwar railway and transport coal situation', 1938, p.7.
2   NA DT 7795A, 'Arigna mineral exploration', memo for executive council, 2 July 1936, p.5.
3   GSRGM 53960, 'Briquette manufacture', Morton to Supplies, 11 July 1941, reply of 6 August.
4   M. White, 'Fifty years of a locoman's life', *Journal of the Irish Railway Record Society*, no. 32 (1963), p.266.
5   GSRGM 53960/10, 'Briquetting miscellaneous', Bredin to Morton, 3 September 1941 re. manufacture by Sisk, Bredin to Ginnety, 20 October 1941, re. an unsuccessful batch from the Kingscourt Terracotta Company.
6   GSRGM 53960/9, 'Purchase of briquetting plants', memo for chairman, 2 September 1942.
7   GSRGM 53960/10, Minute of meeting, 3 April 1946.
8   GSRGM 53960/2, Ginnety to Bredin, 6 March 1942, memo for general manager, 17 April 1942.
9   GSRGM 53673, 'Late running of goods trains', O'Dowd to Bredin, 13 April 1942.
10 *Irish Press*, 15 April 1942.
11 GSRGM 53960/2, 1 May 1942, Ginnety to Bredin.
12 *Railway Gazette*, 4 September 1942, p.216.
13 E. Sauvage, *La Machine Locomotive* (Paris, 1918), p.97.
14 J.H. Dudley, 'Railway fuel problems', *JIRRS*, no. 3 (1947), p.66.

15 GSRGM 53960/2, Report of Lyons, 4 October 1941.
16 GSRGM 53960/9, Ratledge to Reynolds, 1 September 1942.
17 GSRGM 53960/2, 'Purchase of briquette plant from forest patent fuel company',
    passim. For clandestine dealings see correspondence between McMahon and Morton.
    Instructions from Bredin to George Lyons, engineer in charge of dismantling and
    shipping the plants.
18 GSRGM 53960/2, Ginnety to Bredin, 7 February 1942.
19 Ibid.
20 NA DFA P23.1, Note of a phone conversation, 16 May 1941.
21 GSRGM 53206, Minute, 5 May 1942.
22 GSRGM 53960/10, Industry and Commerce to Bredin, 1 June 1942.
23 Irish Press, 30 June, 18 August 1942.
24 C. Wills, That Neutral Island (London, 2007), p.209.
25 Railway Gazette, 17 July 1942, p.66.
26 Weekly circular, 8 August 1942.
27 GSRGM 55196, Supplies to GSR, 7 September 1942.
28 Wills, That Neutral Island, p.252.
29 GSRGM 58480, 'Passenger coaches attached to perishable trains', Bredin to Stewart, 17
    May 1943.
30 See Chapter 5.
31 GSRGM 53960/9, Memo for chairman, 2 September 1942.
32 GSRGM 53960/12, Meadows to Bredin, 2 November 1942.
33 GSRGM 56864, 'Soap rationing'; see also coal daily record sheets (passim) for briquette
    plant closures.
34 Dudley, 'Railway fuel problems', p.68.
35 GSRGM 55566, 'Fuel position appointment of Mr Burnell', minute of meeting, 24
    October 1942.
36 GSR, Inchicore foremens' book, p.29, 30 May 1943.
37 Dudley, 'Problems', p.69.
38 White, 'Fifty years', p.267.
39 K.B. Nowlan and T.D. Williams (eds), Ireland in the War Years and After (Dublin,
    1969), p.36.
40 GSRGM 51598, 'ASLEF protest against notice, Maryboro', notice, n.d., Bredin to
    Ginnety, 7 January 1942.
41 V. Horan, 'Memories', JIRRS, no. 87 (1982), p.333.
42 GSRGM 55202, 'Overtime paid to drivers and firemen'.
43 GSRGM 52212, 'Rostering of enginemen', Sweeney (ASLEF) to Bredin, 24 June 1942,
    minute of meeting, 19 September 1942.
44 GSRGM 52212, Agreement between ASLEF, NUR and GSR, 19 November 1942.
45 Irish Railway Wages Board, Proceedings, 17 April 1942, evidence of C.D. Watters,
    NUR.
46 GSRGM 54475, 'Complaints from enginemen', Larkin to Reynolds, 27 April 1942.
47 GSRGM 54475, McLean and others to Reynolds, 18 June 1942.
48 Horan, 'Memories', p.335.
49 GSRGM 54475, Minute of meeting, 6 November 1942.
50 GSRGM 55590, 'Driver J. Dolan's claim for Sunday payment' describes this case.
51 Locomotive Journal (July 1943), p.143.
52 Irish Railway Wages Board, Proceedings, 17 April 1942, evidence of G.B. Howden,
    GNR.
53 GSRGM 49897, 'Meal and lodging allowances', memo, 8 April 1942.

54 GSRGM 56549, 'Sleeping vans for fairs', Kirwan to Bredin, 1 June 1943.
55 GSRGM 58526, 'Dept. of I & C re. running of certain passenger trains', Kirwan to Bredin, 31 May 1943.
56 GSRGM 52112, Kirwan to Bredin, 20 July 1943.
57 P. Semmens, *A History of the GWR, 1939–1948* (London, 1985), p.33.
58 GSRGM 58522, 'Proposed additional passenger trains', minute, 12 June 1943.
59 GSRGM 58275 'Application to run mixed train, Birr–Roscrea' and 58479, 'Proposed mixed train Athenry–Galway'.
60 GSRGM 58522, John O'Brien to Bredin, 9 July 1943.
61 *Connacht Sentinel*, 13 July 1943.
62 P.M. Kalla Bishop, *Locomotives at War* (Truro, 1980), p.58.
63 *Fayle's Bulletin*, no. 52 (1942), p.26.
64 U. Mac Eoin, *The IRA in the Twilight Years* (Dublin, 1997), p.469.
65 *Fayle's Bulletin*, no. 52 (1942), p.56.
66 R. Uí Ógáin (ed.), *Mise an Fear Ceoil* (Dublin, 2007), pp.37, 121.
67 M.S. Quigley, *A US Spy in Ireland* (Dublin, 1999), pp.136, 189.
68 H.C. Casserly, *Railways Since 1939* (Newton Abbot, 1972), p.11.
69 FB 56.14
70 GSRGM 55806, 'Locomotive failures', Bredin to Tyndall, 16 November 1942, Bredin to Stewart, 23 December 1942.
71 GSRGM 55806, Results tabulated in an Access database is the source of these figures.
72 Inchicore foremens' book, circulars of 9 March and 6 October 1943.
73 GSRGM 52136, 'Strike by fitters, Inchicore', Bredin to Industry and Commerce, 10 February 1942.
74 Inchicore foremens' book, 5 February 1944.
75 Inchicore foremens' book, circular to foremen, 29 November 1943.
76 GSR Chemists Department, CHEM F30, loco failures due to alleged poor quality of coal, Tyndall to Burnell, 3 December 1943.
77 Inchicore foremens' book, circular to foremen, 16 December 1943.
78 CHEM F30, Tyndall to Burnell, 14 December 1943, Burnell to Tyndall, 15 December 1943.
79 CHEM F30, passim.
80 CHEM F30 contains this correspondence.
81 *Locomotive Journal*, June 1943, p.141.
82 CHEM F30, Massey to running superintendent, 27 November 1945.
83 P. Rigney, 'Arigna coal mines and the Emergency', *Breifne*, no. 40 (2004), pp.290–3.
84 J. Horgan, *Enigmatic Patriot* (Dublin, 1997), p.25.
85 GSRGM 53960/2, Meadows to Bredin, 31 March 1942, quotes from Lynn's of Sligo, Arigna colliery and Castlecomer collieries.
86 GSRGM 60370 details the trials on locomotives.
87 GSRGM 60370.
88 GSRGM 60370 contains these exchanges.
89 CHEM F30, Chemist to running superintendent, 4 December 1945.
90 GSRGM 60370, Minute of meeting, 18 March 1943.
91 See Chapter 3, Note 63.
92 GSRGM 54005, 'Cost and tonnage of fuel consumed by locos', Burnell to Bredin, 26 September 1942.
93 GM60370, Ledwith to McNab, 10 February 1943.
94 P. Rigney, 'Report on Arigna coal mines', *Breifne*, 38 (2002), pp.509–16 reproduces this report.

95 GSRGM 60370, Murphy to Bredin, 6 February, 25 February 1944.

96 Rigney, 'Arigna coalfield', p.293.

97 GSRGM 60370, Murphy to Bredin, 3 February 1944.

98 GSRGM 54433, Murphy (Stores) to Bredin, 6 October 1944.

99 NA DT 7795A, Memo for executive council, 2 July 1936, p.6.

100 GSRGM 54433, 'Use of pitch in locomotives', Meadows to Bredin, 22 April 1943.

101 Letter to author.

102 Inchicore foremens' book, memo to foremen, Northern District, 15 October 1943.

103 GSRGM 56700, 'Weekly aggregate figure of coal consumption', 1942/1943 table.

104 GSRGM 60370, See Note 70.

105 GSRGM 54433, Ginnety to Bredin, 17 July 1942.

106 *Irish Times*, 28 December 1942.

107 GSRGM 55538, 'Purchase of slack-burning apparatus from diesel engine company'; GSRGM 56254, 'Loco 354 tests with Mr McAllister's patent grate', passim.

108 GNRGM 200/37 'Book on locomotives and their fuel', Bratt to Howden, 10 August 1942.

109 GSRGM 60370, Murphy to Bredin, 29 February 1944.

110 GSRGM 61576, 'Processing of coal', Bredin to Jennings Gill, patent agents, 15 May 1944.

111 GSRGM 65854, 'World Fuel Conference 1946', report by CIÉ.

112 Interview with Paddy Guilfoyle, late driver, Inchicore, who was fireman on these tests.

113 GSRGM 61576, Reynolds to Benbulben Barytes Company, 23 November 1944.

114 GSRGM, Unnumbered file of daily coal returns.

115 W.H.B. Court, *History of the Second World War Coal* (London, 1951), p.374.

116 Inchicore foremens' book, circulars re. fuel classification. p.97, re. segregation, p.104.

117 GSRGM 53960/12, Table of phurnacite deliveries.

118 GSRGM 53960/12, 'Analysis and test of phurnacite coal ovoids', Reihill to Bredin, 26 May 1942.

119 GSRGM 53960/12, Johnston to Bredin, 11 May 1943.

120 GSRGM 43737/1, 'Increases in steam coal prices', minute of meeting, 14 September 1943.

121 Dudley, 'Problems', p.72.

122 *Irish Railway News*, 30 December 1943.

123 FB no. 53 p.30.

124 FB no. 56 p.8.

125 GSRGM 47744A, 'Theft of keys', Murphy to commissioner, 5 August 1941, commissioner to Murphy, 9 September 1941.

126 GSRGM 50360, 'Theft of coal, Shankill', Bredin to Morton, 2 September 1941.

127 GSRGM 47744, 'Trespass 1941'.

128 GSRGM 53350, 'Trespass 1942'.

129 GSRGM 53350/2, 'Damage to fences, Macroom line', Sheehan to district engineer, Cork, 4 May 1942.

130 GSRGM 53350/6, 'Trespass and theft of keys', report of Garda T. O'Driscoll, Irishtown, 20 June 1942.

131 GSRGM 54540, 'Trees pillaged, mp 23, Bandon section'.

132 GSRGM 54547, 'Larceny of turf, Mullingar'.

133 GSRGM 54529, 'Pillage of briquettes, Inchicore'.

134 GSRGM 53350/11, 'Trespass and damage to sleepers, Wexford south branch'.

135 GSRGM 53350/15, 'Theft of keys, mp 163, Kingsbridge–Cork line'.

136 GSRGM 55561, 'Milepost 35 3/4 stolen'.

137 GSRGM 55578, 'Maynooth: fencing posts stolen'.

138 GSRGM 55519, 'Pillage of turf at Killarney Junction, Mallow', Brazil to Bredin, 15 October 1942.

139 GSRGM 65932/1, 'Theft of coal at Mullingar', memo to general manager, 4 July 1947.

140 GSRGM 65932, 'Theft of coal at Mallow', Heany to traffic manager, 12 March 1947.

141 C. Ó Gráda, *A Rocky Road: The Irish Economy Since the 1920s* (Manchester, 1997), p.17.

142 GSRGM 61581, 'Boilermaker J. Woodfull suggestion re. drop grates', Tyndall to Bredin, 21 April, Bredin to Tyndall, 23 April 1944.

143 N. Rosenberg, *Inside the Black Box: Technology and Economics* (Cambridge, 1982), p.64.

144 F.S.L. Lyons, *Ireland Since the Famine* (London, 1973), pp.557–8; R. Fisk, *In Time of War* (London, 1983), pp.352–85.

145 GNRGM 200/37, Bratt to Howden, 10 August 1942.

146 Nowlan and Williams, *War Years*, p.36.

9

Towards the End of the Emergency

The preparations for the invasion of Europe led to the most severe supply crisis of the Emergency period. Concerns about security caused severe restrictions on all forms of Anglo-Irish communication. The need to stockpile coal for the invasion together with the need for merchant shipping meant there was less coal for Ireland and fewer ships to carry it. Unlike 1941, there was some warning of the impending restrictions, and the Irish had some chance to make preparations. The impending cuts were discussed in the Dáil where Seán Lemass said: 'The term "essential" is an elastic one. We have become accustomed...to do without commodities and facilities which we would have regarded as essential...before the war, but many things which...we have regarded as essential must now be eliminated.'[1] From the GSR point of view the most significant change was that Ireland's coal allocation was almost halved, and was to be of an even worse quality. Even this limited coal allocation was dependent on the continuation of Irish exports of strategic materials to Britain. Sir John Maffey told de Valera of the impending communications restrictions on 28 March 1944. These restrictions were imposed on passenger travel, phone communications, and air travel to Britain. Shipping services from Ireland to Portugal were suspended, many British ports were closed to Irish ships and British-owned colliers were withdrawn from the Irish coal trade.[2] The attitude of the British side was in sharp contrast with 1941. On 30 March 1944 F.H. Boland and John Leydon flew with Maffey from Long Kesh airfield to London for a meeting with the British authorities.[3] Leydon reported that while assurances were given that the measures planned were only of a temporary character, this did not apply to coal because:

> The British are confronted with supply difficulties of the gravest kind ...We were unable to get any assurance as to the duration of the various alterations because...the military authorities will have the last word as to when security requirements will permit return to

present conditions. I think, however, it would not be unreasonable to anticipate such a stage may be reached in say two or three months.[4]

The Irish side were clearly given an indication as to the approximate date of the invasion. They were also told that the weekly coal allocation of 19,700 tons was to be cut to 10,000 tons.

Table 12 Reductions in weekly coal allocation (tons).

Company	Weekly tonnage	A reduction of
Gas companies	1,640	2.500
G.S.R.	3.650	1,300
G.N.R.	600	250
ESB	nil	2,250
Sugar coy	nil	nil
Unallocated	1,000	4,000

Source: NA DFA A59, report of meeting, 31 March 1941.

Leydon continued:

As regards the railways we were told that the coal would be inferior to what we had been getting up to the present... On the unallocated coal we were given to understand that the British desire that certain preferential customers should continue to get their allocation, i.e. Commissioners of Irish Lights, certain creameries which do an export trade of 150 tons, Guinness and other maltsters 400 tons, Goodbody's jute and BOAC. I pointed out that taking account of quality our proposed allocation would be less than one sixth of normal [pre-war] allocation... while they appreciated our difficulties they could not improve on their proposal. I asked for increased petrol allocation as passenger miles of GSR already cut by 50% and I could not see where further savings could be made without paralysing our internal transport. It was suggested to me that the high commissioner should make representations.[5]

On 20 April Leydon wrote to Norman Archer of the British High Commission: 'The economic effects of this dislocation of the country's transport system cannot yet be gauged precisely. But it is obvious that it must be considerable. Cattle fairs in particular are certain to suffer ... The reduction of railway services might be off set ... by an expansion in road services ... [for which] an additional supply of at least 3,500 tons of petroleum a month would be required.'[6]

A crisis had been developing in British coal production since autumn 1943. On 13 October Maj. Lloyd George, Minister of Fuel and Power, outlined to the Commons the supply outlook for the following year. He mentioned the additional demands on British coal production caused by the surrender of Italy.[7] He also expressed concern that aggregate coal output was down compared with the same period in 1942 despite the decline in the number of industrial disputes in this period. Between the coal seasons of 1940–1 and 1943–4 British coal consumption fell by 2 per cent. During the same period, consumption on Britain's railways rose by 11 per cent while consumption in Northern Ireland rose by 2 per cent.[8]

The conscription of labour into the mines is an indication of the severity of the production problems. During 1944, 11,100 forces personnel were reallocated to mining, of whom only 6,400 were ex-miners.[9] The mining workforce was becoming a mixture of the very old and the very young: 'Many of the latter had been plunged into work and into war at the same time, divorced by a generation from their older workmates and told at a time of hardship to keep in line by their own union.'[10] This was not a contented workforce, and the official wartime history of the industry observes that 'no other major British industry carried so many unsolved problems into the war: none brought more out.'[11] Industrial relations problems intensified in spring 1944 when dissatisfaction over wages caused a wave of unofficial strikes in Scotland, Yorkshire[12] and, crucially for Ireland, South Wales. Here it took a week of solid persuasion by union officials to get the 90,000 men back to work in early March, by which stage half a million tons production had been lost.[13] With invasion planning came the need to stockpile coal, with SHAEF[14] demanding quality large coal for use as locomotive fuel.[15] Shortfalls in British coal production meant that the Middle East and the Mediterranean were supplied from India and South Africa by a fleet of 'old crocks unsuitable for service elsewhere'.[16]

Immediately after the London meeting the GSR began drawing up an emergency timetable, which was introduced on 24 April. All services were withdrawn on eleven branch lines and passenger services on four secondary lines. Passenger train services outside the cities were reduced to two days per week and goods train services to four days per week. A restricted suburban service continued to run daily in Dublin, Cork,

Limerick and Waterford. Lemass told the Dáil on 20 April: 'If by limiting services at the present time we can make possible the provision of greater transport facilities to move grain, beet and turf... then it is clearly desirable that we should accept now whatever limitations are necessary... There will be a reduction of...40 per cent in the number of passengers and 20 per cent in the amount of [goods] traffic...A corresponding reduction in the special goods train service [turf, grain, beet, livestock] will [not] be made.'[17] These cuts reduced weekly train mileage by almost a third from 162,000 to 116,000 miles.[18]

The provincial press seemed resigned, with the editor of the *Munster Express* writing: 'In the circumstances we must take a philosophical view [and] ask providence to spare us from unbearable burdens.'[19] The understanding attitude to the service cutbacks taken by the press may be linked to the appointment by the GSR of its first press officer in April 1944. Richard Dowling formerly worked for *The Irish Times* and was described by the *Connacht Tribune* as 'the man in the gap...when the train crisis arose last week. It was the first time...that newspaper men found that they could quickly discover what was happening in Kingsbridge.' Such was the publicity surrounding the restricted services that on the first day of the new timetable the first train to leave Galway provided over 350 seats of which half were unoccupied.[20] In the north-west the *Anglo Celt* noted: 'The alternative services of the GNR are running normally.'[21] In this period many travellers from Sligo to Dublin travelled via Enniskillen and onwards through Clones and Dundalk on the GNR.

On 21 April 1944 Leydon and Norman Archer discussed an Irish request for additional petrol. Irish exports and coal imports played a central role in this discussion, as they had in 1942. Leydon pointed out that 'he could not expect to turn this country into a manufacturing factory for the United Kingdom giving us just sufficient raw materials for imports... Archer then said that the arrangement for letting us have 10,000 tons of coal a week hangs by a thread.' Ian Forsyth of Fuel and Power emphasised how important it was that...

...the UK departments concerned are satisfied with the maintenance of imports from Éire...e.g. cement, beer, rubber manufacture, creamery products, cattle, cattle feed, agricultural machinery, flax and jute yarn, binder twine and cordage, talc, glycerine... continuance of supplies of coal...could only be justified so long as imports from Éire of the above products were maintained.[22]

This extensive range of products reflects the expansion of trade in strategic materials which had developed since 1942 and at least in part explains the co-operative attitude of the British side. In late June, Forsyth stated: 'As an indication of their realisation of Irish difficulties they were prepared... to make available an additional 2,000 tons of coal a week. Every effort would be made to provide coal to the extent to which it could be carried.' The narrowness of the shipping margin and the co-operative spirit in these discussions is shown by the request by the Ministry of War Transport that 'in connection with the Great Southern Railways it would be of considerable assistance if... eggs and condensed milk which are at present shipped from Limerick port could be diverted to Cork for shipment from there.'[23] Times had indeed changed since 1941 when cuts in coal deliveries were punitive, and justified on the basis of non-existent shortages. By 1944 the British difficulties with coal supply were real.

The 'coal year' ran from May to April with the prime stocking season being from late spring to early autumn, when the weather facilitated both extraction and transport.[24] Winter was a consumption season when bad weather and winter illnesses could slow extraction and distribution of coal. The 1944 restrictions came in the midst of the coal-stocking season which meant that shortages would outlive shipping restrictions, and would continue through the winter of 1944/5. However, in contrast to 1941/2, by 1944 the GSR had perfected the management of coal supplies by adjusting their mileage.

Managing coal supplies on an extremely thin margin required detailed knowledge, and daily reports on the coal position of the GSR survive from January 1944 to October 1946. These reports record the daily level of stocks, the output of the briquette plants and sailing information for colliers. At the beginning of 1944 there was a stock of 19,381 tons, or 3.07 weeks' supply.[25] Much of this was raw material for the five briquette plants, which produced approximately 300 tons of fuel per day.[26] Stocks fell to a low point of 12,000 tons by the end of February, but as the stocking season commenced rose 17,964 tons on 30 March, the day Leydon and Boland went to London. An early casualty of the restrictions was the supply of duff, despised by the crews when it first appeared in 1941 but since mid-1942 vital for the manufacture of briquettes. The last cargo of duff was discharged on 17 April 1944, causing production of briquettes to decline to about 160 tons per day. On 31 May the third shift was discontinued and the plants struggled on with whatever material could be got until finally only the Broadstone plant was in operation, using slurry, turf mould and Irish coal to produce briquettes.[27] These ingredients brought quality problems, as seen in a Waterford foreman's report on the late arrival of the Dublin passenger train: 'I examined the fire on arrival here and it was practically out; it consisted of reddened dross. The briquettes used were apparently of bad quality and fell away to dust. The driver states he had great difficulty in keeping the fire lighting and... I do not doubt his word.'[28] As the restrictions began to bite, on 5 April shipping information became erratic as a hold-up on cross-channel telephone calls took effect. All Irish coal was shipped at the nominated ports of Ardrossan and Ayr in Ayrshire, Workington and Maryport in Cumbria and Mostyn and Point of Ayr in North Wales.[29] The coalfields nominated to supply Ireland were in Ayrshire, Cumberland, Durham and Northumberland. All ships sailed to Dublin, leaving the GSR to distribute from there coal that previously had been shipped direct to Cork and Waterford. The cost of internal distribution was estimated at 6 shillings per ton, which was high compared with the 13 shillings a ton it cost to ship the coal from Britain.[30]

Charles Johnston transferred his base from Newport to Maryport in Cumbria, and on 24 May he wrote: 'Spoke to Fuel and Power this afternoon, the opinion there seems to be that we will not revert to normal for some time.'[31] Half of the entire British coasting fleet was earmarked for the invasion of France and British ships were withdrawn from the Irish trade.[32] The return of 27 April recorded: '*Turquoise* was to sail last night from Ayr. This will probably be the last British vessel to operate to here for the moment.'[33] British vessels were replaced by Irish ships that had been debarred from the Lisbon run for security reasons. The Irish ships lacked the suitability of purpose-built colliers and were exorbitantly expensive according to the stores superintendent:[34]

The [Irish] ships... which are temporarily withdrawn from the Lisbon route are now carrying our coal cargoes. In addition we are using the ships belonging to the Dublin Gas Company, Messrs. Heiton and Messrs Lockington of Dundalk which habitually engaged in cross-channel coal traffic. In the early stages the freight rates demanded for the Lisbon ships was 20/- per ton but our discharging agents McKenzies and Co. who were anxious to break the 20/- rate were able to obtain for us the Gas Company and Heiton vessels at the British rate plus 4/- surcharge, which worked out at about 13/- per ton. Following representations, the Department of Supplies have ruled that the rate for the Lisbon vessels is fixed at 13/- and to be retrospective to catch any payments we had made at 20/-...I consider this very satisfactory.

However, there was sometimes nothing to load, and in a typical note on 25 May Johnston reported 'no cargo for *Kerloge*, no cargo for *Moyalla*'.[35]

Despite the cutbacks in regular services, by the end of June the amount of coal issued weekly to locomotives exceeded coal shipments by 900 tons. Bredin summoned a meeting on 29 June to consider remedies for this unsustainable trend. David Stewart, the traffic manager, pointed out that between 80 and 90 per cent of the freight traffic was priority traffic such as turf, coal, cattle, grain and animal feedstuffs. Most of the special trains were for Castlecomer coal and for the residue of traffic which could not be accommodated on scheduled regular services. A suggestion that turf be re-introduced as fuel on turf specials was described as 'highly undesirable from the point of view of efficiency' and senior management was instructed to bring down train mileage.[36] On 2 July the issue to locomotives was cut by 12 per cent to 4,700 tons per day. On 7 July Bredin reversed the previous week's policy on the use of turf and instructed that each loaded turf train should be supplied with two wagons of turf as fuel. What was highly undesirable just a week before had become a necessity. This was the low point in coal supply, and an improvement can be pinpointed to 12 July when instructions were issued that 'owing to improved coal position cancel arrangements for loading turf for locos.'[37]

Passenger services improved slightly when the department allowed the attachment of a single passenger coach to perishable trains on the Dublin to Cork line on condition that it would not displace perishable traffic and would not be advertised. Despite the advertising restrictions, these services attracted passengers and in mid-July were given connections to Tralee, Limerick and Waterford.[38] Suburban services were maintained in Dublin with the help of four Drumm battery trains. However, an exceptionally dry spring lowered water levels in the River Shannon and caused an electricity shortage. Electricity rationing was introduced, and in April the use of electric current for traction was capped at 60 per cent of 1943 levels.[39] In June, when the coal position was at its worst, the use of electricity for transport was banned. These regulations grounded the Drumm trains and the DUTC tram fleet, placing increased demands on GSR steam-hauled suburban services.[40] In contrast, mainline passenger services began to benefit from improvements in coal supply and resumed four-day week running from mid-July. Further improvements in the Saturday suburban services in Dublin were made in October, while a six-day passenger service was restored between 11 and 23 December. Additionally on some branch lines a passenger coach was attached to goods trains.[41]

From August the seasonal traffic of turf, grain and beet began to be carried and on 2 August the daily coal issue was increased to 5,570 tons. This was increased regularly thereafter until 10 October when it stood at 6,200 tons. Deliveries from Irish mines amounted to no more than 900 tons per week or equivalent to two coal boats. Lemass had warned deputies not to 'imagine that there is possible any increase in the output of coal from the Irish mines which would effect more than a very slight change in our circumstances. The total output of all the Irish mines working to the fullest capacity would probably not exceed 4,000 tons a week and that... is the consumption of the Great Southern Railway Company alone.'[42] The weekly mileage shown in Table 13 shows a summer trough followed by an autumn peak as the livestock, turf, grain and beet seasons followed in quick succession.

Table 13 Coal stocks: weekly issue and miles run, 1944–1945.

Date	Stock in tons	index	Stock in weeks	Train mileage	Index	Daily issue tons	
April 44	17,48	100	3.2	163,982	100	5,300	
Sept. 44	11,539	65	2.02	147.000	90	5,700	108
Dec. 44	15,070	85	2.5	166,185	101	6,000	113
April 45	23,318	132	3.9	139,170	85	5,850	110
Sept. 45	27,732	175	4.62	161,894	99	6,000	113
Dec. 45	25,769	146	3.97	182,266	111	6,500	123

The weekly mileage run reached 150,000 at the end of October 1944, which was 30,000 less than in the same period in 1943. During the harsh weather of January 1945 Welsh coal tips and dockside cranes were frozen. Around this time stocks of direct firing coal fell below the critical one-week level, and the daily issue was cut by 14 per cent. The low point for stock was in September 1944, but the low point for mileage run came in April 1945, reflecting the different seasonal patterns of supply and traffic. As supplies improved the need for daily monitoring of stocks disappeared and in September 1946 the daily coal record ceased, at which point the stock stood at 47,000 tons or just over seven-weeks' supply.

As soon as the D Day landings took place some security measures could be relaxed. From 10 July 1944 Irish ships were allowed access to all British ports north of the Bristol Channel,[43] but access was denied to the

Bristol Channel itself until September.[44] Johnston stressed the importance of using these newly won concessions by keeping a flow through the Bristol Channel.[45] In September colliers began to arrive in Cork and Waterford and Rosslare, saving both shipping space and internal distribution costs.

The passenger service was cut in April 1944 to two days a week and the goods service to four, and all subsequent improvements in service can be linked directly to improvements in supply. In July 1944 with the partial relaxation of security restrictions the passenger service increased to four days a week. In September the goods service was restored to five week running, coincidental with the opening of the Bristol Channel and the re-opening of Rosslare as a coal port. In July 1945 passenger services were restored to five-day running and in August to six-day running, coincidental with the return of British colliers to the Irish trade. These close links between shipping and rail services demonstrates the narrowness of the margin between supply and demand.

The demise of the GSR after two decades of existence and the creation of Córas Iompair Éireann has been described in Ó Riain's history of CIÉ.[46] The corporate restructuring had little or no effect on how the railway operated during the last months of the Emergency, but a summary of the main events is given for the sake of completeness and to put in context the appointment of Percy Reynolds in early 1942. On 6 February 1943 Reynolds wrote to Lemass setting out his views on the future of the GSR, suggesting a long-term reorganisation with a new re-capitalised company being established. He asked the minister to indicate a policy that he could announce to the shareholders at the AGM. Reynolds was told that approval of a new policy could not be conveyed within the timescale requested. (The tenth Dáil was coming to the end of its life under constitutional time limits.) At the company's AGM of 3 March Reynolds outlined the difficulties facing the GSR – stating that plans for a restructuring of the company could not be postponed – and requested government action.

The authoritative account of subsequent events comes from the report of a tribunal of enquiry into dealings in GSR stocks, established in November 1943 to examine movements in the GSR stock price during the earlier part of that year. This report has a section entitled 'Inner history of events leading to the capital reorganisation proposals' which fills the gaps left by the lack of surviving records.[47] Discussions on the fate of the GSR continued between Reynolds and the department and on 27 February 1943 Lemass indicated that he had arrived at a tentative conclusion that a new re-capitalised company would be established that would compulsorily acquire both the GSR and the DUTC. Confidential discussions on these proposals straddled a general election held on 23 June. The result of the election was a decrease in support for Fianna Fáil and Fine Gael and an eleventh Dáil where Fianna Fáil formed a minority government, due in part to the inability of the opposition to unite.[48] Discussions continued between Reynolds and the civil servants and proposals were considered by the cabinet at its meetings of 15 and 19 October and approved on the latter date. The government decision was conveyed to the shareholders on 24 October 1943.

From mid-August dealing intensified in GSR shares, and despite discussions on restructuring, the stock exchange did not suspend dealings in the shares.

The increased level of trading was described as 'absolutely abnormal, a boom, absolutely hectic and inexplicable'.[49] Following a parliamentary question put by an independent deputy in November, a tribunal of enquiry was established to investigate the dealings and 'the extent, if any, to which any such dealings were attributable to the improper use or disclosure of information'.[50]

Table 14 Dealings in GSR shares on Dublin Stock Exchange.

Period	GSR shares purchased
32 weeks to 14 August	550,000
10 weeks to 23 October	634,000
4 weeks to 20 November	815,000

Source: GSR shares tribunal report.

The Transport Bill was introduced in the Dáil on 2 May 1944 by Seán Lemass. He said the legislation was designed to facilitate a long-term transport policy and had no relationship to the transport difficulties of the Emergency. He stated that by 1938 the government had recognised that the legislation of 1932 and 1933 had failed in its objective of securing the financial health of the railway companies and in particular of the GSR. His speech went on to synthesise the attitude of the government to the GSR and is as relevant to the events of February 1942 as of March 1944.

[The government] had no power under statute to enforce changes in the management or the organisation of the GSR. It had no evidence that such changes would be made by that company on its own

initiative... [or that such changes] within the framework of the GSR
would be sufficient to overcome the bad traditions of the organisation
or to promote with sufficient speed the development of a sound
outlook within it, upon its own responsibility to the nation and its
functions in relation to national economic and social development.[51]

The powerlessness of the government was rectified by the use of
Emergency Powers legislation in 1942. Percy Reynolds had been installed
in the manner of a commissioner in a delinquent local authority or a
commissar in the Red Army to ensure a 'sound outlook'. However, these
changes had only been achieved using emergency legislation, which
would lapse on the return of peace. Unless new transport legislation was
enacted, the government risked a return to the 'old' GSR, with what
Lemass had described as its bad traditions.

The passage of the bill was delayed by 'events', as Harold MacMillan
might have put it. The opposition put down a motion to defer consideration of the bill until the tribunal of enquiry into share dealings reported.
When this matter was put to the vote the government was defeated by one
vote. The Transport Bill had forced an election, which allowed Fianna Fáil
to go to the country when the opposition was in disarray. Fine Gael was
weakened, the Labour party was in the throes of a split and the new Clann
na Talmhan was untried.

The government returned after the election with an increased majority
and continued with its programme. One of the first legislative tasks of the
new Dáil was a new Transport Bill and the Transport (No. 2) Bill was
introduced into the Dáil on 12 June, the second day's sitting of the twelfth
Dáil. The bill contained no changes other than alterations of the dates
rendered necessary by the delay.[52] The GSR and DUTC would be absorbed
into the new company and their shareholders would receive stock in the
new private company, Córas Iompair Éireann. The government retained
the right to nominate the chairman contained in the 1942 order while the
shareholders elected the directors. The passage of the bill through the
Oireachtas was predictable. The Labour party wanted nationalisation, Fine
Gael supported private enterprise and sought to make capital out of
previous Fianna Fáil promises to nationalise the railways, while some,
particularly in the Seanad, sought additional compensation for
shareholders. The tribunal reported and found that none of the share
dealings were irregular, although John O'Brien, principal officer with
responsibility for the GSR, resigned and was replaced by Thekla Beere.

On 31 December 1944 the GSR ceased to exist. The manner of its departure had been established in 1942, with the 1944 act giving a peace-time framework to a piece of Emergency legislation. At an operational level, the new corporate structure brought little change and the rail and road services struggled to cope with Emergency shortages. A more significant operational milestone was reached on 28 December 1944 when the GSR lost its twenty-year record of fatality-free operation. The Dublin to Cork night mail train collided with a cattle train at Straboe level crossing, six miles south of Portarlington, and a postal sorter was killed. The subsequent enquiry found that the primary cause of the accident was that the driver and fireman of the mail train passed a signal at danger. The secondary cause was the failure of the guard of the cattle train to take appropriate precautions when his train stopped. However, the conditions imposed by the Emergency also had a significant bearing on the accident. The cattle train had taken six hours to cover the forty-one miles to Portarlington, where the fire was cleaned. Having left with a fresh fire, the train got three miles when it had to stop to build up pressure. Upon restarting it got no further than a further two and a quarter miles before having to stop again to clean the fire. The failure to display the correct red light on the end of the goods train and the shortage of paraffin oil was also mentioned in the report of the enquiry.[53] The conditions prevailing since 1940, with stops in mid-section to clean fires, unprotected by signals, and the distraction of crews by badly performing locomotives increased the hazard of a serious incident and the circumstances eventually combined to cause a fatal accident.

The British cabinet sub-committee on Éire met for the last time on the evening of D Day with a one-item agenda – the Irish request for a supplementary oil supply. The Dominions Office memo noted how allowances had been made to Éire...

> ...to allow her to export to us the agricultural products which we needed...recently we had to make cuts in coastal shipping and close certain ports...coal supplies to Éire had been temporarily reduced by over 50%...It is proposed that 3,500 tons of fuel oil [extra] be allowed as long as coal restrictions remain plus 1,000 tons of lubricating oil.[54]

This response was conveyed unofficially to Leydon two days later.[55] In early October the British expressed a willingness to restore the 'pre-security' coal allocation of 21,300 tons a week provided the Irish could provide ships to carry it. However, there were not sufficient Irish ships to

achieve this. Leydon stressed to the British how all available shipping –
even schooners – had been pressed into service and that an Irish shipping
vessel had been taken off the North Atlantic run even though this would
cause problems for wheat imports. He requested that more of Ireland's
allocation would come from South Wales due to the better loading
facilities there.[56] Smith's sympathy with the Irish case can be seen in his
note to the Ministry of War Transport that 'Leydon mentions various
difficulties which stand in the way of his carrying the present figure of
15,000 tons per week, and we should like if we could to find some way
out of these difficulties... we would like to get back to the figure of
21,300 tons per week ... Would there be any chance of putting in some
British tonnage?'[57] While this was not yet possible, the Department of
Supplies continued to press for small incremental improvements aimed at
speeding the turnaround of ships, such as turning up the navigation lights
in Preston to peacetime strength and speeding up the security clearance of
Irish ships.[58]

A coal famine was expected in Europe at the end of the war, but the
extent of the problem in France was not appreciated until spring 1945. Up
to then there were few railways to operate and most of the mining areas
were still under German control.[59] As Allied communication lines
lengthened, more traffic was put on the reopening railway system,
increasing the demand for French mined coal. So severe was the resulting
shortage that steam-hauled passenger services had to be suspended in
France between January and March 1945 with a skeleton service being
provided by diesel railcars.[60] In April 1945, with France getting only 35 per
cent of its pre-war needs after military requirements were taken into
account, it was realised 'that all was not well with France's coal
supplies'.[61] These difficulties impacted directly on Irish coal supplies;
Charles Johnston reported on...

> ...the lack of output from the British mines, the increased
> consumption cross channel and increased export to Europe... There
> was very little coal being got from the French mines... The future
> outlook was not bright... the quality of coal... being supplied to
> British railways was inferior to that normally used.[62]

By August 1945 French production of 630,000 tons was augmented by
400,000 tons of British and US imports.[63] US coal was transported across
the Atlantic in deep sea ships and was trans-shipped in Britain into small
channel colliers as a port capable of handling deep sea ships did not

become available until November 1944 after the fall of Antwerp.[64] Such small ships were normally used to supply Ireland. The urgency of coal supply within liberated Europe can be seen in the establishment of a solid fuels section of SHAEF, staffed with officers from a coal background who 'went into the French mines before the last Germans were out of the mining camps [and] started these mines...while they were still under enemy shell fire'.[65]

The end of the war in Europe brought changes to the shipping situation and in late May 1945 Dulanty wrote that 'ten British colliers have been operating on the coal trade with Ireland...carrying 8,500 tons [of] our present allocation of 17,000 tons.' The daily coal returns show ships that had traditionally served the GSR returning to the Irish Sea, releasing Irish ships to trade with Iberia and transport supplies for Ireland that had accumulated in Lisbon. Gilmour Jenkins informed Dulanty that 'while it is not possible to give any binding understanding, the probability is that during the good weather season we shall be able to continue the assistance we are now giving.'[66] After the fall of Germany, the European supply situation worsened further as 'on 4 May it had been [the military's] duty to kill Germans and destroy the material resources of Germany...but since 5 May it had all at once become their duty to save the lives of their enemy...but it was six months to the winter and all its north European severity.'[67] The effort to feed, clothe and heat the German people during the winter of 1945/6 was described as the 'Battle of the winter'. It was anticipated that if food and fuel was not made available, civil unrest would involve the British in police actions, which would delay the transfer of troops to the Far East. Therefore, 'the rescue of Germany from famine and anarchy was dictated not by sentiment but by self-interest.'[68] The coal situation mirrored that of 1940 when the burden of supplying coal to the defeated powers fell on the victorious side. Poland and Germany, two of Europe's major pre-war coal-producing nations, had been laid waste by war. As Court states: 'Europe could contribute little to its own [coal] requirements and was caught in the vicious cycle of being unable to restore transport services until someone supplied the coal. Britain was to be that someone.'[69] This meant that coal supplies remained scarce and fuel prices remained high until well after the end of the war. This can be seen in the price charged by the GSR for turf mould that had accumulated at stations. The 1944 price of 2/6 per ton climbed to 7/6 per ton in 1945, remaining at that price in 1946 and not dropping to 1/ per ton until 1947.[70]

When the pre-invasion restrictions were imposed in spring 1944, the GSR had been struggling with bad coal for three years, and many of their previous policy assumptions came under question. In February 1941 Bredin had told the Engineering and Scientific Association of Ireland: 'In a country such as this in easy reach of the finest coalfields in the world, there can be no doubt that for many years to come the steam locomotive will be the most economical and satisfactory unit for general rail traction.'[71] By 1944 this 'finest steam coal in the world' was but a memory in Ireland and showed no signs of being available in the foreseeable future. Between 1940 and 1944 the cost of fuel increased by 170 per cent on a cost per ton basis and by 337 per cent on a cost per mile basis.[72] In 1945 the GSR used almost 70,000 tons more coal per annum to operate a service of four million miles less than in 1939.[73] In April 1944, as the coal supply position was at its lowest point, the GSR decided to move from coal to oil. On 13 April, in the midst of the pulverised fuel experiments, the chief draughtsman prepared a report on oil burning. This included a review of international practice, especially in South America, where the Buenos Aires Great Southern had the most extensive fleet of oil-burning locomotives in the world.[74] While it was decided not to proceed at that time as there was no prospect of securing oil supplies, the project was revived in early 1945. Much of the experimental work had been undertaken during the Emergency. The modifications made in the locomotive firebox for the pulverised fuel experiment were similar to those needed for oil burning.

A more significant long-term move in the direction of oil fuel was towards diesel traction. In his 1941 address to the Engineering and Scientific Association of Ireland (ESAI) Bredin had said: 'It is a popular belief with many people that the cure [for the economic ills of the railway] is to replace steam locomotives by diesel engines. I am going to attempt this evening to show you how unsound such a belief is.'[75] The transition from steam to diesel was much less developed on European railways than on their US counterparts. While railcars had been successfully developed during the 1930s by the GNR and the County Donegal Railways, among others, there were no comparable prototypes for mainline locomotives. Bredin said that 'up to [2,000 hp]...a well designed diesel unit has lower net operating costs than any other form of rail traction...But the initial cost saddles the machine with enormous interest and depreciation charges and frequently makes the gross operating cost greater than that of an equivalent steam locomotive.'[76] The huge increase in fuel costs between 1941 and 1944 altered the cost equation, but there were few operational mainline diesel locomotives in Europe and none in Britain.

On 21 April 1944 Bredin approached the Dublin agent of the Sulzer brothers, seeking proposals for the supply of prototypes for mainline and shunting locomotives and a railcar.[77] This initiative had not been discussed by the GSR board. Sulzers were an established manufacturer of diesel locomotives and had supplied countries as diverse as France, Argentina, Siam and Algeria during the 1930s. Their workshops in Winterhur were untouched by wartime destruction. Any armaments work they had undertaken was for the Germans and was declining. They would not be occupied with armaments manufacture for the war against Japan. Additionally – although this was not known to the GSR – they held some diesel units whose sale had been disrupted by the war.[78] The initial Sulzer design for the GSR, shown in Plate 7, was based on locomotives supplied to Siamese Railways in 1938. In Siam, as in Ireland, security of fuel supply prompted the adoption of diesel locomotives as wood-burning steam locomotives were depleting the forests.[79] A move towards diesel traction was well under way in the United States, the cradle of diesel locomotive development. In August 1945 the New York, Ontario and Western Railroad announced its intention to fully convert to diesel traction.[80] This company's coal costs were 75 per cent above the average of US railroads, due to its distance from coalfields or ports.[81] In fact the following December the New York and Susquehanna Railroad became the first US road to totally dispense with steam traction.[82]

The widespread introduction of diesel traction was planned by the GSR before D Day. The decision to make the heavy capital investment in the uncertain technology of diesel locomotives was motivated by an uncertainty over fuel supply, which would have been clearer to Irish locomotive engineers, given their wartime experience, than to engineers employed by railways with access to better and more secure supplies of coal.

Although the GSR was planning a move to diesel locomotives, it was clear that in the short and medium term steam would be the predominant form of traction. On 2 March 1945 Bredin approved plans for the conversion of a goods locomotive for oil burning and ordered that it be treated as a matter of urgency.[83] Bredin was requested by the Department of Supplies for an estimate of his future oil needs, and indicated a requirement of 46 million gallons of oil for steam locomotives, together with 25 million gallons for as yet undesigned diesel electric locomotives, dwarfing the 4.6 million gallon annual requirement of the road fleet of CIÉ.[84] This radical strategy involved the complete abandonment of coal as an energy source, and constituted the adoption of Dean Swift's advice to 'burn everything English except their coal' on a grand scale, displacing 240,000 tons of British coal per annum. In accordance with this decision, goods locomotive 264 was converted to oil burning and by the end of May

1945 had completed tests. While fuel costs were over twice as high as with coal, it was security of supply rather than cost that motivated the experiments.

The end of hostilities brought little improvement in coal supplies, which depended on continuing good weather for shipping. Train punctuality worsened in late 1945. In November the general manager was advised that 'this increase [in fuel consumption] is attributed mainly to the cessation of the manufacture of briquettes on 16/11/1945. In May 1945 supplies of duff were cut off as duff was required for British and Continental use and since May we have been working off our reserve stock of duff which is now exhausted.' The report continued: 'The present inferior quality of coal has brought about a situation which is almost as bad as at any time during the Emergency. The timekeeping of trains has disimproved... Overtime payment to train and engine crews has increased.'[85]

Table 15 Late running trains, June 1945–January 1946.

Month	June	July	Aug.	Sept.	Oct.	Nov.	Dec.	Jan.
	20	25	22	19	30	74	73	94

Source: CHEM F39 late train returns.

In February 1946 Bredin wrote: 'We have been passing through a very critical period regarding loco fuel supplies... the supply position has been serious for the last few weeks... I anticipate that except for a very severe break in the weather we shall not have to reduce rail services.'[86]

The development of diesel traction by CIÉ was part of the Emergency experience. While the patchy survival of evidence makes it difficult to trace with absolute precision, it is clear that key decisions were made before the end of the war. In April 1945 CIÉ informed Sulzers that 'the company has disposed of the question of the supply of diesel electric shunting locomotives.'[87] On 3 September 1945 the Dublin representative of Metropolitan Vickers called on Frank Lemass, assistant general manager, to discuss the prospect of orders for diesel locomotives. Lemass replied: 'When I saw your representative... I explained to him that my chairman... was at the time in London and it was quite possible that our diesel electric requirements as regards prototype models would be fixed up. The chairman has now returned and he concluded arrangements for the supply of prototypes for all our requirements in diesel electric traction.'[88] Before the end of the war CIÉ had procured the design and manufacture of prototype diesel electric shunting and mainline locomotives. The delivery of these seven units (five shunters and two mainline) was delayed by material shortages until 1947 and 1950 and falls outside the scope of this work. At the first AGM of CIÉ Reynolds announced a plan for the construction of diesel locomotives in Inchicore using imported engines and electrical equipment. In April 1946, *Diesel Railway Traction* featured a report titled 'Éire to build its own diesel locomotives' and in August it reported: 'Post-war programmes, in Éire especially, will involve extended application of diesel power.'[89]

In January 1945 services were restored on all lines where they had been restricted or terminated in April 1944, with the exception of the Shillelagh and Killaloe branches, which remained closed. The end of the war brought increased expectations of the return of peacetime conditions, and although passengers did not experience any improvement until summer 1946, in June of that year Sunday seaside trains were introduced – a month earlier than in 1945. The trains served Dublin, Cork, Waterford, Limerick (to Foynes) and Wexford (to Rosslare). In July a second service each way per day was introduced on mainline routes.[90] The *Connacht Sentinel* reported: 'It will be possible for Galway people to leave home on the morning train, do business in Dublin and return home that night.'[91] The timing of the fastest express between Dublin and Cork in 1939 was three hours thirty minutes. The Emergency timing was six hours forty minutes while the acceleration of July 1946 brought it to four hours fifty minutes.[92] The improvements, although a far cry from 1939 conditions, marked an end to the Emergency.

However, uncertainty over coal supplies continued and in March 1946 Percy Reynolds told the first AGM of CIÉ: 'Our coal stocks are low and the situation does not show any sign of improving. The quality of coal we are getting is as bad as it ever has been.'[93] The Department of Industry and Commerce were approached for a supply of crude oil to place oil-burning prototype 264 in regular traffic. The request was initially declined,[94] but on 16 September 1946 the locomotive entered service. Although the operating costs were 16 per cent higher than for an equivalent coal-burning locomotive,[95] for the first time since 1941 the company had developed an effective alternative to coal. While the locomotives used in other fuel experiments were reconverted to coal burning as soon as the experiments were concluded, locomotive 264 was kept out of use for almost a year until oil supplies became available. This decision was not taken lightly, as 264 was of a class described as 'the most important heavy goods engines on the system, of good design and [requiring] little maintenance... essential to the working of beet and cattle specials.'[96] Keeping such a valuable locomotive out of traffic shows that the oil-burning system that had been developed was a success. The chief draughtsman told CIÉ's public relations officer in 1946 that during the Emergency a senior British scientist credited with the development of the British flame thrower had visited Inchicore, and having examined the performance figures said that there was little scope for improvement. This is yet another example of high-level technical contacts between senior British administrators and the GSR.[97]

British coal supplies deteriorated rapidly due to the exceptionally severe winter of 1946/7. On 20 November 1946 Frank Lemass, the new general manager, dictated from his sick bed an authorisation to convert 'two decent-sized locomotives, one passenger and one freight, to oil burning for crew-training purposes' and instructed the chief mechanical engineer (CME) to find out all that was possible about oil burning on British and American railways, if necessary sending someone to Britain to glean what they could. Tyndall indicated that thirty locomotives could be converted quickly and the board approved his proposal on the same day.[98] The crisis of 1946/7 has been described elsewhere and involved a radical cut in services more serious than anything experienced during the Emergency, with passenger services being suspended for a number of months.[99] One hundred locomotives were converted to burn oil based on the prototype developed in spring 1945. Such an extensive and speedy conversion programme to oil burning was only possible because of the extensive experimentation with a range of solid fuels that had been undertaken during the Emergency.

For the GSR, 1944 was the most challenging year of the Emergency. Services were cut to the bone for most of the spring and summer and reached a low point in mid-July. This round of cuts never made its way into the collective historical memory partly because the public had by now grown 'Emergency weary' and partly because the cuts were publicised widely in advance in Dáil debates and newspaper reports. The invasion of Europe and the end of the war brought, if anything, a worsening in coal supplies. This led the GSR to take a strategic decision in spring 1944 to move away from coal as a locomotive fuel. This move was grounded in the Emergency experience and involved two technological innovations – the adaptation of steam locomotives to burn oil and the development of diesel electric traction. These developments in motive power policy represented a break with British practice which remained focused on the steam locomotive. The conversion of a prototype oil-burning locomotive in spring 1945 had its roots in previous experiments with pitch and pulverised coal and paved the way for an extensive conversion programme during the winter of 1946/7. The decision to move from coal anticipated the long-term decline in the British coal industry which would lead to problems with the quality of locomotive coal supplies almost to the end of steam traction on CIÉ.

The wartime experiences of the GSR convinced management of the necessity of developing diesel locomotives even though they were as yet untried in Europe. This was a more radical step than the Dutch decision in 1945 to electrify their railways. Mainline electric traction was highly developed in Europe in 1945, but mainline diesel traction was not. The most rapid adoption of the diesel locomotive in the post-war years was in the US, with steam locomotives eliminated on most major railways by 1956 and the last steam stronghold, the Norfolk and Western Railway, withdrawing its last steam locomotive in 1960. In Europe substantial orders for steam locomotives were placed in the immediate post-war period. Ireland conforms with a North American rather than a European model with the decision to move towards diesel traction being taken in the darkest period of the Emergency – April 1944. At the beginning of the Emergency the GSR was criticised for its slavish following of British locomotive practice. By the end of the period, this had changed. British Railways did not commit itself to a diesel future until 1955 and built its last steam locomotive as late as 1960. In contrast, despite a number of false starts, CIÉ placed two large orders in 1950 and 1954 for diesel locomotives and railcars which culminated in the elimination of steam traction in March 1963.

Notes

1 *Dáil Debates*, vol. 93, col. 1283, 20 April 1944.
2 NA DFA A59, Maffey to de Valera, 28 March 1944.
3 NA DFA A59, Report, Boland to An Taoiseach, 3 April 1944.
4 NA DFA A59, Undated report by Leydon on meeting of 31 March 1944.
5 Ibid.
6 NA DFA P33, Leydon to Norman Archer, 20 April 1944.
7 C.R.S. Harris, *Allied Military Administration of Italy, 1943 –45* (London, 1957), p.102.
8 W.H.B. Court, *History of the Second World War Coal* (London, 1951), p.388.
9 Ibid., pp.246, 304.
10 Francis and Smith, *The Fed,* p.415.
11 Court, *Coal,* p.375.
12 *Times,* 12 April 1944.
13 H.D. Francis and D. Smith, *The Fed: A History of the South Wales Miners' Federation* (London, 1980), pp.411–12.

14 Supreme Headquarters Allied Expeditionary Force.

15 Court, *Coal*, p.375.

16 C.B.A. Behrens, *Merchant Shipping and the Demands of War* (London, 1955), p.341.

17 *Dáil Debates*, vol. 93, cols 1284–6, 20 April 1944.

18 GSRGM, Unnumbered file, 'Statement of weekly mileage and fuel cost', 1944.

19 *Munster Express*, 21 April 1944.

20 *Connacht Tribune*, 18 April 1944, 22 April 1944, 29 April 1944.

21 *Anglo Celt*, 22 April 1944.

22 NA DFA P33, Leydon to Boland, 21 April 1944, Forsyth to Leydon, 17 May 1944.

23 NA DFA P33, Minute of meeting, 23 June 1944.

24 Court, *Coal*, p.389.

25 These returns are contained in an unnumbered file and are referred to hereafter as 'coal returns'.

26 Coal returns. An average of 303 tons per day was produced over twelve days, 13 to 26 January 1944.

27 GSRGM, 53960/10, Minute of meeting, 9 June 1945.

28 CHEM F30, McIlveen to running superintendent, 11 June 1945.

29 NA DFA A59, Jenkins (War Transport) to Leydon, 2 May 1944.

30 GSRGM 61847, Murphy to Bredin, 23, 27 June 1944.

31 GSRGM 50542, Memo, 9 May 1944, Johnston to Murphy, 24 May 1944.

32 Behrens, *Shipping*, p.400.

33 GSRGM Coal returns, January1944, March 1946.

34 GSRGM 43737/1, 'Increases in steam coal costs', Murphy to Bredin, 19 May 1944.

35 GSRGM Coal returns, January1944, March 1946.

36 GSRGM 54005, 'Cost and tonnage of fuel consumed in locomotives', minute of meeting, 29 June 1944.

37 GSRGM 53300/24, 'Working of turf specials, MGW', Bredin to running superintendent, 7, 12 July 1944.

38 GSRGM 61551, Bredin to Ferguson, 23 May, Ferguson to Bredin, 18 July 1944.

39 *Irish Times*, 1 April 1944.

40 *Irish Times*, 8 June 1944.

41 GSRGM 61551/12, 'Revision of train service 17/7/1944', Kirwan to Bredin, 20 October, board minute 5489, 11 November, Beere to Bredin, 15 November 1944.

42 *Dáil Debates*, vol. 93, col. 1292, 20 April 1944.

43 NA DFA A59, Note of telephone conversation, Braddock to Leydon, 8 July 1945.

44 NA DFA P33, Maffey to Walsh, 30 August 1944 re. an allocation of South Wales anthracite for Irish maltsters: 'The anthracite will be sent to the Mersey for shipment.'

45 GSRGM 50542, Johnston to Reynolds, 15 September 1944.

46 M. Ó Riain, *On the Move* (Dublin, 1995), pp.28–37.

47 *Report of the Tribunal of Enquiry into Dealings in GSR Stocks Between the first day of January 1943 and the eighteenth day of November 1943* (Dublin, 1944, p6792), pp.20–4.

48 C. Wills, *That Neutral Island* (London, 2007), pp.330, 336.

49 *Report of the Tribunal of Enquiry into Dealings in GSR Stocks*, pp.10–11.

50 Ibid., p.4.

51 *Dáil Debates*, vol. 93, cols 1786–7, 2 May 1944.

52 *Dáil Debates*, vol. 94, col. 110, 12 June 1944.

53 Department of Industry and Commerce, *Report of Investigation of Accident at Straboe near Portarlington, 20 December 1944* (Dublin, 1945), pp.6–7.

54 BNA CAB 72/25, Minute of meeting and memorandum for meeting, 6 June 1944.

55 NA DFA P33, Note of phone call, 8 June 1944.

56 NA DFA P23, Leydon to Campbell, 6 October 1944.
57 BNA MT 59/1282, 'Coal shipments to Éire', Smith to Gorick, 14 October 1944.
58 BNA MT 59/1282, Memo to Bennett, 25 October 1944.
59 F.S.V. Donnison, *Civil Affairs and Military Government, North West Europe, 1944–1946* (London, 1961), p.398.
60 *Railway Gazette*, 12 January 1945, p.93, 9 March 1945, p.242.
61 Donnison, *Civil Affairs*, p.399.
62 GSRGM 53960/10, Minute of meeting, 6 April 1945.
63 *Railway Gazette*, 24 August 1945, p.189.
64 Donnison, *Civil Affairs*, p.121.
65 C.J. Potter, 'Europe's coal problem', *Proceedings of the Academy of Political Science*, 21, 4 (January 1946), p.30.
66 NA DFA A59, Dulanty to Gilmour Jenkins, 30 May, Gilmour Jenkins to Dulanty, 5 June 1945.
67 Donnison, *Civil Affairs*, p.231.
68 Ibid.
69 Court, *Coal*, p.375.
70 GSRGM 50715/5, 'Turf mould at stations', passim.
71 E.C. Bredin, 'The steam locomotive of today and alternative forms of power for railway traction', 10 February 1941, p.16 (copy in file).
72 GSRGM 65854, 'World power conference', CIÉ report, August 1946.
73 'World power conference', 1946 report, p.5.
74 GSRGM 63665, 'Oil-burning locomotives', minute, 13 April 1944.
75 Bredin, 'The steam locomotive of today', p.1.
76 Ibid., pp.23–4.
77 PEC 6/11, Bredin to Sulzers, 21 April 1944.
78 PEC 6/11, Sulzers to Bredin, 28 October 1944.
79 Sulzer Brothers history & production details available at http://www.derbysulzers.com/sulzer.html
80 *Railway Gazette*, 14 September 1945, p.289.
81 *Diesel Railway Traction*, August 1945, p.71.
82 *Diesel Railway Traction*, December 1945, p.125.
83 GSRGM 63665, Minute of meeting, 2 March 1945, Bredin to mechanical engineer, 2 March 1945.
84 GSRGM 63655, Bredin to Department of Supplies, 23 May 1945.
85 GSRGM 63665, Memo for general manager, 5 December 1945.
86 GSRGM 65480, 'Running of goods trains', Bredin to Stewart, 20 February 1945.
87 PEC 6/11, Lemass to Sulzers, 21 April 1945.
88 GSRGM 65042, 'Metropolitan Vickers Export Co.', Lemass to Graty, 28 September 1945.
89 *Diesel Railway Traction (DRT)*, April 1946, p.37, August 1946, p.100.
90 GSRGM 65110, Stewart to Bredin, 21 May 1946, Luke diary, section O.
91 *Connacht Sentinel*, 29 October 1946.
92 GSR and CIÉ working timetables.
93 *Irish Independent*, 15 March 1946.
94 GSRGM 63665, Bredin to Supplies, 7 March, Supplies to Bredin, 14 March 1946.
95 GSRGM 63566, Industry and Commerce to Lemass, 5 September 1946, Tyndall to Lemass, 20 September 1946.
96 IRRS archives, memo re. steam locomotive stock, running superintendent to CME, 17 June 1953.

97   IRRS archives, Leslie Luke notebook.
98   GSRGM 63566, Note dictated over telephone, Lemass to Tyndall, 20 November, Tyndall to Lemass, 18 December 1946, board minute 1569.
99   V. Horan, '1947 and the oil burners', *JIRRS*, no. 96 (1985), pp.337–51.

Conclusion

The 'Emergency Historical Record' was produced in 1945 under the auspices of the Taoiseach's Department. It states that:

> The difficulties of the 1939–45 period were due to a great extent to the mismanagement of the Great Southern Railway in the years preceding the Emergency and also to a lack of funds which led to deferred maintenance. Many different types of locomotive and road vehicles were in use so that spare parts presented an acute problem. There were serious arrears of track maintenance and wagon repairs even at the outbreak of the Emergency. In the case of the road services there had been a low standard of maintenance and an almost complete lack of local depots suitable for overhaul and repairs. There was also a shortage of vehicles, equipment spare parts and other materials.[1]

This bizarre Orwellian passage fails to mention the failure of the coal supply, which was the cause of most problems with railway operation during the Emergency. Shortages of materials did not prevent the commissioning of the briquette plants, the experiments with alternative road and rail fuels or the development of a successful prototype oil-burning locomotive. Arrears of track maintenance continued to accumulate, but the branch lines closed in April 1944 were re-opened later in the year as coal supplies improved. Spare parts continued to be manufactured for locomotives and rolling stock and the manufacturing of spare parts for lorries and buses was undertaken. The GSR became a predominantly freight railway and the figures for goods wagon availability were as good as those in Britain. We can only speculate as to why the 'Emergency Historical Record' is so misleading. The controversy over the coal shortages and the failure to stockpile materials in advance had been well aired in the 1943 election and were perhaps too political to be recounted in an internal departmental history. Perhaps it suited neither the department nor CIÉ to draw too much attention to the origins of the company in Emergency Powers legislation. The 1944 Transport Act gave a peacetime legislative format to Emergency Powers Order 152 of February 1942 which allowed the GSR to be taken over. For administrators this represented an opportunity to solve the 'railway problem', which had been on the agenda of every government since the foundation of the state.

The GSR came out of the 1939 to 1945 period in a much dilapidated state due to arrears of maintenance. The report books of first-line supervisors such as locomotive foremen and boiler inspectors show equipment worn out, often to a frightening extent.[2] However, the railway recovered rapidly from this period of dilapidation. While railway managers in most European countries ordered new steam locomotives to replace those destroyed or worn out during the war, CIÉ went the route of diesel traction. This decision was taken as a direct consequence of the Emergency fuel crisis. CIÉ thus became an early adopter of diesel traction, which strengthened the long-term position of the railway system in the face of revived post-war road transport.

Problems with arrears of maintenance in the war years and after were not unique to Ireland. British railway companies experienced similar problems during the inter-war years. Much of the carriage stock of the LMSR and LNER was described as 'ancient and getting shabby' or being 'a long way behind standards that were acceptable'. The LNER captured the world rail speed record of 126 mph in 1938 but in the same year the auditors had to qualify their certificate because of inadequate provision for maintenance.[3] Indeed the wartime record of British railways differed between companies where it was 'noticeable that the LMS and LNER [London and North Eastern Railway] adapted well to the changing traffic circumstances whereas the Great Western was quite unable to do this'.[4]

The main expectation of most citizens of their railway system is that a train will turn up on a reliable and punctual basis to transport them or their goods at a reasonable price. Subject to this, citizens care little about ownership, capital structure or governance. The GSR failed in its side of the bargain to the passenger for about twelve months after July 1941. After that point it succeeded in running slow passenger trains that were punctual most of the time. Despite a near failure with the turf harvest of 1941, the GSR never broke its bargain with the freight customers. Livestock was exported, the beet factories ran, the grain harvest was moved and urbanites had access to turf, even if it was often soggy. The fulfilment of this bargain was due in the main to the efforts of the engineering staff and locomotive crews of the GSR.

The Emergency experience of the GSR was by no means unique. It was similar to the wartime experience of railway companies in other jurisdictions, especially neutral countries. While Switzerland, with its extensive electrified network, is an obvious exception, many parallels may be found between the GSR and RENFE in Spain, CP in Portugal, SJ in Sweden and the various companies in Argentina – all of which had relied on Britain for coal in the pre-war years. Unnoticed by the general public, these parallels could be readily seen in the columns of the *Railway Gazette*. They ranged from the pressure on the railways to use unsuitable alternative fuel, as in Argentina, to the key role of the railway in bringing alternative domestic fuel to the cities, as in Sweden, and the mid-war recriminations directed at the railway company for not having bought more coal in 1940, as in Portugal. These similarities have gone unremarked, as most historical treatments of this period are based on a study of high politics or of trade policy at a high level rather than on the flow of commodities.[5]

Coal was a central tool in the bargaining process between states during the war. The period from 1939 to 1941 saw a sudden reversal of the pre-war situation of too few customers for too much coal. Coal went into short supply as war economies geared up, and both sides used this shortage in negotiations with neutrals, as had happened during the First World War when coal was used by Britain as a bargaining tool with Norway, and similarly by Germany with Holland. Just as Britain sought to use coal as a lever in dealing with neutrals for what the official history describes as 'good political reasons', Germany used its position after 1939 as sole exporter in mainland Europe to shape its foreign trade policy with Switzerland and Sweden. In wartime trade the considerations are seldom the market prices, as buyers are generally price takers. The considerations might instead be the need to leverage more supplies of a given commodity (such as wheat in the case of Guinness) or the need to deny a commodity to an enemy (such as was the case with Portuguese wolfram). Trade does not cease in war – it assumes new forms and often takes on a new urgency.

The imposition of trade sanctions by Britain in December 1940 gave an opportunity for advocates of Irish fuel self-sufficiency to put their theories to the test. The main plank of Irish energy self-sufficiency was the Ardnacrusha hydro-electric power station. A similar station on the Liffey was partially commissioned in 1942 but the war meant it was not fully commissioned until 1947. Timber, the main alternative fuel in Sweden and Portugal, was too scarce in Ireland to be of significance. The TDB was a young organisation and there was insufficient time to bring its development work into mainstream production before the outbreak of war due, inter alia, to the stranding of key equipment in Germany. Most of the turf harvested in Ireland during the Emergency was done so by traditional hand methods. The period showed that while turf might serve some markets, it could not, even in combination with Irish coal, replace imported coal. Some experiments in turf burning had begun before 1939 under the auspices of the TDB, but the Emergency turned the entire country into a gigantic outdoor fuel laboratory. This process proved the proposition of Sir John Purser Griffith that the most effective way of using turf was to burn it on the bog and transmit the energy to the end user. The main evidence of this can be seen in the post-war network of turf-fired power stations. The Emergency tested the expanded Irish coal-mining industry, but as Lemass told the Dáil in April 1944, the combined output of the Irish mines could only meet the needs of the GSR.

The main role of the railway in Emergency energy policy was to act as the national grid for turf. The task was simplified in 1942 when production was shifted towards the midland bogs. This was in marked comparison with the hastily improvised 1941 season with its disorganisation and poor linkages between the different components of the turf logistics machine. A different role had been envisaged in late 1940, with the widespread use of turf as a locomotive fuel being planned. However, within a year it was realised that harvesting labour and transport were not infinite and priorities had to be set. C.S. Andrews, the turf evangelist, was the bearer of this message to the GSR when he instructed the company to stop buying turf to allow sufficient supplies for the use of the domestic consumer.

Wagon shortages and capacity problems which plagued the GSR in its handling of the turf harvest were also suffered by the British railway system which struggled to keep London and southern England supplied with coal. The Swedish railway system was severely taxed by the need to transport timber from the north of the country to urban centres. A number of railway systems, notably Sweden and Switzerland, expanded their electrified networks during this period. The use of electricity on the GSR was limited to the technological cul de sac of the Drumm battery railcars. The final judgement on the effectiveness of native fuels came in the immediate post-war years when coal shortages were more severe than in the Emergency period. In this period the mainstay of railway services was oil and 100 locomotives were converted to burn it during the bad winter of 1946/7. This demonstrates the limitations of Irish coal or turf and the various devices designed to adapt them to the steam locomotive.

In terms of British policy the most striking theme to emerge was the relative autonomy of the Ministry of Fuel and Power in pursuing its own policy on coal exports, be they to Argentina or Ireland. Having spent most of the 1930s maintaining Britain's share of global coal markets, the ministry seemed to view the use of coal in diplomacy with a jaundiced eye. Had it wished to paralyse the GSR, it could have embargoed the export of briquette plants in late 1941 but did not do so. The reason for this attitude is obscure but it began with shipments of phurnacite from mid-1942 and was followed by the granting of an extra coal allocation in December of that year, when civil servants subverted a cabinet decision on the export of coal to Éire. Civil servants are unlikely to act in this manner without an expectation of support from their political masters, and with a Labour dominions secretary and a Liberal minister for fuel and power civil servants counted on the support of their ministers in pursuing actions supportive of the war effort even when these actions conflicted with a cabinet decision. This bizarre episode can only be explained by the coalition of forces within the British ministries concerned, the demonstrable failure of the sanctions policy to achieve its effects and the development of common economic interest across the Irish Sea. These common interests are easily visible in the case of the Ministry of Food – more food for British tables. The motives of the Ministry of Fuel and Power are explained by its mandate to promote the use of low-grade fuels. A laboratory was needed to demonstrate that low-quality fuels were in fact usable and the GSR was that laboratory.

The GSR was widely seen as a failure by 1938 and this view was confirmed by the events of 1941. The collapse of services and the controversy over increased bus fares meant that the days of the company were numbered. However, to this commercial and political failure was counterposed the engineering and operational success in the period of the Emergency and immediately after when the management of the railway experimented, innovated and bargained their way through and kept the Irish economy turning over. This should not be taken for granted, as can be seen from the extreme difficulties encountered by the French railways in the immediate post-war period and the loss of an entire sugar beet harvest. In their experimentation and dealings, GSR managers made full use of their professional expertise with the broader body of railway professionals in the English-speaking world. Perhaps the most significant factor working in favour of the GSR was that it had its own representative, Charles Johnston, on the ground in Britain. Johnston played a key role in maintaining and building a relationship with the Ministry of Fuel and

Power which allowed the GSR to be portrayed as a body that had something to offer the Allied war effort, be it food or experience in the use of inferior coal which could be deployed by the Ministry of Fuel and Power in its dealings with reluctant British consumers.

The appointment of A.P. Reynolds as chairman neutralised the board and the management in the debates over the future of the GSR, a significant consideration given the scale of the task that was faced. The choice of Reynolds can be seen as a political one – from a Fianna Fáil viewpoint he was a safe pair of hands. An alternative view was that he was an experienced transport manager and that the government considered that new blood needed to be brought into the GSR to tackle what Lemass called its bad culture. Support for this viewpoint can be seen in Reynolds' attempt to headhunt W.A. Smith from the Ministry of Aircraft Production to Inchicore and in the pattern of external appointments to CIÉ management. The view was that the railway needed an infusion of new blood at senior management level. Reynolds was succeeded by T.C. Courtney of the Department of Local Government, who was in turn succeeded by George Howden of the GNR. Similarly, when the post of chief mechanical engineer, vacant since 1942, was filled in 1948 the candidate was O.V.S. Bullied, the talented if eccentric retired CME of the English Southern Railway. The post-war experience of CIÉ was controversial, with yet another report on transport being commissioned by the inter-party government. This led in turn to the dismissal of Percy Reynolds and to the 1950 Transport Act which nationalised CIÉ, completing the work of the 1944 act.

For most European states the wartime management of the railway system was a simple matter as the railways were either state owned, as in Germany, were nationalised during the war, as in Spain where RENFE was created in 1941, or were brought under government control for the duration, as in Britain. The financial weakness of the GSR made the government initially reluctant to impose control, as it might lead to its assuming ownership of a bankrupt company. However, the powerlessness of the government in the face of a number of crises forced it to take control of the GSR under emergency legislation. This exercise of control was undertaken as much with an eye to post-war policy as to the immediate requirements of the Emergency economy.

The Emergency experience exposed the fallacy of the proposition that a steam-powered railway system could provide reasonably cheap and efficient transport using the fuel available on the island of Ireland. The experience of these years brought it home to railway engineers that the future for Ireland's rail network lay with a total conversion to diesel traction. This marked the move of the Irish railway system out of the British sphere of influence and into a space where European and American thinking exercised equal strength of influence.

Notes

1   NA EHR 2 memo, 'Internal transport', from Industry and Commerce to Department of An Taoiseach, October 1945, p.2.
2   IRRS archives, Northern District boiler inspection book, 1946/7, 1947/8.
3   M. Bonavia, *Railway Policy Between the Wars* (Manchester, 1981), pp.77, 89–90.
4   Ibid., p.21.
5   Notable exceptions are Ollson's work on German coal and Swedish ore and Bourgeois' work on Switzerland.

Appendix I

Coal and Other Priority Traffic Liable to Disruption by the Turf Programme[1]

	Wagons per day
Castlecomer	30
Arigna	30
Ballylinan	6
Rossmore / Carlow	3
Slievarda ex Laffansbridge	2
Company Briquette distribution	35
Phosphate ex Ennistymon	12
Machinery ex Wexford	15
Sand ex Newbridge	24
Sand ex Courtmacsherry	10
Scrap iron	5
Hides and skins	5
Round timber	35
Firewood	25

1   From GSRGM 53300/18. Minute of meeting 12 May 1943

Appendix II

Arrangements for Evacuation of Rolling Stock[2]

Southern Command

Limerick: all stock from as far west as Tralee, Foynes and Bruree to travel east through Limerick itself and concentrate in Roscrea.

Cork: On West Cork line all traffic to stop on the code word and to go eastward picking up stock and then cross the city to Glanmire station before going northwards.

Other Cork lines: Cobh and Youghal to be cleared northwards to Cashel branch. Fermoy loco to clear to Mallow and northwards.

Kerry: All westward traffic to stop and return, picking up stock. Tralee and Fenit stock to go to Limerick via Newcastle West. Killarney, Cahirciveen and Kenmare trains to head eastwards loading stores in Killarney if possible, trains to be held in Mallow beet sidings then northwards. Tralee and Dingle to go to Tralee where locos would be immobilised.

Western Command

All stock on the lines to concentrate in Claremorris or Ballinasloe depending on their location. 'The narrow gauge lines in Leitrim and Donegal are now so little used that it is scarcely worthwhile taking action.'

Eastern Command

The direction of the invasion made planning difficult, but it was proposed to concentrate as much as possible in Kingscourt. As to the GNR, it was indicated that action would be taken in Dundalk through the LDF, and that: 'It is not proposed to take up the matter with the GNR owing to the particular circumstance of that company.'

Curragh Command

All stock from Waterford, Wexford and Rosslare was to move to Bagenalstown and Kilkenny. No engine to be kept in steam overnight in Dungarvan. Locomotives to be always in steam in Waterford, Wexford and Rosslare, placed to leave at short notice hauling all other mobile locomotives. All rolling stock east of the Slaney to move to Wicklow.

Appendix III

Closure of Lines and Curtailment of Services from 24 April 1944

Passenger services ceased:

Sallins to Tullow
Inny Junction to Cavan

Clonsilla to Kingscourt
Waterford to Macmine Junction

All services cancelled:

Bagenalstown to Palace East
Portlaoise to Mountmellick
Birdhill to Killaloe
Goolds Cross to Cashel
Fermoy to Mitchelstown
Banteer to Newmarket

Tralee to Fenit
Crossdowney to Killeshandra
Woodenbridge to Shillelagh
Schull to Skibereen
Clara to Streamstown

---

1   MA EDP 66, Memo – Railway rolling stock removal and immobilisation, 5 March 1942.

Bibliography

Archives

National Archives of Ireland:
Taoiseach S Series
External Affairs
Finance Supply Series
Emergency Historical Record Series

National Archives, London:
Cabinet Sub-Committee on Éire (CAB 72/25)
Ministry of War Shipping (MT Series)
Ministry of Food (MAF Series)
Treasury (T Series)
Ministry of Fuel and Power (POWE Series)

Irish Railway Record Society, Heuston Station, Dublin:
GS&WR Secretary's Office files
GSR General Manager's files
GSR Chemist's files
GSR Board Minutes
GSR Miscellaneous Collection (contains documents generated at local
    depots)
GNR Mechanical Engineer's files (see Paddy Mallon collection below)
GNR General Manager's files
GNR Locomotive Superintendent's files, Belfast

Córas Iompair Éireann, Heuston Station, Dublin:
GSR Board minutes
MGWR Board minutes
CIÉ Board minutes

Military Archives, Cathal Brugha Barracks, Dublin:
Emergency Defence Preparation (EDP) Series

Louth County Archives, Ardee Road, Dundalk:
Paddy Mallon Collection, GNR Mechanical Engineer's Letter index

books, 1940, 1941, 1942. This gives an indication of the contents of correspondence which in many cases does not survive.

Official Publications

Irish Official Publications:
Boithre Iarainn na hÉireann – Tuarasgbhail an Choimisiuin do Cheap an Rialtas Sealadach (Dublin, 1922)
Reports of the Tribunal of Enquiry on Public Transport, 1939 (Dublin, 1941), p.7634
Report of the Tribunal of Enquiry into Dealings in Great Southern Railway Stocks between the First Day of January 1943 and the Eighteenth Day of November 1943 (Dublin, 1944), p.6792
Report on Transport in Ireland (Dublin, 1948), p.9201 (Milne report)
Report of Investigation of Accident at Straboe near Portarlington, 20th December 1944 (Dublin, 1945)
Dáil Proceedings

British Parliamentary Papers:
Report of Commission of Enquiry into Irish Railways, 1910 cmd 5247
Irish Coal Industry Committee 1919, *Minutes of Evidence with Appendices Thereto* (Dublin, 1920), Q.1840
Coal Mining – Report of the Technical Advisory Committee, 1944/45, iv: cmd 6610
Irish Railway Wages Board Proceedings

Newspapers, Periodicals and Trade Press

Bulletin of the International Railway Congress Association
Colliery Guardian
Cork Examiner
Diesel Railway Traction
Dublin Opinion
Economist
Fayle's Bulletin
Evening Mail
Irish Independent
Irish Industry
Irish Press
Irish Times
Locomotive Magazine (Trade press, main emphasis on locomotive technology and engineering products)

Locomotive Journal (Official organ of the Associated Society of
   Locomotive Engineers and Firemen)
Railway Gazette (Trade press with a broader systems emphasis)
Railway Review (Official organ of the National Union of Railwaymen)
Railway Yearbook 1922
Weekly Circular, GSR / CIÉ, 1938–46

Interviews and Correspondence

Interview with Paddy Guilfoyle, locomotive driver, Inchicore (1937–86),
   15 November 2002
Jim Martin, engineer, Turf Development Board / Bórd na Móna
   (1941–82), 24 July 2004
Correspondence with Val Horan, locomotive driver, Athlone (1943–86),
   branch secretary, ASLEF

Books

Abbenhuis, M.M. *The Art of Staying Neutral: The Netherlands in the
   First World War* (Amsterdam, 2006)
Andrews, C.S. *Man of No Property* (Dublin, 1982)
Arnott, R.P. *South Wales Miners* (London, 1967)
Beattie, R. *The Death Railway* (Bangkok, 2006)
Beaumont, J. *Rails to Achill* (Usk, 2002)
Behrens, C.B.A. *Merchant Shipping and the Demands of War* (London,
   1955)
Bell, A.M. *Locomotives: Their Construction, Maintenance and
   Operation* (London, 1937)
Benson, J., Neville, R.G. and Thompson, C.H., *Bibliography of the
   British Coal Industry* (Oxford, 1981)
Bew, P. and Patterson, H. *Seán Lemass and the Making of Modern
   Ireland* (Dublin, 1982)
Blake, J.W. *Northern Ireland in the Second World War* (Belfast, 1956)
Bonavia, M. *The Organisation of British Railways* (London, 1971)
Bonavia, M. *A History of the LNER, 1939–1948* (London, 1983)
Bonavia, M. *Railway Policy Between the Wars* (Manchester, 1981)
Bourgeois, D. *Business Helevetique et Troiseme Reich* (Zurich, 1998)
Brown, M. *Evacuees: Wartime Evacuation in Britain 1939–1945*
   (Stroud, 2005)
Bullock, A. *The Life and Times of Ernest Bevin*, vol. 2 (London, 1967)

Burgos, D. and Lozano, I. *Los Railes del Exilio-Ninos de Morelia: Un Éxódo a Mexico* (Madrid, 2007)

Butler, J.R.M. *The War at Sea*, vol. 1 (London, 1954)

Buxton, N. *The Economic Development of the British Coal Industry* (London, 1978)

Canning, P. *British Policy Towards Ireland, 1921–1941* (London, 1985)

Carroll, J.T. *Ireland in the War Years* (Newton Abbot, 1975)

Casserly, H.C. *Railways Since 1939* (Newton Abbot, 1972)

Colville, J. *The Fringes of Power: Downing Street Diaries 1939–October 1941* (London, 1985)

Conroy, J.C. *A History of Railways in Ireland* (Dublin, 1928)

Conry, M.J. *Dancing the Culm: Burning Culm as a Domestic and Industrial Fuel in Ireland* (Carlow, 2001)

Córas Iompair Éireann, *Locomotive Fuel Economy* (Dublin, n.d.)

Court, W.H.B. *History of the Second World War Coal* (London, 1951)

Crowe, C., Fanning, R., Kennedy, M., Keogh, D. and O'Halpin, E. (eds), *Documents on Irish Foreign Policy, vol. IV, 1932–1936* (Dublin, 2004)

Daly, M.E. *Industrial Development and Irish National Identity* (Syracuse, 1992)

Daly, M.E. *The Buffer State: The Historical Roots of the Department of the Environment* (Dublin, 1997)

Devernais, E. *La Locomotive Actuelle* (Paris, 1948, 3rd edition)

Donnison, F.S.V. *Civil Affairs and Military Government in North West Europe, 1944–1946* (London, 1961)

Douglas, R.M. *Architects of the Resurrection: Ailtirí na hAiseirighe and the Fascist 'New Order' in Ireland* (Manchester, 2009)

Farmar, T. *Heitons: A Managed Transition, 1818–1996* (Dublin, 1996)

Fisk, R. *In Time of War: Ireland, Ulster and the Price of Neutrality* (Dublin, 1983)

Flanagan, P. (ed.), *Steaming Through a Century: The 101 Class Locomotives of the GS&WR* (Dublin, 1966)

Forde, F. *The Long Watch: The History of the Irish Merchant Marine in World War Two* (Dublin, 1981)

Francis, H.D. and Smith, D. *The Fed: A History of the South Wales Miners' Federation* (London, 1980)

Gillingham, J. *Industry and Politics in the Third Reich* (London, 1985)

Girvin, B. *Ireland in the Second World War: Politics, Society and Remembrance* (Dublin, 2000)

Girvin, B. *The Emergency: Neutral Ireland, 1939–45* (London, 2006)

Grey, T. *The Lost Years* (Dublin, 1997)

Hammond, R.J. *Food: The Growth of Policy* (London, 1951)

Harris, C.R.S. *Allied Military Administration of Italy, 1943–45* (London, 1957)

Harvie, C. *A Floating Commonwealth: Politics, Technology and Culture on Britain's Atlantic Coast, 1860–1930* (Oxford, 2008)

Hodgson, J. and Williams, J. *Locomotive Management from Cleaning to Driving* (London, 1928 (first edition, 1908))

Horgan, J. *Seán Lemass: The Enigmatic Patriot* (Dublin, 1997)

Institute of Civil Engineers of Ireland, *Emergency Fuel* (Dublin, 1942)

Jefferys, K. *The Churchill Coalition and Wartime Politics* (Manchester, 1990)

Kalla Bishop, P.M. *Locomotives at War* (Truro, 1980)

Kearns, K. *The Bombing of Dublin's North Strand, 1941* (Dublin, 2009)

Kennedy, M. *Division and Consensus: The Politics of Cross-Border Relations, 1925–1969* (Dublin, 2000)

Kennedy, W. *Shipping in Dublin Port, 1939–45* (Edinburgh, 1998)

Keogh, D. and O'Driscoll, M. *Ireland in World War Two* (Cork, 2004)

Kreis, G. *Switzerland and the Second World War* (London, 2000)

Leitz, C. *Nazi Germany and Neutral Europe* (Manchester, 2000)

Lyons, F.S.L. *Ireland Since the Famine* (London, 1973)

McLysaght, E. *Changing Times* (London, 1978)

McCann, F.D. *The Brazilian–American Alliance* (Princeton, 1973)

McMahon, D. *Republicans and Imperialists: Anglo-Irish Relations in the 1930s* (London, 1984)

McShane, C. *The Locomotive Up to Date* (Chicago, 1900)

Manning, M. and McDowell, M. *Electricity Supply in Ireland: The History of the ESB* (Dublin, 1984)

Maume, P. *The Long Gestation: Irish Nationalist Life, 1891–1918* (Dublin, 1999)

Medlicott, W.N. *The Economic Blockade* (London, 1959)

Mierzejewski, A.C. *The Collapse of the German War Economy: Allied Air Power and the German National Railway* (Chapel Hill, 1988)

Mierzejewski, A.C. *The Most Valued Asset of the Reich* (Chapel Hill, 2000)

Mierzejewski, A.C. *Hitler's Trains: The German National Railway and the Reich* (Stroud, 2005)

Milward, A.S. *The New Order and the French Economy* (Oxford, 1970)

Milward, A.S. *War, Economy and Society, 1939–1945* (London, 1977)

More, C. *Skill and the English Working Class, 1870–1914* (London, 1980)

National Union of Railwaymen, *Irish Railway Agreements 1919–1923* (London, 1925)

Nowlan, K.B. and Williams, T.D. *Ireland in the War Years and After, 1939–1951* (Dublin, 1969)

Offer, A. *The First World War: An Agrarian Interpretation* (Oxford, 1989)

Ó Gráda, C. *Ireland: A New Economic History, 1780–1939* (Oxford, 1994)

Ó Gráda, C. *A Rocky Road: The Irish Economy Since the 1920s* (Manchester, 1997)

O'Halpin, E. *Defending Ireland* (Oxford, 1999)

Ó hEithir, B. *Over the Bar: A Personal Relationship with the GAA* (Cork, 2005)

Ollson, S.O. *German Coal and Swedish Fuel, 1939–1945* (Goteborg, 1975)

O'Nolan, K. (ed.), *The Best of Myles: A Selection from Cruiskeen Lawn* (Dublin, 1968)

Ó Riain, M. *On the Move: Córas Iompair Éireann, 1945–1995* (Dublin, 1995)

O'Sullivan, C.J. *The Gas Makers* (Dublin, 1987)

O'Sullivan, M. *Seán Lemass: A Biography* (Dublin, 1994)

Ottley, G. *A Bibliography of British Railway History* (London, 1983)

Pimlot, B. (ed.), *The Second World War Diaries of Hugh Dalton* (London, 1986)

Purdom, D.C. *British Steam on the Pampas* (London, 1977)

Quigley, M.S. *A US Spy in Ireland* (Dublin, 1999)

Rosenberg, N. *Inside the Black Box: Technology and Economics* (Cambridge, 1982)

Ross, D. *The Willing Servant: A History of the Steam Locomotive* (Stroud, 2004)

Sauvage, E. *La Machine Locomotive* (Paris, 1918)

Savage, C.I. *Inland Transport* (London, 1957)

Semmens, P. *A History of the GWR, 1939–1948* (London, 1985)

Supple, B. *The History of the British Coal Industry. Volume 4, 1913–1946: The Political Economy of Decline* (Oxford, 1987)

Tonnaire, J. *La Vapeur: Souvenirs d'un Mecano de Locomotive, 1932–1950* (Paris, 1982)

Uí Ógáin, R. (ed.), *Mise an Fear Ceoil* (Dublin, 2007)

Van der Zee, H. *The Hunger Winter* (London, 1982)

Walters, R.H. *The Economic and Business History of the South Wales Steam Coal Industry* (New York, 1977)

Wardale, D. *The Red Devil and Other Tales from the Age of Steam* (Inverness, 1998)

Rt. Hon. the Earl of Woolton, *Memoirs* (London, 1959)

Wills, C. *That Neutral Island* (London, 2007)

Wright, T. *Coal Mining in China's Economy and Society* (Cambridge, 1994)

Wright, W.R. *British-Owned Railways in Argentina: Their Effects on Economic Nationalism* (Austin, 1974)

Wylie, N. *European Neutrals and Non-Belligerents During the Second World War* (Cambridge, 2001)

Articles and Chapters

Andrews, C.S. 'Some precursors of Bórd na Móna', *Journal of the Statistical and Social Inquiry Society of Ireland (JSSISI)*, 24, 2 (1952), pp.132–55

Bezilla, M. 'Steam railroad electrification in America 1920–1950: The unrealised potential', *The Public Historian*, 4, 1 (Winter, 1982), pp.29–52

Bredin E.C. 'The steam locomotive of today and alternative forms of power for railway traction', 10 February 1941. Copy contained in GM 42656

Brookfield, H.C. 'A study in the economic geography of the pre-war coastwise coal trade', *Transactions and Papers of the British Institute of Geographers*, no. 19 (1953), pp.81–94

Caruana, L. and Rockoff, H. 'An elephant in the garden: The Allies, Spain and oil in World War II', National Bureau of Economic Research working paper 12228

Case, C. 'Handling and consumption of coal', *Journal of the Institution of Locomotive Engineers*, no. 143 (1938), pp.249–312

Chadwick, W.J. 'Turf production in County Tipperary (North Riding)', *Transactions of the Institute of Civil Engineers of Ireland*, 68 (1941–2), pp.145–75

Clements, R N. 'Turf-burning locomotives', *Journal of the Irish Railway Record Society*, no. 7 (1950), pp.64–71

Clements, R N. 'The locomotive exchange of 1911', *Journal of the Irish Railway Record Society*, no. 71 (1976), pp.281–301

Clarke, C.W, 'The combustion of inferior coal on Indian railways', *Journal of the Institute of Locomotive Engineers*, no. 183 (1945), pp.3–39

Cox, E.S. 'A modern loco history', *Journal of the Institute of Locomotive Engineers*, no. 190 (1946), pp.100–71

Crompton, G. and Jupe, R. 'An awkward fence to cross: Railway capitalisation in Britain in the inter-war years', *Accounting Business & Financial History*, 12, 3 (2002), pp.439–59

Currivan, P.J. 'Engineman's son', *Journal of the Irish Railway Record Society*, no. 65 (October 1974), pp.261–81, no. 66 (February 1975), pp.20–35, no. 67 (June 1975), pp.63–79

Da Costa, J. 'Low-grade fuel in Indian locomotive practice', *Journal of the Institution of Locomotive Engineers*, no. 166 (1942), pp.64–92

Delaney, D. 'English and Irish railways', *Journal of the Irish Railway Record Society*, no. 106 (June 1988), pp.388–96, no. 110 (October 1989), pp.106–20, no. 112 (June 1990), pp.237–43

Dudley, J.H. 'Railway fuel problems', *Journal of the Irish Railway Record Society*, no. 3 (1947), pp.66–72

Duffy, M.C. 'Technomorphology and the Stephenson traction system', *Transactions of the Newcomen Society*, vol. 54 (1982), pp.55–78

Fishlow, A. 'Productivity and technical change in the railroad sector, 1840–1910', NBER working paper, 1966

Geoghegan, H.C. 'A plea for Irish mines and minerals', *JSSISI*, 12, 83 (1908), p.141–61

Gill-Cummins, M. 'They kept the home fires burning: The story of turf production on the Kildare–Offaly bogs in the 1940s–1950s', *Journal of the County Kildare Archeological Society*, vol. 19 (2003), pp.300–14

Hartley, H. 'William Arthur Stanier 1876–1965', *Bibliographical Memoirs of Fellows of the Royal Society*, vol. 12 (November 1966), pp.488–502

Hogan, M.A. 'Producer gas for internal combustion engines', *Transactions of the Institute of Civil Engineers of Ireland*, 69 (1942–3), pp.71–134 (also published in pamphlet form)

Horan, V. 'Memories', *Journal of the Irish Railway Record Society*, no. 87 (1982), pp.326–36

Horan, V. '1947 and oil burners', *Journal of the Irish Railway Record Society*, no. 96 (1985), pp.337–51

Jensen, W.G. 'The importance of energy in the first and second world wars', *Historical Journal*, vol. XI (1968), pp.538–44

Kettle, L.J. 'Irish coal and coalfields', *Transactions of the Institute of Civil Engineers of Ireland*, 66 (1921–2), pp.51–108

Kettle, L.J. 'Ireland's sources of power supply', *Studies*, no. 11 (1922), pp.61–75

Leckey, J. 'CIÉs first diesel programme', *Journal of the Irish Railway Record Society*, no. 86 (1981), pp.275–7

Mangan, C. 'Plans and operations', *Irish Sword*, no. 19 (1993–4), pp.47–56

Martin, J.J. 'The winning and utilisation of milled peat for briquetting and power generation', *Transactions of the Institute of Civil Engineers of Ireland*, 72 (1945–6), pp.29–54

Mierzejewski, A.C. 'The Deutsche Reichsbahn and Germany's supply of coal, 1939–45', *Transport History* [Great Britain], vol. 8 (1987), pp.111–25

Murphy, P.G. 'Reconstruction of the Pigeon House electricity station', *Transactions of the Institute of Civil Engineers of Ireland*, 62 (1939–40), pp.142–75

O'Rourke, K. 'Burn everything English except their coal: The Anglo-Irish economic war of the 1930s', *The Journal of Economic History*, vol. 51 (1991), pp.357–66

Owen, A. Review of 'Evacuation Survey: A Report to the Fabian Society', *The Economic Journal*, 50, 200 (December 1940), pp.502–5

Potter, C.J. 'Europe's Coal Problem', *Proceedings of the Academy of Political Science*, 21, 4 (January 1946), pp.28–40

Purdom, D.S. 'Argentine railway workshops in wartime', *Journal of the Institute of Locomotive Engineers*, no. 163 (1941), pp.344–457

Raymond, R.J. 'World War Two and the foundation of Irish Shipping', *Éire Ireland* (1984), pp.48–76

Ribeill, G. 'Les chantiers de collaboration socials des federations legals des cheminots (1939–1944)', *Le Mouvement Social*, no. 158 (1992), pp.87–116

Rigney, P. 'Report on Arigna coal mines, 1942', *Breifne*, no. 38 (2002), pp.509–16

Rigney, P. 'Arigna coal mines and the Emergency', *Breifne*, no. 40 (2004), pp.290–3

Rigney, P. 'Easter week 1916 and the Great Southern and Western Railway', *Journal of the Irish Railway Record Society*, no. 160 (2006), pp.459–61

Rigney, P. 'Military service and the GS&WR staff, 1914–1923', *Journal of the Irish Railway Record Society*, no. 161 (2006), pp.459–61

Rooth, T.J.T. 'Limits of leverage: The Anglo-Danish trade agreement of 1933', *Economic History Review* [Great Britain], vol. 37 (1984), pp 211–28

Shields, B.F. 'An analysis of the financial and operating statistics of the

GSR and GNR, 1938–1944', *Journal of the Statistical and Social Enquiry Society of Ireland*, vol. 17 (1945–6), pp.540–64

Smyth, W.A. 'My service on Irish Railways', *Journal of the Irish Railway Record Society*, no. 83 (1980), pp.117–28

Stevenson, D. 'War by timetable? The railway race before 1914', *Past and Present* no. 162 (February 1999), pp.163–94

Warner, A. 'Peat production: Some mechanical methods', *Transactions of the Institute of Civil Engineers of Ireland*, 69 (1942–3), pp.39–69

Weidenhammer, R.M. 'A national fuel policy III: Bituminous coal, postwar prospects', *Journal of Land and Public Utility Economics*, 21, 3 (August 1945), pp.232–5

White, M. 'Fifty years of a locoman's life', *Journal of the Irish Railway Record Society*, no. 32 (1963), pp 259–69

Internet Resources and Conference Papers

Kristiansen, T. 'The Norwegian merchant fleet during the First World War, the Second World War and the Cold War', Paper delivered to ICMH conference, Rabat, August 2004

Wheeler, D.J. 'The Price of Neutrality: Portugal, the Wolfram Question, and World War II', *Luso-Brazilian Review*, 23, 2 (Winter 1986), pp.97–111

Theses

Bradley, R.J. 'The Emergency Scientific Research Bureau: An analysis and evaluation of the scientific and technical impact of the ESRB', unpublished PhD thesis, Trinity College Dublin, 1992

Field, M.M. 'The politics of turf, 1939–45', unpublished MA thesis, University College Dublin, 1990

Muldowney, M. 'The impact of the Second World War on women in Belfast and Dublin: An Oral History', PhD thesis, Trinity College Dublin, 2006

Index